Allen Curnow
Collected Poems

Allen Curnow
Collected Poems

Edited by
Elizabeth Caffin
& Terry Sturm

AUCKLAND
UNIVERSITY
PRESS

First published 2017
Auckland University Press
University of Auckland
Private Bag 92019
Auckland 1142
New Zealand
www.press.auckland.ac.nz

Poems and author notes © Tim Curnow, 2017
Introduction and remaining notes © Elizabeth Caffin, 2017

ISBN 978 1 86940 851 0

Published with the assistance of

ARTS COUNCIL OF NEW ZEALAND TOI AOTEAROA

A catalogue record for this book is available from the National Library of New Zealand

Book design by Katrina Duncan
Typeset in Adobe Caslon
Jacket design by Sarah Maxey

Endpaper design by Betty Curnow. The design was commissioned by
Denis Glover of The Caxton Press for his book of poems *The Wind and
the Sand: Poems 1934–44* published in 1945 on his return from the war.

Printed in China by 1010 Printing International Ltd

In memory of

Terry Sturm
scholar and teacher
and of his great spirit of generosity

CONTENTS

Introduction   I

Valley of Decision, 1933   5
Three Poems, 1935   18
From Another Argo, 1935   22
From A Caxton Miscellany, 1937   23
Enemies, 1937   25
Not in Narrow Seas, 1939   39
From Recent Poems, 1941   54
Island and Time, 1941   56
Sailing or Drowning, 1943   84
Jack without Magic, 1946   100
At Dead Low Water, 1949   106
Poems 1949–57, 1957   116
A Small Room with Large Windows, 1962   137
Poems from the 1960s   142
Trees, Effigies, Moving Objects, 1972   151
An Abominable Temper, 1973   173
An Incorrigible Music, 1979   193
You Will Know When You Get There, 1982   227
The Loop in Lone Kauri Road, 1986   267
From Continuum, 1988   285
The Game of Tag, *from* Early Days Yet, 1997   293
The Bells of Saint Babel's, 2001   319

Notes   356
Bibliography   375
Author's Note from *Collected Poems*, 1974   376
Index of Titles   378
Index of First Lines   381

Appendix: www.press.auckland.ac.nz/en/curnow-collected-appendix.html

Introduction

Allen Curnow (1911–2001) is widely acknowledged as New Zealand's most important English-language poet, respected in his own country from early in his career and highly praised internationally in his later years. Producing poetry for almost seventy years, he was not however a prolific poet and his work bears the marks of intense concentration and dedication. He was deeply influenced by his father, an Anglican vicar and himself a poet; and his work is imbued with the twin traditions of English poetry and the Church of England.

His early work shows his awareness of contemporary poetic practice in England and the United States but was often a conscious and complex attempt to address the local context. Some of these poems, frequently ambivalent approaches to New Zealand identity and myth, are among his best known. But Curnow as a poet was always on the move and from the 1950s his work became more personal, though never confessional, and philosophic, dealing repeatedly with the encounter between language and the observed world, with mind and perception, and with memory. The dazzling and original poetry of his middle years responded to the experiences of travel, history and politics in unexpected ways, while recollections of childhood pervaded his rich later works.

Painstaking and prolonged labour created each poem, always seen in a wider context of thought about literature and its place in the world. Allen Curnow also played a major role as critic, commentator and anthologist, as well as a much-loved writer of light verse under the penname of Whim Wham.

From time to time he took backward looks at his own work and the starting point for this volume is the *Collected Poems, 1933–1973* (1974). This was the second and the most extensive retrospective collection that Curnow produced in his lifetime. It includes the texts of all collections published up till 1973 (excluding a few early poems and obviously avoiding duplications). Some of the poems however were extensively revised for that volume. Further small revisions were also made in the later selections of his work. Throughout the present book the last version of every poem has in all cases been preferred, as Curnow would have wished.

While Curnow continued to innovate and experiment, to shift attention and alter focus, his work yet has a remarkable consistency and integrity. He seems to have thought of it as a whole — but always from the present perspective. In his Author's Note to the 1974 *Collected Poems* he defended his common practice of revision:

> Even after forty years some poems carry between or under the lines their own instructions for revision. These instructions a poet must read as well as he can. His choice is between ignoring them and acting on them, and if he acts, he takes the risk of exceeding them. I think it is a good risk to take. If he doesn't revise, he is in effect concealing something from the reader: some part of his own better understanding. . . .*

However as the years passed the poems furthest away from the present moment lost interest to him; and in the next anthology, *Selected Poems* (1982), published by Penguin, the first three volumes were omitted, while selections only were included from *Island and Time* (1941), *Sailing or Drowning* (1943), *Jack Without Magic* (1946) and *At Dead Low Water* (1949). And in the next retrospective collection, *Continuum* (1988), his tenacious grip on the present was reinforced by including only collections from 1972 on, presented in reverse chronological order so that a group of new poems opened the book. Emboldened, he chose for the second Penguin *Selected Poems* of 1990 an even more radical order, recent poems circling round early poems 'touching the history and identity of my country'. While in the final anthology, *Early Days Yet: New and Collected Poems, 1941–1997* (1997), the reverse order is again used with the selection strongly favouring more recent poems.

This collection attempts to give a comprehensive coverage of Curnow's work. It includes all published collections following a conventional chronological order of first publication. The poems up to 1974 are presented in the order used in the 1974 *Collected Poems*. The remaining poems are ordered as in the individual collections. This book does not include early poems published in journals and periodicals but these are available in the online Appendix: www.press.auckland. ac.nz/en/curnow-collected-appendix.html. In addition to the text of the 1974 *Collected Poems* there are a couple of poems from the 1930s that appeared in

---

* The full text of the 'Author's Note', 1974, is reproduced on pp 376-77.

Caxton anthologies grouping several poets. I have also included an interesting group of poems from the 1960s partly on the grounds of their own literary merit but also to show that though no major collection appeared in these years, the poet was not idle. Among these is a glimpse of the master of light verse in 'On the Tour' and two poems that re-emerged in different forms in the 1972 volume, *Trees, Effigies, Moving Objects*.

The Notes, which are extensive, reproduce all of Curnow's comments on individual poems, made sometimes on different occasions, along with relevant quotations from his Author's Notes. (Some of his notes from *Early Days Yet* might seem superfluous to New Zealand readers but were written expressly for the book's simultaneous publication by Carcanet in England.) I have also added comments of my own when that might illuminate or explain.

The online Appendix collects the first versions of three early collections, *Valley of Decision*, *Enemies* and *Not in Narrow Seas*; the last of these originally appeared in the journal *Tomorrow* in 1937–38. Other uncollected poems from journals *Kiwi*, *Phoenix*, *Canterbury College Review*, *Tomorrow*, *Book*, *New Zealand New Writing* and later *Cornish Review* also appear. When in the 1930s individual poems were sometimes signed with the penname Julian, this has been indicated. The full text of a long verse letter to fellow poet, publisher and dear friend Denis Glover, absent in wartime, is of interest as only part of it, called 'Spring in Wartime', appeared in *Sailing or Drowning*. There are also two celebrated satirical broad-sheets, of 1957 and 1958, attacking the Auckland City Council in a row about the relocation of the University. The final poem in the online Appendix is part of a commissioned chapter on Curnow's schooldays at Christchurch Boys' High School.

Light verse by Whim Wham will not be found here as Curnow always insisted in keeping him separate from the serious poet; in any case Terry Sturm has done him full justice elsewhere (*Whim Wham's New Zealand: The Best of Whim Wham 1937–1988*, ed. Terry Sturm, 2005). Nor are there any selections from his verse dramas, important but somewhat forgotten works which deserve an edited volume of their own.

During the many years in which Terry Sturm was writing his literary biography of Allen Curnow he was also assembling the materials for a Collected Poems. Sadly he did not live to complete this task and I, as Curnow's last publisher, have been privileged to inherit it. My greatest debt therefore is to Terry, acknowledging his sensitive and judicious approach, his care and his deep knowledge and understanding of Curnow's poetry. Much of the work was done: an initial selection was made, the order and version of the poems established, omissions decided. A fundamental division into main text and appendix was also clearly indicated, the appendix providing further subordinate texts useful to scholars.

I must acknowledge the strong support of Tim Curnow, literary agent and copyright owner of Curnow's work, who encouraged me to take on this task and assisted me on the way; and also Linda Cassells, Terry Sturm's widow, who kindly provided Terry's files, both of the collected poems and the biography, and answered all my queries promptly and efficiently. I thank Alex Calder and Mac Jackson, both of the English Department at the University of Auckland and colleagues of Sturm, for their good advice. I am grateful too to Sam Elworthy, who succeeded me at AUP, and for the skill of the AUP staff, and especially Katrina Duncan and Anna Hodge. I would also like to recall with deep affection the friendship of Jeny Curnow, Allen Curnow's widow, and to regret she did not live to see either this book or the biography in print.

Wellington, 9 November 2016

VALLEY OF DECISION, 1933 (1974)

SEA CHANGES

Strange times have taken hold on me,
strange seas have locked across my eyes,
thick in the twilight undersea
unheard-of-silence heard these cries.

Out of the glimmer of green waters
the ringing deafness of dark seas,
such dim-begotten sons and daughters
of love and cold-flesh death are these:

Uncertain are they hunting on
and all their faith's inconstancy;
they are who touch and straight are gone
yet have no other where to be.

RENUNCIATION

Darken, eyes, toward the day,
look well on neither flower nor tree:
I have given a springing world away
for worlds which I believe to be.

The motion of this ill belief
I cannot speak, lest every word
whine to a soft attenuate grief
and every flower burn out a sword

surgeon's or angel's keen to cut
body from soul, one two, one two.
Eyes, darken; whining mouth, be shut
till I have cleaner work for you.

ET RESURREXIT

Servants of God,
how do you stand
to their witness,
eye, ear, hand?

Eternal heaven
as the eye can see
is wing's upon wing's
tautology.

As the ear can hear
there is no song
but of brute birth
and mortal tongue.

All the hand knows
for a fast friend
is blind first touch
and a last as blind.

How does that heaven
of yours agree
with this, life's in-
most certainty?

We teach it this way,
sons of men:
on the third day
He rose again.

VENTURE

He had begun to look within
and midnight high the walls flew up,
God was a breath of blazing cold
before the morning winds begin:

and now he was a timeless king,
now dust of all kings ever rode
over such walls and dropped their dead
and knew they were not anything:

now rounding eye on eye he saw
the breathless builder on the walls,
the blazing cold, the towering bone
was God within as God before.

'Be damned these aching walls' he said,
'be sunk this fire to natural hell.
'I looked within, only to find
'what eyes are pricking in my head.'

So he went by and looked without,
to find the old and equal sight,
but there was fog and a few stones,
a dazed wind puffed the dust about,

and a strange face he knew was cold
(so white) said to him with half lips,
'Now you have learned to look within
'there's nothing here that is not old.'

He saw the steep flight of the wall,
the blazing cold, the breath of God:
now king, now dust, whatever's crushed
between the thumb and the eyeball.

VALLEY OF DECISION

Come to the cliff, look over,
see your years flake down,
man, you'll discover
truth is a ghost town

fallen out of time
from this cliff top,
truth is the dizzy climb,
the sheer drop.

Proud hour, creeping minute
flake, fall, strew
the ghostly polis, in it
your lies come true;

hopes, loves, reasons,
times of your life,
all weathers and seasons
shredded over the knife

edge of this chasm —
shape and substance
a twitch of the eye, a spasm,
a dusty dance

idly neither here nor
there, a breath
trapped, do you need more
to please death?

Come to the cliff, look over,
see your years flake down,
man, you'll discover
truth is a ghost town.

AT THE BRINK

When I have seen a perfect flower
or stood a little by the sea
love on this beauty there begets
the pain of clouded sight in me;

for perfect things must needs be dead
or live alone in perfect praise,
and one bright day is but the seal
of countless deaths of countless days.

The poets and their nightingales
both sing, two voices in one song;
but matched against eternity
the music does not echo long.

Can there be light beyond the day,
the common sun of lovely things?
Beauty's a creature of the mind.
No nightingale, but poet, sings.

Beauty's a tree that walks by night,
the farthest sentinel of sense,
dark hope of an enduring light
in an eternal transience.

MATINS

Pray God and quiet take
for this day's part
of His desiring, make
greater your heart

to brim the joy and shame
the hours repeat
as Light in pity's name
kneels at your feet

and sues you, offering
quick love before you:
birds at your rising sing:
angels adore you.

He gives you suns to burn:
beauty for beauty
give then, your best return
candles for duty.

HIS DECEIT

And so the world makes you unquiet too,
so cold upon your pride of being man:
you too have thought how there is nothing new
under the sun, since under-sun began;

so you lean hard upon your hands in prayer,
your grace of life, your fleshhood all denied
saying, 'Lord, indeed for these I have no care.'
God in his beauty curse you for your pride.

FOUR WALLS

The street's a fixed stare on the pointless night
black focus of the nearest dark, direct
sharp style of limits whose shrewd architect
shaped in the circling flux of mortal sight

a walled city against the infinite ways
where spirits mount nor ever make an end
of star on star, high towers to defend
our finished hours and finely rounded days:

these are brave walls about our narrow peace,
between them measured seconds rule our feet;
the swinging littleness we pace nor cease
to labour comfort from our spare deceit:

yet star on star the motion of ascent
shadows across the difficult content.

BEHOLD NOW BEHEMOTH

See the wide-footed, pendant-bellied beast
called Behemoth, burst loose the river weeds
in cloudy mud-mist down the stream; he feeds
grunting, suck-sucking Jordan with his feast
of grass; slow swings his low eyes to the east,
blinks as the sun strikes, turns away; he needs
no such clean light, shafting the trodden reeds;
logs it in water-holes till day has ceased.

Drowse and be comfortable; lie, Behemoth
under the cross-stick shadow, tremulous veil
heat-vibrant, quick in the slant-broken stems.
So has he made you; bone and sinew both
of iron, that his image man may quail
at sight of you, and clutch his garment's hems.

THE SPIRIT SHALL RETURN

Often the things I see are tired,
the sounds I hear lag halting back;
I lump the world along with me,
a body in a shouldered sack

that huddles with its mortal weight
the loaded wrist against my throat;
the silence runs upon my soul,
the dust has fingers on my coat.

The rising dust that pulls me down
knows well I walk the road alone,
or the road walks, where I might be
entombed, and straining at the stone.

Stars that lit Jacob's ladder once
drop out of heaven to the dust
or heaven itself is there, and there
the treasuries of moth and rust;

I lump the world along with me
though heaven is eaten, and the night
poured out upon the sea of glass
obliterates the Light of Light.

This way's the only narrow way,
swagging the body of this death,
to know this life, and that I live.
Dust unto dust, the preacher saith.

THE AGONY

Stammering wind this night
gustily utters
its deaf-mute cries
and the rain
trapped fingers tapping wakes me
under the windowless rock
outside this house.
There, there again!
Out there alone somebody sighed,
a scrabbling sigh of sharp unpartnered
pain:
     so dark,
dark in the heart, and still
the sighing wind, the rain
dropping, dropping,
the bloody sweat down-dropping,
oh God!
can pity be worth so much?

SCREENED

He dressed his love in a fine dress
praising its swing and suppleness:

they laughed to see the boy at play
and said, he had a pretty way;

and he dipped to a dainty kiss,
said, this my love, my love is this:

content they were to see the slow
meet of the flesh so lightly go —

good and his evil went their round
and shoulder-looking knowledge frowned.

HOST OF THE AIR

Out of the living pit
deep under the moon
beat to the fiend's tune
round the tall back-lit
scarp of the moon flame
they whom God gave no name.

Earth, water and fire
labour and breathe them out,
twist they a man with doubt
and a knife at his desire,
they are the piercingest
pain without a breast.

Who knows that he is known
by name to Christ his Lord,
his peace, his sword?
Each son of man alone
walks with a wind of wings
of the nameless things.

STATUS QUO

If these stuck clods were blasted wide
the rubble raked apart to give
the sun below, they'd spill their pride
and learn of worms the way to live.

THE SERPENT

The plague's about along the street.
In proud decay the dead go by
and, failing flesh on lagging feet,
move on the many marked to die:

there is no mourning day and night,
nor simple tears nor common sorrow,
since death today strikes at the sight
and reaches for the heart tomorrow;

so no-one sees the shrouded men
about their business through the day
dividing to their dust again,
for whom there is no other way,

for the one dust has nourished them
and thickened round their clodded feet;
so earth will earth at last condemn
to earth's last pitiable retreat.

Christ take the whip of knotted cord,
flay out the money-changing dead!
Christ bring the labourer's reward,
the burning thirst on Dives' head!

See where the healing serpent stands,
Christ lifted up — his felon's crown
crush on our heads, and set our hands
to turn the whole world upside down.

APOCALYPTIC

Yet a star will speak
and the swift wheels which spatter
bright hours with idle dirt
the wheels which whirl and hurt
will gasp off at the hub:
yet a star will speak.

The smoke of their burning
chokes the song of the day,
incense of quick decay,
still the wheels whining pray
God burn us up, burn up.
The smoke of their burning.

Man, blood in your head
flies thick with the spin of the rim
round with you bound and broken
while a star has not spoken.
Does it sparkle behind the ball,
man, blood in your head?

There is no loosing hands,
the hour is the power which moves,
the very pivot is space
in whose gift's no grace
for there is no tangent,
there is no loosing hands

till a star speak to a man
and two shall join to him
and the pain die in the burning
and the seized wheels cease turning:
guard our strength as we may,
till a star speak to a man.

POWER OF THE MANY

Against these eyes where is a man to hide?
Cover him close to friend with the worm inside,
cover him close by the intimate lips of the worm
where the bed is soft, for he hates anything firm.

The eyes have a hard way with a waking man
in their force, forcing sleep down the throat till he can
breathe his best in the mothering coil of the worm
where the bed is soft, for he hates anything firm.

'Fill his heart, Christ, that he wake and walk in sight
'of the cloud by day, the untouchable flame by night,
'so the withering eyes recoil from the wakened man
'heartened, hardened for heaven, so that he can
'straighten his way from the smothering loop of the worm
'where the bed is soft, for he hates anything firm'.

ON RELIEF

They gave your hands a grubbing-tool
and you have learnt to use the thing:
you thought, a man's a bloody fool
who starves when work is offering.

And there's a stiffness in your eyes
that is not earth nor bodily pain;
your eyes give nothing to the dust
though foot and hand shake out the chain:

this iron marks you man, bound low
under a mad king's blind control,
who wills you change, you would or no,
his mass-compassion for a soul.

THREE POEMS, 1935 (1974)

ASPECTS OF MONISM

I

This was untrue, that there is division
between body and mind, making sin
and matter for secret speaking or derision
out of an act where sight and strength begin:

this believing, I could not give you alone
body's touch and power, nor want of you
warm sense only, since these are known
but as form of thought, weapon of will to do.

So pity is born of power, love of subjection —
blood is swift to learn and the mind slow —
did I think before, would there be recollection
by the mind of error when it did not know?

Now it is too late to save the deceit;
it is death or whole acceptance of the vision
of beauty gone down full-eyed in defeat
earth receiving her. There is no division.

II

Nothing passes, all is the one moment
possessing richly world's breadth; and the clear
succession, which is illusion, of jewelled hours
is a burning peace in the eyes of one woman;
and it is time there was an end of asking.

III

In the dawning eye only has the sun its being,
waking to dawn in a man's body, burning
as ultimate knowledge looked fairly in the face;
and where lastly is the act of seeing?

And the day has one white foot on the very far
first step from darkness, and a white arm takes
the sea in a bowl held upward in a glory.
There is no earth nor any other star;

only, they have claimed arrogantly
that it is possible to see the sun
and the rising wonder and the burden of lightening
consciousness. How should they see

into the bodiless unity, scatter the strength
which is both sight of the eyes and utmost vision
from the first sun step to the end in darkness?
If any god has led us to this length

there is a temple to be overthrown
before any man can wake with earth's waking
or answer the love which crosses the sea at morning
or visit the mountains and be known.

IV

So with me you must come into certain places
where the blood of earth runs clear
in a slim green plant and in a standing tree
and there are no separate death-hardened faces

dividing in a dream the shadow of a man;
then it may be life will look on life,
eye into eye and see no difference,
but earth, love, death, lost in a single span.

RESTRAINT

For pity of your own heart, think
of the way you would choose:
I shall tell you of its certain end
and what your heart may lose:

you may have at last slight memory
of seas crossed, other lands,
strange speech, strange faces
and the work of strange hands.

For a time your heart will plead with you
for space in which to see
the sun rise upon dark places
that were lost utterly;

but there will be silence in a while
and another memory
of a dream broken and beauty left
at the border of the sea:

there is one sun the world over
and the one heaven's blue;
and one heart risen with the morning
can light the world for you.

Many cities and new marvels
only blind the eyes
which a flower might have perfected
the hour before it dies:

never look long at a flower —
a moment, at the most —
for fear your heart walk desolate
in a cold land lost.

THE WILDERNESS

Soul, put on now as vesture
well-chosen word and gesture;
let good manners attend you
and common speech defend you:

the stars your enemies,
the tall malicious trees
and the sunlit flesh of her
who is life's doorkeeper

know where you will tread;
be cold then, as if dead,
and beauty may desert you
nor find where to hurt you.

From ANOTHER ARGO, 1935

DOOM AT SUNRISE

Pain like cold fire binds the brows of the earth
now the armed angel-morning burns to birth,
the steel sinks in hearts hot with hurrying
down dusty pavements where the tram-bells ring;

ward how they will thrusting up blind walls
the blue bow bends, dips, the shaft falls
into an eye bare unwitting at a crack
into a pinched ear, on white breast and back.

Cold snow pain strung tight from peak to peak
loins of earth angel-lightened, who shall speak
replying to love out of emptiness
to beauty from wrench'd lips?
the poised peaks will not fall on us,
the folded wings of rock not cover us
in this our day of doom striking.

Some have been struck dead instantly
or mad, to drum the head against a tree;
yet love, a breath piercing the dumb pain
will drive the steel, with a spark, back again.

INHERITANCE

I

He will not walk in the sun, the young life
after birth in cloud of fear, in secret guilt;
cold mist about his feet is fear pursuing.
The cup is lifted, neither drunk nor spilt.

He will not press towards any mark
being taught backward-looking, a windless hate.
His instruction is adequate, a safe prescription,
and he enjoys smut, will come to school late.

Now see him climb to well-grown beauty,
striving at football, body wild with release.
Fear follows. A girl waits at frosty nightfall,
life's light creeps like a thief's lantern
while they two seek groping the entailed
estate of forebears who laughed and died.

II

Cleanliness, tidiness and expedient caution
white plaster and raw new wood,
and an index-system and central heating;
of such is the kingdom of God on earth.
Life has been drained, dried into cells,
a dwindling current, pocket electricity.

Here now life at maturity, the completed product
(no crooked eclipses for glory has departed);
the swivel chair throne of benign success,
Caesar's sceptre a gold fountain-pen
and still the world cringes.

Honour to the builders of this fame:
pale schoolmasters who broke the fine spirit,
employers preaching sound business methods —
all authors of fear who forgot fear.

III

Pray for him now that he will not forget
altogether the vast peaks and valleys of fear.
If the heart is not dying yet,
in that desolate country wandering among
sudden horrors and impending despair,
a harsh nobility may perhaps be won.

ENEMIES, 1937 (1974)

NEW ZEALAND CITY

Small city, your streets
lack legend, lead nowhere
proud shrined, notorious
for a church or a brothel.

Your potentates cringe,
nobody notices.
Nations do not quote
your newspapers. London
has spawned. Here are banks
in the egg, Beaverbrook
foetuses, Chamberlain
foetuses, toy trains,
mud pies and sandpits,
an unstained sky.

Yet the cloud
curdles in the wind
pitted with blue
or the cloud returns
laden, still laden
after the rain

and many coats hang
from a hanger or shoulder
and pens by the thousand
scratch like rats' teeth
busy in the wall

and a rubbery squeal
tells the tarseal
that a man goes home
at evening which must follow
any toil's end.

Land of new hopes
with a thousand years'
despair, of children
with senile faces,
this land, these islands:
the shadow of Europe
falls, over the fallen
walls of an empire:
the planet called Asia
spins visibly
from here, small city,
to the naked eye
some worlds away
in the northern sky:
and eastward the white
hospital where
the sick breathe air
conditioned air
and dollar by dollar
the beads are told there.

Serf to them all
for pleasure or pain;
betrayed to the world's
garret and gutter,
sold for the export
price of butter.

RECALL TO EARTH

Together let us regain the earth's friendship.
The poplar spire topped by no cross
may be our temple tower, of delight in wind
or of roadside riches no loss.

Fear, iron-eyed chauffeur of ambition,
drives daily to the gold-lettered door
him whose property increases and multiplies,
like every private pontiff and public bore.

Monkey chatter in the newest manner
offends your spirit. Foolishness harries you.
Will you play bridge? Tongues fence, lips mince.
Trapped handshake, mechanical howdyadoo.

Shall we put up with it no longer than
body and soul can bear? Life gets to its feet, —
Excuse us, the wind is waiting, the unpaid sun
babysits for us in another street.

CHIEF END

Drag a star down to the office table —
what sort of light is that to work by?
Rising wind will confuse important papers
not contributing to efficiency.

Get up at daybreak, seek bed at dusk?
So little time there would be for pleasure.
We shall save money and buy a car
and cultivate a right use of leisure.

FACTORY AT NIGHT

This light both whip and burden to your eyes
that wince, being tender yet. After the glory
of wide-armed sun at morning, leaves warmed through,
the blood's green quickened, the day dies
not gratefully for you,
but a mocked day dawns on the plaster,
strokes of an idiot's brush;
oil streams, steel slides faster
and faster the shadows rush
under the whipping lights
overhead under and over again.

Fish out of water, these eyes,
and the net is pain.

COLONIAL OUTLOOK

Night, will not night identical draw down
merciful shutter on our unimportance
as (one imagines) mountainous dark will drown
organic millions in dreamy pretence
of works relaxed by deathly creeds, in sleep?

So many thousand fewer paved miles
so many fewer turns of shuddering tyres
so many fewer strong, remote smiles
(with us) shield rout of refugee desires;
insignificant conflict, late begun,
and comic disaster — surely bitterness
and fear have here as central impetus?

Our beds empty, streets a desert no less
than in the other provinces of the sun:
yet we remain, dog-at-heel, obsequious.

A WOMAN IN MIND

I

I have lit a single lamp
and laid my fire beneath
for cold faint-sun days
of frost and cloudy breath.

Her eyes my early lamp
in this winter of the heart;
her body, limbs burning,
holds bitterness apart.

Shadows prank my walls;
outside, rain is flying:
ere my light and my fire die
I too shall be dying.

II

Your face between my hands
and your eyes open to me,
it is as if I stood
beside a great sea;
for nothing is so still
or perfect in its pride
or such deep semblance, as
the flesh I stand beside.

III

My hands worship
you with suppliant touch
in whatever part seeking
to know you bodily.

Nothing is withheld
from us in our free
city of love, we conceal
not from any sense.

To shrink from flesh
is to offend the spirit —
who can divide them
one from the other?

Now you receive
hand at breast and thigh,
I suppliant; but soon
equal communion.

IV

As the green music compassing
all earth that listens in the spring
so is the semblance when your nearness
shakes taut and void to broken clearness
and music, music cries to be
about the way you walk to me.

V

Who am I
that I should own
so fair a field
and meet, for yield?

That in this earth's
deep, sweet warmth
my seed should stir
(the sun loves her)

drinking bright rain
in womb of tenderness,
god's gate, the same,
Mary without blame?

Since it is mine
this earth, her flesh,
bears that which I
wanting, should die.

VI

By pain outspoken
a precious thing is broken,
peace destroyed by pain
no words can bring again.

May sun never bless me
and loud winds oppress me
if from me is heard
a destructive word.

Shut my mouth upon your breast;
now I have confessed,
on my lips let move
breath only of love.

VII

In the time of your conceiving
which shall be in spring
we shall die with flowers, together
in all our blossoming.

A rose shall ask your lips
close, as never before
when summer has deepened
and life is at the door.

Autumn shall bring us then
leaves' grace in falling,
wind-lightened, lost suns
without pain recalling.

Winter, not an enemy
to earth's true lover,
but womb of new sowing,
shall cover us over.

MOUNTAIN ELEGY

I

Immaculate wing unfolding slowly enfolding
white light, sun wakening the great bird roosted
on the broken edges of a thousand feet.
Portent of flight till mountain dawn withholding.

Nightlong dreamless motionless among intermittent
huge migrations of wind, loud hosts in passing
leaving louder silences, bird upon the cliff
knows morning in each cell, light palpitant.

Morning has no audible herald at this height:
all is translated, song into flight;
trumpet note into arrogance of light
bannered fiercely through the passes,
as striking fire from new-split gem
leaps at the haggard eastward masses
cracking gold from the heart of them.

II

Voiceless but the only articulate
motion on earth's frozen lip,
beautiful for invisible mate
the wing trembles to the tip;

if dumb space did not intervene
drowning familiarities,
could be heard lightly the dark lean
claws finding grip to rise.

Ascending cry across the blue.
Upward the wing'd glory breaks
and suddenly morning is in view
which is not till the creature wakes.

III

The eye is now withdrawn, extreme reach of self
and extreme sacrifice, in rhythmic reasonless flying;
nothing heard or seen, everything heard and seen,
that topmost life realised once in dying.

Life has crept above the broken edges, has leapt
assured into remote clasp of snow and sun
which after all live but by living blood, waiting
on the reviving wing for their day begun.

IV

Smears of a dark hand,
piecemeal evening
swarms from lower land
to the breach hasting,
shuddering wings

forget high-noon fire,
on low crag at rest
searching no higher.

Sapphire clouded
white garment torn
young body shrouded
bright hair shorn.

Slowly
          enfolding light
only articulate
                    nightlong
                              dreamless.

Death is most in mind
in this mountain evening without wind.

ENEMIES

Detestable gutter child, if you knew
how we hate you, I and my kind,
you would scramble bawling with terror
to that refuge behind
the sodden stinking privy at the back
of the two rooms stuck by the railway track.

SLUM

Walking in the garden of our Father
I find evil places; it is rather
as if honouring death we
had planted here Gethsemane.

Though Christ came from God, he
taught us the love of death and agony.

The garden wall is iron, its soil
is dust choking those who toil;
boards rot in the shadow, some few
are aware of a heart rotting too.

Christ loved mankind it is true,
but said 'the poor you always have with you.'

Almsgiving knows no pity;
charity collected in the city
is self-defence of deep hate
bribing the enemy from the gate.

As Christ taught we feed our enemies
fearing the unblunted enmities.

Between the factory and
the filthy house I stand
a moment, seeing a woman sitting
glance at me over her knitting;

better forget sixpenny charity
when the poor carry their hate honestly.

We have agents behind the lines,
peddlers of promise, seers of signs,
preaching that the starving should not covet
good things, bringing Moses' law to prove it:

yet Moses' case is scarcely comparable
with these who have no manna for the table.

Walking in the garden one sees
so many of our enemies,
hearts fix'd strength undecay'd,
that I wonder that we are not afraid:

but we are safe until the day
our weapons show obvious decay.

REMAINDER

I go home with my wife
and we talk about you
who go home with your wives,
possibly mentioning us.

We all went into the sea
muddy soup stirred not
only by feet but wind
also, long ladle of ocean.

Up again Aphrodite
neat in wool and rubber;
lumps out of the soup;
shake off the drips.

Such is our contact;
faith our mainstay, you
possibly mentioning us.

ORBIT

With so great wonder, at times fear,
I hear and see the distraught people
in twitching panic tread the collapsed hours
(time's rhythm wrench'd, rush'd with pale speed,
time in time machine-maddened): I must keep
heart's beat by you who follow the sun
whose blood keeps time of the sun the governor;
spite of chaos' steam and steel writhing
heart learns of you right motion,
season's swing, curve of rejoicing comet,
remote, holy obedience of the stars.

THE LEAVES DEAD

Drained flesh and hardened
by winter wind and water
leaves fill, with poison
part of their own nature;

blown from safe mooring
above heavy water
up heaven's wind-tunnel,
leaves fill the chamber
of sight, with death-yellow
spume lightly hardened.

Mud, leaf-rot, water
mix under a tree,
dissolution found in them
part of their own nature.

PAID WELL

No more burns the fire within the word.
Use stiffens the rhythm, effaces the image
which came and went like flame.

Great waters
are come upon the world, all cold
untroubled by birth and death alike.

NOT IN NARROW SEAS, 1939

Dedication
To him who can distinguish
In an unfeigned anguish
What is general
From what is personal,
Who has heard optimism
Crash in the last chasm
And knows hope more near
His heart's despair.

Towards mid-day, on December 13, in the year 1642 — the year of English revolution, of the death of Galileo, and the birth of Newton — the eyes of a sailor, straining over the waters of the Pacific, saw about 60 miles to the eastward 'a great land uplifted high'...

...The Dutch christened the shore thus uncertainly glimpsed New Zealand...

... Canterbury (was settled) by J. R. Godley (later of the War Office) and an Episcopalian pilgrimage in 1850. For some years these provinces were proudly conscious of their nationality and their virtue; the obliterating passage of time, alas! has merged them with their fellows in a common mediocrity...

... Yet in the midst of converging cables, shipping and wireless communication, it has remained always isolated; and in that verdant isolation perhaps lies the remote secret — if there is one — of the national life ... and it may be that in the 20th century the making of new nationalities is an anachronism, as it certainly is a danger.

— J.C. Beaglehole, *New Zealand: A Short History* (1936)

STATEMENT

In your atlas two islands not in narrow seas
Like a child's kite anchored in the indifferent blue,
Two islands pointing from the Pole, upward
From the Ross Sea and the tall havenless ice:
Small trade and no triumph, men of strength
Proved at football and wars not their own:

So much and the soft weather you may call your own
And the week-end bach by the salt healing seas,
Deep soil and shingle-slide to try your strength
Under the sun or dark-to-thunder blue;
Under your impudent feet the glacier's ice
Stirs like the hour-hand as you stumble upward.

In the little city's scattered smoke look upward
Feeling the various active fields your own
And your terrible equity in the blazing ice:
Forgetting the bondholder over the seas
And the foreigner's far cry, his bending blue,
And fear in a fast car finding its own strength.

Look upward. Now comes near a test of strength,
You at the desk and in the street look upward,
Both the county chairman and the airman in blue,
Take courage for these also are your own:
The pay envelope and the letter overseas,
Shame at night and ambition that is like ice.

The girls' feet crackle on the pavement ice,
A little warfare with superior strength,
To the Office. Enemies have crossed the seas
And hold the passes that enfold you upward,
Over Cook's peak and the lakes still your own
The aircraft crawling in the ill-mapped blue:

Not in a life your triumph nor the blue
Empty of fear, from the high chasmed ice

To the sheep lands, cattle lands that are your own:
Inheritors of an unrejoicing strength,
Driving, driven to market, heaving upward
A dust, your landfall's cloud mark and the sea's:

Therefore I sing your agonies, not upward,
For the two islands not in narrow seas
Cringe in a wind from the world's nether ice.

I

In a little artificial port with five jetties, overseas shipping waits to
be loaded with the primary products from which the Dominion derives
its wealth. This is a natural point from which to begin a study of the
birth, life and growth of a nation now nearly 100 years old. Attempts
are being made to establish a culture similar to that which Europe has
taken 1000 years to build; but the real ambitions of this people are
naive enough — 'a radio, perhaps a car.'

    The water is burred with rain.
    Men scrape rough iron, squatting
    On the slung plank, setting
    Knee and toe to the ship's flank.

    Rust and dust and the keen
    Wind strapping the ankle;
    Chips from the chisels sprinkle
    Down to the blue mud.

    There are five wharves.
    Today the port is quite full.
    They will load mutton and wool
    As soon as the rain stops.

    The Minister believes
    The price is sufficient to cover
    Labour costs and something over
    For a radio, perhaps a car.

II

At the time of writing it is more than 80 years since the Canterbury
Province of New Zealand was settled. There arrived in the port
(then not equipped for the handling of mutton carcases) in 1850, four
sailing vessels, bearing the persons, livestock and other goods of the
settlers. From the shore of the harbour, a seven–miles gulf of ancient
volcanic formation, they climbed to the hilltop and looked out over 100
miles of plain: a country they were to conquer without force or danger.

> Eighty years since salted sails
> Dropped among these hills
> And the iron water closed on
> The anchor's dry iron.
>
> Bedding and tents and stores
> Littered the frontiers
> Of a country taken
> To be stripped and broken.
>
> Not leap of capture theirs,
> But as who safely dares,
> Seizing without sword
> Front garden and backyard.

III

For many months they had been at sea. It was a pilgrimage under
the blessing of the Church of England, more definitely religious in its
professions, perhaps, than any since the Mayflower.

> Strut on the beach loos'd nervous limbs
> And they praised God with bad hymns,
> Quavering in a huge volcanic crack
> With the iron water at their back.
>
> Doubtless their liturgy had prayer
> For establishing truth and virtue there,

For the wind clipping the reverent scalps
Howled the joke to the high Alps:

'We shall not blacken this land O Lord,
Thou hast given us without sword;
Our weapon and our lust lie at home
And in peace for peace we are come.'

IV

*Apparently there was a chance here for a clean break. The dark
places of industrial England, its poverty and diseases, were left behind.
Only the best had been taken, it seemed, of the English tradition. The
liturgy of the Church of England, immigrants of picked stock, sufficient
capital to provide for material needs and their development.*

Escape in seeming from smoke and iron,
The hammered street and the hot wheels,
Clanging conquest of the deep-rich hills.

Left behind the known germ and poison
Breeding and soaking in decrepit soils.

Jerusalem is built as a city
That is at unity in itself,
Built with liturgy and adequate capital
Dwelling of the elect, the selected immigrants.

V

*Iron, first introduced to the islands when the ships dropped anchor
offshore, soon becomes more firmly established. It must be noted that the
traditional courage of pioneers becomes, in social terms, merely the
furious sorties of man confronted with the unknown. Frustration drives
men to seek a new country; but the savagery of the new land threatens an
even more terrible frustration; so that fear swallows creative effort; and
the sole effective desire remaining is to conserve and extend the illusion*

of life in the old world. So the cycle is completed in time, and the
original frustration is perpetuated.

Blood in the climbing limb
No fear checking the pulse,
Pulls mountains down flat,
Erects cathedrals.

The superior race, Lo!
The pass in a twinkling
Yields the advancing column
A top-gear incline.

Green grows the bungalow
At the courageous heels,
Valour makes home for fear
Under hesitant sails:

A beginning, a beginning
A fresh start in life
With a blue-new shovel
And a rusted belief.

Iron for axe and hammer
Iron for rod and nail
Iron for the door-knocker
Like the head of a bull.

Where the first anchor's cable
Slackened into sleep
Iron threads rock for prison
Bars on the harbour slope.

VI

*The Church is quick to follow the imperial lead. Shrewdly, she
acquires property, and ownership is thus sanctified. The Gospel, it
might be imagined, would seek to find realisation in the building of a
new social order. But the Church is chiefly concerned with re-establishing
and conserving an order in which she has learnt to flourish. Any
departure from that order is disquieting to her. It has been noticed that
religion thrives best among the poor in spirit and in body.*

     The bishop boundary-rides his diocese
     Carrying the sacraments at saddle-bow;
     The church equestrian christens peak and river
     Where land is cheap and the reapers are few.

     Years after where his lordship braved the ford
     Less hardy saints cross bridges in a gig:
     Good rents assure their stipends, not even
     Judas so providently kept the bag.

     A faith worthy of empire; ere the four
     Earliest migrant vessels put to sea
     The wise company granted God permission
     To work His passage to the colony.

     Certified seed in a prepared soil —
     What land would not give the approved return?
     Here's no renewal of the world's youth,
     But age-soured infancy, a darkened dawn.

VII

*The pleasant work of exploring and building proceeds, making the
country fit for civilised people to live in.*

     Woman who wakes beneath casewood and canvas
     Salutes sunrise excellently painted,
     Warm familiar among unfamiliar
     To which heart unwilling consented.

Waking next morning, moving curtain, she
Sees front plot fenced, path in place;
The cloud, the mountain-terror tamed now
Framed to taste for parlour chimneypiece.

Not lessened the offensive against fear,
Eye cracking distance, foot on ford and steep;
Each to his tools his trade and his journey,
Restoring reason, the known scene and shape.

VIII

*For the young child a different destiny is expected. His
surroundings are clean, hardly-broken country. For that reason it is
assumed that he has a rich, unassessed heritage. In fact, as time has
demonstrated, his heritage is already bought and sold at market price.
If there is any gain it is not here. Even those to whom they are politically
sacred admit that ownership and trade have brought their inevitable
attendant evils. These are more potent here, where there are fewer
escapes by culture or tradition from the economic cycle of strength,
work and food.*

Child of the stolen country
Tumbling on the raw clay,
By the fence of the green wood
Given to play

With terrible idle earth,
Mountains and two seas
Opposing with patience
Endless enmities —

Child, old evil sprouts
Along the new track
From home's front door
To privy at the back
And where scrub is cleared
Round the neighbour's shack.

46

Not your destiny nor
This land's your shaping:
The sowing yours
Another's the reaping.

(The seed itself tainted
In the excited soil,
Yellow the trampled ford
Where the floods boil.)

Cancel the vision and
Wipe prayer from lip:
God comes not to market
Nor saints by ship.

IX

*In a brief conversation the Teacher explains to the Pupil the
meaning of empire. God and the flag are one, national pride being
(by naive admission) the solution of all social opposites and discrepancies.
Only the wind serves still to remind the patriot that the fight for liberty
continues; the pupil apparently convinced by Authority, is still
somewhat corrupted by the wind. The wind, it will be observed, has
the last word.*

Teacher: Haul the flag to the top of the mast,
Let it break there proclaiming brightly
The imperial message for this is the day
For remembering the nation our creator:
Honour the motherland as privilege and duty.

Pupil: See how the deep gusts out of the mountain
Snatch at the flag as if they hated it.

Teacher: Do not speak of hatred of the flag.
It has God's cross, see, in the white and red.

Pupil: It is a sinful wind that does not love
          The flag that bears God's cross.
          Eighty years ago this flag was brought
          To struggle upon this pole today
          Over a million heads microcosm
          Of the nation which colonised these islands;
          A greatness not to be straitened,
          Not by wind and ocean beaten off.

Teacher: That is today's lesson, Move on, please
          And see the convenient state prepared for you
          From the field the mountain and the shingly river.
          Walk by the sundial in the front garden,
          The double garage, the gravelled backyard.

Pupil: The flag flies high over that large building,
          Four floors glassed and terraced, idle lawns:
          I suppose that is the Governor's residence?

Teacher: That is the mental hospital where 5000
          Live, poor loonies, getting the best treatment.

Pupil: God's cross over the kingdom of the mad.
          The mad are a great nation to extend
          Their empire to the islands of the sea.

Teacher: The wind blew out their brains. We take the tram
          (A municipal enterprise of some importance)
          To another quarter of the growing city,
          The bungalows in rows smartly painted
          And the educated citizen returning
          After work with a friend to make four at bridge.
          Tourists have declared that the standard of living
          Is higher than anywhere in Europe.

Pupil: Two rooms lift rusted iron, a kennel roof
          By the fleshy brick of the twine factory.
          This, I take it, the penal settlement.

Teacher:	One of the poorer suburbs, the colony
	Of those who heard the wind, the enemy:
	Such refuse heaps make disposal a problem
	But the contractors it is said are doing well.

| *Pupil:* | God's cross over the kingdom of the poor. |

The Wind:	The flag rides rattling at the hoist
	At prison and at madhouse door;
	I swell'd their sails and what's the end?
	The poor insane and the insane poor.

X

*The new country must be aware of the dangerous extent to which
it is only a flattery by imitation of the old. Being a flattery it tends to
imitate in the grosser respects only. The street scene, the cheap
entertainment, are all faithfully reproduced. The values whose death
is celebrated everywhere under buildings of iron and concrete, are no
more apparent here than in the old countries. There is reproduction,
but not resurrection.*

Jaunty hopes that play
Against the cynical scene:
New land New Zealand
Dancing before the throne.

Now while the gilt is fresh
In our intimate theatre,
Listen and you will hear
The old, old gags recur:

Apprenticed to this stage
We thumb the greasy script:
Here we foreknow laughter,
There we shall have wept.

Who tinkers with the lines?
It makes no difference:
The old play that catches
Nobody's conscience.

Reproduction, reproduction
Of the curved, the angled, the tangible
Street measurable block by block:

Never resurrection
Of entombed pity, only discernible
Vanity of the practised trick.

Sensitive the film senselessly
Unrolls the death-embracing images:
Island and ocean a theatre

Screening a weary self-flattery
Where colour and where courage is
Costumed secondhand, in character.

XI

Having matched itself against the rest of the world in a game at which the rest of the world is by experience superior, the infant nation suffers an increase of frustration. Therefore it assumes a proprietary pride in the natural phenomena of the country. These, as well as the fruits of the soil, must be sold, to enable the nation to continue living just a little beyond its means. Foreign films and motor-cars (without which life is obviously intolerable) must be paid for. Mountains and other pleasant places must be, if necessary, blasted with facilities to satisfy the scenery-swallowing appetites of wealthy visitors from abroad. With such assets and others, the Government may borrow abroad to provide increasing facilities for civilised comfort: generally speaking, no other interpretation of civilisation is commonly admitted.

Naked goes the land
Under the sweating hand
Of the lover of a night,
While the procuress
Has eyes on a dress
Of innocent white.

You are on a holiday trip, sir,
And what do you think of our country?
Let us discuss beauty
And various scenic attractions:
Tell me our alps excel
Switzerland and the Rockies.

Interviewed by *The Blast*
Sir Bradford classed
Our mountain scenery
With Switzerland's best
Was deeply impressed
Is at present the guest
Of Dean Horn at the Deanery.

(O lord, O lord, lord, O lord
Make them say the encouraging word.)

Spirit, O spirit of the first-comers under sail
Where lost, you spirit?
                    Under a movie-theatre seat
Later disposed of by the police at auction.
However, there is ample pleasant distraction
Many arts of frustration to emulate
At 3½ per cent on a borrowed smile.

XII

Yet, out of the orgy of imitation, there will in time be born men of spirit. So far the country has not been able to contain its great spirits; that, perhaps, is because there have been none great enough to expand the country till it is able to sustain them. Poets, painters, musicians, scientists will suffer agonies in a country serving under gross masters. But out of their sufferings the wheat lands, the cattle country and the sheep country may be born again. At present, however, an artist can only suffer, and record his suffering; hoping to make others suffer with him the necessary pains of first self-knowledge.

> Where Van Gogh struck his seed
> Flat France twirled with pain:
> To these Pacific boulders
> There will come men
>
> Put to such planting
> After the rusted harrow
> Mining among mountains
> With their seed of sorrow:
>
> The vertical ice, the dry
> Shriek of the kea
> A howl of misery like
> The cornfields of Auvers.

EPILOGUE

> *A pickaxe and a spade:*
> For this is insolent country,
> James Cook's pig-farm
> Without rule or road.
>
> *And eke a shrowding sheet:*
> For the brown singing people
> Lift nobody off from Te Reinga
> So heavy, alone and late.

A house of clay for to be made:
I shall write long letters home,
I shall mind my English accent,
I shall read, and read.

Let winds and tempests beat
On 1000 bungalows,
To our sad suburban funeral
Drag followers on foot.

Then down I'll lie
As cold as clay
True love and false
both pass away,

The empire and the empty lands
The iron and the golden sands
Dredged and dumped
With the wheezing sea clay.

ROOKS OVER RICCARTON

Stormily high the rooks soar
Like aircraft whirling off to war.

Now in the thunder-hinged gates
To us the wind alone dictates,
The wind that roars but never hates:

No private engines of defence
Cover us on the unmanned immense
Frontiers of intelligence,

Where, the sky striding, wonder goes
Faster than fear, and the heart knows
An anger no longer asking blows.

None here make their splendid stand
For life, liberty, or land,
Their fathers' house a-quake on sand;

But here furious no more,
Braving the big sky before
In ruinous raid the mad rooks soar.

ACHIEVEMENT

Their Pole attained, bones
Sealed in ice remain
Embalmed, integral:
The bright unbroken cells
Contrive no new foulness
Where death his trophy holds
With easy violence.

THE BATH

Two steaming knees
Bright coffin'd in the bath
Where beauty lies
Laving the body of her death,
Her fronded hair.
Knees turn up, turn down,
In lust, in prayer,
She soaps away the stain.

STRATAGEM

Fear made the superior sea
The colour of his new car;
From a window in the hillside
He saw the sky bare
All but the handhold of a cloud
On a derelict gate. Ashamed,
He knew the weedy fog showed
His mother's hair uncombed;
And all for that the snaking road
In low gear climbed.
Before night he punished them,
The bright scenes hostile,
By a boy and girl in the
                    young broom.
He told that story well.

ISLAND AND TIME, 1941

…The air of their islands is mainly fresh from the sea, and the rainfall
abundant from the mountains whereon it condenses, from which, in
some places, a violent sirocco results. Their present condition depends
on the state of peoples a great distance off, and their communications
with these. As yet they have no future of their own; and when at
length one confronts them, they shall awake to find where they lie,
and what realm it was they so rudely and rashly disturbed.

— D'Arcy Cresswell, *Present without Leave*

SENTENCE

Tentative the houses
Unhaunted over tombs;
Wind shakes the standing
Timber, shakes rooms
Where cold under *rimu*
Rafters they discover
The wind wet with change, and
The stranger for lover.

THE UNHISTORIC STORY

Whaling for continents coveted deep in the south
The Dutchman envied the unknown, drew bold
Images of market-place, populous rivermouth,
The Land of Beach ignorant of the value of gold:
    Morning in Murderers' Bay,
    Blood drifted away.
    It was something different, something
    Nobody counted on.

Spider, clever and fragile, Cook showed how
To spring a trap for islands, turning from planets
His measuring mission, showed what the musket could do,
Made his Christmas goose of the wild gannets.
    Still as the collier steered
    No continent appeared;
    It was something different, something
    Nobody counted on.

The roving tentacles touched, rested, clutched
Substantial earth, that is, accustomed haven
For the hungry whaler. Some inland, some hutched
Rudely in bays, the shaggy foreshore shaven,
    Lusted, preached as they knew;
    But as the children grew
    It was something different, something
    Nobody counted on.

Green slashed with flags, pipeclay and boots in the bush,
Christ in a canoe and the musketed Maori boast;
All a rubble-rattle at Time's glacial push:
Vogel and Seddon howling empire from an empty coast
    A vast ocean laughter
    Echoed unheard, and after
    All it was different, something
    Nobody counted on.

The pilgrim dream pricked by a cold dawn died
Among the chemical farmers, the fresh towns; among
Miners, not husbandmen, who piercing the side
Let the land's life, found like all who had so long
    Bloodily or tenderly striven
    To rearrange the given,
    It was something different, something
    Nobody counted on.

After all re-ordering of old elements
Time trips up all but the humblest of heart
Stumbling after the fire, not in the smoke of events;
For many are called, but many are left at the start,

And whatever islands may be
Under or over the sea,
It is something different, something
Nobody counted on.

THE DANCE

If music may save
Then dance to what you have,
To the wind in the angle
Of an old tin shed
To the whistling of a river
To the creaking of a bed
To the rattle of shingle
To the whisper of sand
To the tractor in the paddock
To a mouth-organ band.
    Over the bones of an ear
    Goes wind, goes fear.

Will you come, curse
You? Nothing could be worse
Than standing drumming
While the dancers disperse
Than a turf unbroken
Than roses in a row
Than an old man reading
Than a new radio
Than a long itching finger
Than nothing left to know.
    Over the bones of an ear
    Goes wind, goes fear.

FANTASY ON A HILLSIDE

Sun's hammer swinging at the skull
Starts a lark singing off the hill,
Pacific stoops a broad blue back
Lower, the higher loops the track;
    Eyes brim, tilt,
    More sea is spilt
Over the rolling convex floor
Between the sky-sill and the shore.

Marooned I gaze, marooned I climb,
Pouring seas to bottomless Time
Whose vaporous chasm will not float
Knotted raft or hollowed boat:
    Horizon's brink
    Should stretch, I think,
With height, and I, with strides immense,
Climb easily into continents.

TIME

I am the nor'west air nosing among the pines
I am the water-race and the rust on railway lines
I am the mileage recorded on the yellow signs.

I am dust, I am distance, I am lupins back of the beach
I am the sums the sole-charge teachers teach
I am cows called to milking and the magpie's screech.

I am nine o'clock in the morning when the office is clean
I am the slap of the belting and the smell of the machine
I am the place in the park where the lovers were seen.

I am recurrent music the children hear
I am level noises in the remembering ear
I am the sawmill and the passionate second gear.

I, Time, am all these, yet these exist
Among my mountainous fabrics like a mist,
So do they the measurable world resist.

I, Time, call down, condense, confer
On the willing memory the shapes these were:
I, more than your conscious carrier,

Am island, am sea, am father, farm, and friend,
Though I am here all things my coming attend;
I am, you have heard it, the Beginning and the End.

DRY WEATHER

Like dry grass burning, nerves
Flicker and spring in my skull;
Now Plato burns, now the sea,
Now lips, now leaves, now all.
Not too close, lest pain
Make tinder of the flesh,
I run behind the running smoke
On the cold soft ash.

ST THOMAS'S RUINS

Bishop George Selwyn grew tired of wood;
Like Solomon he desired permanent materials,
Home comforts for his traveller God,
Cypress and spire, background for burials.

So rock hardly cool from the crater
Assumed devout posture; column and arch
Housed the Lord fittingly and to the better
Credit of His bride the Church.

But ocean weather sucked the ill-mixed mortar
In as many years as the Norman's nave
Had centuries falling; sand, faith's deserter,
Made paste for rain to grind his groove.

Ubi episcopus, ibi ecclesia. The storm
Outgunned in grace the Bishop's praying,
Blew to his knees the seed of this cabbage-palm
Whose tufted rood transfixes the toy ruin.

TIME AND THE CHILD

The Child: Now that I am born, Sir, I suppose
You intend to put me to some use;
You who have given both the place and the hour
Give also some peculiar power
And how best to employ it.

Time: To live and die.
This warm sun will make the minutes fly.

The Child: I like the sound of that. But I am told
That when your own fingers, Sir, have rolled
This earth round once, the sun removes his face

To other children in another place.
What have you for me to do when that deep
Shadow sits in the window?

Time: Why then, sleep,
A trick of mine that makes the minutes go
Faster than light in darkness.

The Child: I want to know
What life and sleep are like. I saw my own face
Yesterday in a mirror, it stood in space
As separate as the sun.

Time: That is an illusion
That can cause nothing but confusion.
Has no-one told you it is a dangerous thing
To imagine a shadow is continuing
In any place?

The Child: Sir, there are people here
Who go about so solid and so clear,
So like a picture painted with wind and fire,
You will not be impatient if I inquire
If life and sleep are beautiful like these?

Time: No more than sand, mountainsides, and trees.

The Child: But they look different.

Time: They live and die.
With the warm sun I make the minutes fly.
Wind and fire vanish and blood runs dry.
I am sorry.

The Child: Then there is nothing else
Except those various minutes that like bells
Dissolve stroke into stroke. Sir, that must be true.
But what about these walls, this window too
Where the river lies along our iron fence

And mountains swim in the river. Is it sense
That these do not continue?

Time: All pretence.
Do you know that there are a thousand such
Rivers, and can your river matter much?
If you would see which way the minutes dance
There are rivers more significant in France
Than ever ditched this yellow island clay.
I speak of events and do not try to deceive.

The Child: Sir, that is more than I can ever believe.

Time: It is not required. Island and continent
Roll in the sun through the minute and the event;
Man, his hour, his marvellous thought descend
Through perpetual beginning and perpetual end.
Boy, if you can make that teaching known
You shall have a house stronger than stone,
You shall have the Danube and the Mexique Bay
And all the secular fury of Europe as well.

The Child: And what comes after that, Sir?

Time: Time will tell.

SONG

A bridge and a bronze creek
And below that a lake
And below that a swamp
And a smoking camp
Where man and his iron bathe
In the sweat of the earth

And above that the feet
Of the forest, the weight
Of the living towers,
And above that the powers
That turn the sun and the weak
Rocks with heat shake,

And between hanging
An invisible bird singing
Between the roof and the root
Lightly lips his flute;
Between the womb and the seed
The song is made:

'Who would live here
Let him be all fire,
Let him not flinch
From the shuddering slim branch,
Let him dare all alone
The direct sun;

'On the rock beneath
There goes death,
Iron in his hand
And his path planned,
Who heaps high the load
And plies the goad:

'Who would sing, the sea
Is his enemy,
Better dies than be cursed
With that harsh thirst
By which the throat is wrung
Too dry for song.'

POLAR OUTLOOK

They arctic we antarctic;
Colder the southern cap, emptier the seas;
Horizon more emphatic
Stamps out one by one our flickering days.

Immature form, no nerves
Twangling a meaningful music; stimulus
Stops at a full gut; waves
Cast up such creatures when the southerlies pass.

No loving analysis of country,
Mountain or basin split, named, beautified,
Or noble house that a century
Stained with better than lamb's or rabbit's blood:

Tour us, tour us with funnels
Yellow and scarlet marching up the mist-
Filled lank-fronded channels;
By a prince's, by a peer's name we shall be blessed.

HOUSE AND LAND

Wasn't this the site, asked the historian,
Of the original homestead?
Couldn't tell you, said the cowman;
I just live here, he said,
Working for old Miss Wilson
Since the old man's been dead.

Moping under the bluegums
The dog trailed his chain
From the privy as far as the fowlhouse
And back to the privy again,
Feeling the stagnant afternoon
Quicken with the smell of rain.

There sat old Miss Wilson,
With her pictures on the wall,
The baronet uncle, mother's side,
And the one she called The Hall;
Taking tea from a silver pot
For fear the house might fall.

People in the *colonies*, she said,
Can't quite understand . . .
Why, from Waiau to the mountains
It was all father's land.

She's all of eighty said the cowman,
Down at the milking-shed.
I'm leaving here next winter.
Too bloody quiet, he said.

The spirit of exile, wrote the historian,
Is strong in the people still.
He reminds me rather, said Miss Wilson,
Of Harriet's youngest, Will.

The cowman, home from the shed, went drinking
With the rabbiter home from the hill.

The sensitive nor'west afternoon
Collapsed, and the rain came;
The dog crept into his barrel
Looking lost and lame.
But you can't attribute to either
Awareness of what great gloom
Stands in a land of settlers
With never a soul at home.

THE SCENE

Bush falls like waves, there is little you can hear
    But the stumbling flight of pigeons
And the buried anger of a truck's first gear
Pounding in gorges the heat-massive day.
Here among shaggy mountains cast away
    Man's shape must be recast;
    Whatever he imagines
Here on the unpeopled diffident scene between
Tasman's great stones, Pacific's gradual sand;
    Whatever is possessed
Between borders of blackened punga, beyond the town
Where tarred roads into the scrub run blind.

On hills above harbours the old habit of cities
    Persists, as the exile unpacks
Small necessaries on nameless island jetties.
Hands reach north for warmth, out of the south
Come storm and silence like a blow on the mouth;
    Inland the remote passes
    By which Time protracts
Forms of failure, instruments of collapse,
Bare will the measure of all, iron at the heart,

67

The unmoved moving faces
In streets gliding like the riding lights of ships
Ill-found, reef-destined even as they depart.

Sheep jostle under a loitering pillar of dust
   Ignorant of the course set
Over the hazy plain to the ultimate coast
And the tossed carcase, and still the drover knows
What township will be reached at the day's close;
   Time's principals decide
   How and where shall be met
Down by the viscid sea the high prosperous hulls
History sends hither for a spendthrift gesture:
   Ever the returning tide
May bear no ships, a sickening shriek of gulls
And the rabbit's tooth free of the steep pasture.

But festive on sale day come farmers driving
   With the great gold-haired pigs
And tottering calves in trailers, early arriving
At favoured hotels, merchants' and agents' doors;
Sons are photographed, leaving for the wars,
   And these maintain the price.
   Here will be one who begs
One season more to bind his difficult acres
Devoured by rivers or blind with early snow;
   Man's still equivocal face
Brave in cloudbursts, disordered by figures
When clerks confirm what the winds overthrow.

Measurement of mountains, measurement of waters,
   Power pulled from the lake,
Where never trod centaur nor strolled satyrs
Creating and mocking man's measureless shape.
Who mustering up creeks saw the lion leap?
   Who in the riverbed
   Saw earth open and shake?
Such instants hover at the fringes of trade
As ships swim and aircraft out of Time like birds;

Passion, pity, and dread
Consigned south out of Time, for islanders made
Whom the world's waste so royally rewards.

Build then, build by the too roomy sea
    For conference with Time
Who kicks down hovels but loves ceremony
And, seeing some piteous splendour here, may land
Bringing gifts, the beginning and the end,
    That is, all man's desire
    That ever learned to dream.
Some day thought will startle the bush like scarlet,
The pillar of dust stand in the road a spinning
    Stiff legendary fire,
Ships come spanking home and passion make solid
Man's shape again with the end and the beginning.

MORNING MOON

There goes the morning moon
Dawn-dull, fire's day-colour,
Bleeding her light away again
As the night's compassion,
Slipping from breast and brain,
Leaves the dry waking pallor.

EXPECT NO SETTLEMENTS

Expect no settlements or certainties
From volleys in deserts, explosions by rivers;
By no such loud and bloody exorcism
Will thunder quit the hills, sourness the plain;
Now hopes go little beyond remission of taxes

Dangerous are tongues that wag of the desperate coast
To which all bear their obsolete equipment.

I have emplaced cannon at all my windows,
At midnight sharpened arrows with a carpenter's file,
By digging under a pear tree found poor shelter;
Do you think there is energy unspent in battle?
No place I visit but has twist or scar of violence,
Though here's no war gear, regimental number,
Or picking over of the dead for burial.

Now that events zoom on with throttle wide,
Permitting one passage where a million clamour,
Now fronts dissolve and pestilence burns clear
Its lines of access to the spirit within,
Banish from this house the current fury;
Anticipate ruin, blank reversal of prayer;
Part death from doom, making it possible.

CRASH AT LEITHFIELD

Mischievous earth and sky were at their worst
That summer's day when they worried him to death
Down off his clattering biplane perch, the first
Last flutter of his only wings and his brief breath.

Low he flew, inexpert nerve straining,
Lens-curved Pegasus Bay — more Icarus he
Raw to wings made trial of his training
Thirty miles on the white seam of land and sea.

Leithfield and lupins, lower, till the roar
Lay flat as a tractor on the brackish land,
Stiffly gasping at each gust of the nor'
Wester. Imminence of engine's sound

Started eyes darting up in township and farm;
Suddenly machine turned man between earth and sun,
Struggling in sucking airs. Could ignorant alarm
Read in his wingtips what was urgent to be done?

Lower, like bird in wave-trough, gustily rearing
Inland, wing flashed sunnily; steep and slow
His wild pilotage had the farm women fearing
What faith in their darling's daring might undergo.

Did he know before they knew the instant had passed
When a touch might start the capable smooth climb?
Did he know which deafening second was the last?
Was there pause in purpose, then the downthrust of Time?

Steadily, gaily tilted to the sun, droning
Still under power, engine and gale together,
To naively cruel earth too swift declining,
To the haystack's and the gum-tree's windy weather;

And the crash, how gentle it was, how cool the cloud
Black-billowing like loam, and silent —
Ah, silence queerer than all — how small, not loud
When this was, we thought, to have been so violent.

And they were still sitting in the aeroplane
Said the baker's driver who sped to be in at the kill,
While it was burning; he said again and again
Both of them were sitting, they are sitting there still.

Some took home bits of scorched fabric and some
Said they thought he was trying to land, and all that day
We watched or heard aircraft after aircraft come
Like foul birds over the dead, and none to drive them away.

QUICK ONE IN SUMMER

Glass handle mugs the barman polishes
And his eye, his amber eye,
Swims in the dusty gulf with flies
Whose sun is skylights high
Slammed by the Pacific-lurching gale;
That timeless sea clocks in,
Rolling safe-conduited for those
Whose hour is closing-time.

Here they come who lean and laugh
Tranced by a dirty glass,
All in that strange sea-dimension
Where Time and Island cross.
What if the weather is hot and wild
And walls creak in the wind?
Sweat has its salt as well as the sea,
Blood runs away like sand.

LAKE MAPOURIKA

The lake's a merry bitch.
She smiles at everyone
With an eye like fire and needles;
Her buoyant breast the sun
Paws and pets, and her secrets
Where young men dive and spill
Their heat in weedy water's
Dark unremorseful chill.

COUNTRY SCHOOL

You know the school; you call it old —
Scrub-worn floors and paint all peeled
On barge-board, weatherboard and gibbet belfry.

Pinus betrays, with rank tufts topping
The roof-ridge, scattering bravely
Nor'west gale as a reef its waves
While the small girls squeal at skipping
And magpies hoot from the eaves.

For scantling *Pinus* stands mature
In less than the life of a man;
The rusty saplings, the school, and you
Together your lives began.

O sweet antiquity! Look, the stone
That skinned your knees. How small
Are the terrible doors; how sad the dunny
And the things you drew on the wall.

A VICTIM

*Jan Tyssen, one of the four Dutch killed by Maori when
Tasman anchored in Murderers' Bay in 1642*

No prey for prowling keels, the south
We found a monster risky to rouse
That at the first approach bared teeth
And slew four with terrible blows.

I, Jan Tyssen, company's sailor,
Shipped aboard Zeehaen from Batavia,
Gerrit Janz master; signed to follow
Bully Tasman, lands to discover.

Java to Mauritius were orders, then
Southward far to the fabulous coast:
Glory to captains, to our masters gain;
To us reward as pleased them best.

Grim under earth the gale-black sea
Spat us between ice-tainted lips;
Heemskirck, Zeehaen, denied that way,
With fair winds eastward bore our hopes:

Mountains stood up (I, Tyssen, now
Remember all thickly through the black
Swoon of the savage's thrust) below
Clouted, thin lipped, a dull surf spoke.

This land we coasted, came on a bay
Calm where canoes slid slim at sunset;
Wary we waited, heard a hollow voice cry,
None came near, nor omen of onset:

Morning brought more canoes; we made
Offer of mirrors, good iron pots,
As orders were; only the tide
Plucked by paddles, and hoarse shouts

Answered. I, one of seven, was told
'Take Zeehaen's boat, pull to your ship'.
(Ah, with what bells is my brain filled
That I forget!) We crossed the gap

Green between hulls. Like devils drove
Cruel of our kind the dark-limbed crew;
Blood bloomed and vanished where the wave
Mouthed for the fruit of us they slew.

I, Tyssen, first blood to the south,
Turned Tasman from that hateful haven.
Your history's cold, and cold's my death,
Past pity, past anger, past forgiving.

SESTINA

Not by voyages or accidents of ships,
Not by waves or the larger rhythms of the sea,
Are your islands mapped, measurable in Time;
Cook's fluent keel made crisp the bushy shore
Simple for seamen, but the projected life gropes
Where rocks in no chart rooted maliciously move.

Nebulae of ocean round which the thin tides move
Like a wavering of mist; here days are ships.
Under mountains, on beaches, a flat life gropes
After that taller dimension; beyond the sea,
Beyond the weeping reefs and sand-cragged shore,
Seeks some vertical structure, cities of the stature of Time.

Gulf'd from those tall cities, twice gulf'd from Time,
Strange even to each other these live and move
Where Waimakariri trowels the silted shore,
Where the harbours and foothills feed their seasonal ships;
Sure is the musterer's foot, safe the passage by sea,
But gust-crazed in gorges man unmeasured gropes.

On the wrong side of legend each man gropes
In the never-navigated currents of Time:
O even should the glittering surf fold back the sea
Far as the Americas, making fools of ships,
Still would the marooned in starving fancy move
Mountains all of glass on the Time-curved shore.

Wreckage mocks history, makes huts on the shore;
Continents pull like moons where the pilot gropes
By dials false to the day; island-bound ships
Wallow in treacherous gulfs this side of Time,
All instruments failing; stars indifferent move
Over fleets scattered on the dead-buoyant sea:

For since every sea has become a strange sea
Where cities and states founder, and every shore

Has dripping crevices where tide-creatures move,
From island to island man's dumb shape gropes
Hoping to recover some discarded gold by Time
Buried in beaches with the wooden bones of ships;

And now maps are folded, now infrequently ships
Counterfeit days, cruising off the fluid shore,
Can look-out leap, crying islands, solid in Time?

WILD IRON

Sea go dark, dark with wind,
Feet go heavy, heavy with sand,
Thoughts go wild, wild with the sound
Of iron on the old shed swinging, clanging:
Go dark, go heavy, go wild, go round,
    Dark with the wind,
    Heavy with the sand,
Wild with the iron that tears at the nail
And the foundering shriek of the gale.

SECOND SONG

Time who takes what he can use
    Takes our body and blood
For some enormous ignorant hour
Neither our fear nor fury chose;
Neither the purpose nor the power
Heaven might manage or accuse
    Lays ambush on this road.
      Now is the same as never
      Where Orion hangs head down.

Uttermost ocean like a mirror
    Images man's face
Screwed and dwarfed to island size,
Less wonder and more terror;
With peering prison-slitted eyes,
With madness marching nearer
    Than in a roomier place.
        Now is the same as never
        Where Orion hangs head down.

Shadows of cities, shadows of men
    Possess what Tasman found,
Shadows of shadows mock the old
Crime of nation tried again;
Shepherd and flock together sold
Straggle, and lean dogs whine
    On man's and no man's ground.
        Now is the same as never
        Where Orion hangs head down.

IT IS TOO LATE

It is too late
To be known, to be great;
Wire hoops the hills, and
Closed is the land:
Now it is absurd
To be seen, to be heard;
Nobody dreams of first,
Second, best, worst.

In no sense terrific
Or proud in Pacific,
Think a dropped cream-can
Will rouse Japan;
Discard the highest

Mountain, the dryest
Summer, the coppered steeple,
And the Maori people:
For these are only
Games for the lonely;
And the trader in freaks
Lost bottom seeks.

Walking weary
By the Waimakariri,
I cannot colour that stream
With wreck's red steam;
Nor picture shelter
Hell's crypt, fear-swelter,
But as stripe of pines
On brown skylines.

What the films show,
What the wires know
Is real, but who read
With nervous greed
Each stencil thrill,
Cry, Kill boys kill,
And of the most perilous
Post are jealous —
As if blood ran
Or breath were drawn
Or any seed sown
To be great, to be known.

Time: National, the word, is a sign among you,
Everywhere nation is talked and taught;
In one-man schools, at public luncheons,
They speak of a nation, never of islands,
As if by repeated incantation
Some god might be persuaded
To descend and transfigure,
Making every man bigger.

Island: The third and fourth generations
Begin to speak differently,
Suffering mutations,
Cannot help identity;
Nation's their only sign
Meaning man and brother,
Telling power, till Time
Discover another.

Time: Man and brother, power,
Flourishing in the same
Place in the same hour
Have no other name,
Till thought bravely stand
Where fear grimacing stood,
And the savage island
Renounce both power and blood.

Island: Show me, Time, behind
Your sea-dark curtain,
What is in your mind
Of which I may be certain,
Some luminous remote direction,
Fair wind and sky's protection.

Time: Step forward, Jew, from those
Of the nation God chose:
Prophesy to the plains

To the coast of heavy rains
To the Waikato and the white
New alps antarctic bright.

The Jew: Fierce nomadic enterprise
Made me a nation;
Came then God's enemies,
Captivity, persecution;
Babylon enslaved me,
Islanded among
Storms, doom'd to a sea
Of infinite wrong.
Bitter after exile
I returned home,
Yet in a little while
Fell prey to Rome:
Many were dispersed,
Many renounced God
Whose promise reversed,
Like poison in the blood,
Remained —

Island: You were promised too?
We are exiled like you;
But the Promise will come true.

Time: Pay attention to the Jew.

The Jew: Promise turns poison,
Curses occur in prayers,
When islanders seek a nation
Thousands of years.
Never be flattered by
The white buildings, the roads:
I had a temple high
Whose inner room was God's;
That pride to vindicate,
That glory to restore,
I am betrayed to hate,
Endlessly at war.

Island:	Surely there are others, Brave men and brothers Exalted by their nation After a different fashion?
The Jew:	Long or short endurance — There is no other difference. Though gun and gas are stronger My warfare is longer.
Island:	Ah, heroic, my friend, Your independence to defend.
The Jew:	That is, war without end. Long since I have sought peace But my enemies, crazed With fear, will not cease. Pitifully I am amazed Hearing islanders claim A destiny and a name.
Time:	There speaks my oldest citizen. Man and brother he knows, Nation and power he knows. My sea-curtain falls again. What more need I disclose?
Island:	You think you have frightened me. I demand the glory and the tragedy. Call me New Zealand. The name And the endless war I claim.
Time:	But your desired safe direction, Fair weather and sky's protection? The land was taken and is given, it will be the worse To fabricate a promise that turns a curse.
Island:	Fold your sea-curtain. Look, History has given me a book

Brighter than this ghostly conversation:
Land, power, and love of nation.

Time: The blasphemous interpreter
Pretending Time's ghostly sight
Deceives in the last chapter
Which I, not he, shall write;
Which I have already written
In no eventual sense:
Time writes, and has forgotten,
Before your books commence.

Island: Then, sir, if the books are lies,
What better can you advise?

Time: I have lifted my sea-curtain, have shown
In what wild waters God's chosen are thrown,
By what traces of torment a nation is known.

Island: Tasman found, Cook mapped;
Cities were planted, forests stripped;
Grandfather, father, and son
Have called me their own.
Surely there is something beyond
Plundering, possession of the land?
Show me some landmark feature,
Not the past again, but the future.

Time: You would get no further if I did.
The future from the past is hid.
What good would it do if I spoke
Words at which your ears would break,
Your eyes explode, your spirit die,
Confronting the eternal Why?

Island: I will not be frightened —

```
Time:    Be safely enlightened
         By ghosts, by actual presences.
         Live and build, build and live,
         Sing, repair your fences.
         Nation is a hazardous sign
         When great peoples expect
         Mutation and, torn by Time,
         That sign reject.
         Let pity and love exclaim,
         Meaning man and brother,
         Telling power, till Time
         Discover another.
```

NO SECOND COMING

Whose fancy fakes such crusted stuff
As sea's cold pickle keeps for ever
Betrays his blood to Time-in-death;
For him the island slims no lover
Nor shall Pacific's rhyming throes
Her belly-water break, from under
Five thousand miles of blossoming ooze
Venus be born with pearl and thunder.

SAILING OR DROWNING, [1943]

DISCOVERY

How shall I compare the discovery of islands?
History had many instinctive processes
Past reason's range, green innocence of nerves,
Now all destroyed by self-analysis.

Or, out of God the separated streams
Down honeyed valleys, Minoan, Egyptian,
And latterly Polynesia like ocean rains,
Flowing, became one flood, one swift corruption;

Or, the mad bar-beating bird of the mind
Still finding the unknown intolerable
Burst into a vaster cage, contained by seas,
Prisoned by planets within the measurable;

Or, Gulliver with needles, guns, and glass,
Thrusting trinkets up from the amazing hatches,
Luring doll kings and popes off palm-tree perches,
Sold them the Age of Reason from the beaches;

Dazzle no more in the discoverer's eye
When his blind chart unglazes, foam and flower
Suddenly spilt on the retreating mirror,
Landfall undreamed or anchorage unsure.

Compare, compare, now horrible untruth
Rings true in our obliterating season:
Our islands lost again, all earth one island,
And all our travel circumnavigation.

NINE SONNETS

I   IN MEMORIAM

2/Lieutenant T.C.F. Ronalds

Weeping for bones in Africa, I turn
Our youth over like a dead bird in my hand.
This unexpected personal concern
That what has character can simply end

In my unsoldierlike acknowledgement
Cousin, to you, once gentle-tough, inert
Now, after the death-flurry of that front
Found finished too. Any why should my report

Cry one more hero, winking through its tears?
I would say, you are cut off, and mourn for that;
Because history where it destroys admires,
But O if your blood's tongued it must recite

South Island feats, those tall snow-country tales
Among incredulous Tunisian hills.

II   OUT OF SLEEP

Awake, but not yet up, too early morning
Brings you like bells in matrix of mist
Noises the mind may finger, but no meaning.
Two blocks away a single car has crossed

Your intersection with the hour; each noise
A cough in the cathedral of your waking —
The cleaners have no souls, no sins — each does
Some job, Christ dying or the day breaking.

85

This you suppose is what goes on all day.
No one is allowed long to stop and listen,
But takes brief turns at it: now as you lie

Dead calm, one gust in the damp cedar hissing
Will have the mist right off in half a minute.
You will not grasp the meaning, you will be in it.

III   SAILING OR DROWNING

In terms of some green myth, sailing or drowning,
Each day makes clear a statement to the next;
But to make out our tomorrow from its motives
Is pure guessing, yesterday's were so mixed.

Papa, Atea, parents of gods or islands,
Quickly forgave the treacherous beaches, none
So bloodily furrowed that the secret tides
Could not make the evening and the morning one.

Ambition has annulled that constitution;
In the solid sea and the space over the sea
Explosions of a complex origin
Shock, rock and split the memory.

Sailing or drowning, the living and the dead,
Less than the gist of what has just been said.

IV   POLYNESIA

Surf is a partial deafness islanders
All suffer from, committed to the land;
A resonant hades, traversing, the fathers
Left cold or sweltering a world behind;

A drumming, drumming, drumming till there leapt
Fully afforested from the well of ocean

Valley and peak; the glove of blindness clapped
On trusting eyes; perpetual collision

Indistinguishable in those eyes,
Of salt of tears within and spray without;
Currents not warm or cold, of abstract seas
By any sense unfathomed, but where float

Small gods in shawls of bark, blind, numb, and deaf,
But buoyant, eastward in the blaze of surf.

V   THE NAVIGATORS

O rational successful hands that swept
Sea treasures up, by sunlight as in fog
Fumbling for islands, is there no wave big
Enough to wash your red ones green? O kept
In suavest history, gloved, quite dark how dipped
In red lagoons, the bright stain like a flag
Flowing and floating. Cradled in the vague
Currents where cables mumble murder slept

And sleeps, but dreams, hands that will not come clean
In endless dumb show utter what they did;
Because it was their rational violence
To think discreet discharge of guns would add
Island on island, that the seas would fence,
And time confirm them, in a change of scene.

VI   THE FALL OF ICARUS

The painting by Brueghel the Elder

The glistening coast, field-labour and sea-faring,
Stood like a crystal brimming with fine weather;
When he went down in flames all held together,
True to earth's ancient compact against caring:

The sun that flayed him warmed the ploughman's back,
The wind that stunned him swept the carrack on
Through the gay archipelago where none
Pitied or even noticed his bad luck.

Among the headlong pilots no revenge
Was wild enough for that indifference:
Wings flogged the fairway, made the seascape wince;
But when the flames that flagged each prouder plunge

Guttered, a mere breeze whisked off the stain.
At once the scenery was itself again.

VII   THE OLD PROVINCIAL COUNCIL BUILDINGS,
       CHRISTCHURCH

The steps are saucered in the trodden parts,
But that doesn't take long to happen here;
Two or three generations' traffic starts
In stone like this to make time's meaning clear.

Azaleas burn your gaze away below,
Corbel and finial tell you when to stop;
For present purposes, it does to know
Transport is licensed somewhere at the top.

Children of those who suffered a sea change
May wonder how much history was quarried
And carted, hoisted, carved; and find it strange
How shallow here their unworn age lies buried

Before its time, before their time, whose eyes
Get back from a stopped clock their own surprise.

VIII   TO M.H. HOLCROFT

That silence in the hills suggested neither
Prayer Book nor Year Book nor our games could save us,
For all the manly noise we made together;
Plainly the mountain would not move or move us.

The dead were burying their dead so deep
No roots could reach them; mostly we behaved
As if the country shamed us with a shape
Too trite or terrible to be believed.

Now all the history that did not happen
Begins, and stings like an unfrozen wound;
Beaches are barbed, the obvious roads lie open
Towards those foothills, Monte, where you found

Spiritual powers, but root and rock to grip;
For islands, an intelligible hope.

IX   AT JOACHIM KAHN'S

A quartet of Beethoven

Your 'innermost Beethoven' in the uttermost isles,
Half angel and half 'plane attains his peak
In weather like these southerlies that strike
But let your glass wall stand; his ceiling smiles;
He outclimbs all. Your room contains controls
To track in dazed skies an invisible wake
And pull his signals down just where you like,
It happens, among these unconnected hills.

The stone-deaf islands may resolve their pain
Easily, however distance howls them down,
By adaptation towards the albatross:
To rise on a stilled wing; or, on these tuned
Strings ride gales to patience; or, to cross
Motionless horizons as if not marooned.

SPRING, 1942

A Letter to Sub-Lieutenant D.J.M. Glover, R.N.Z.N.V.R.

I walk to the Bryndwr bus
By the Wairarapa Stream,
Where a boy too young for an angler
Hooks trout too small to take;
With a Handel air in my head
(The radio just turned off)
And a book I shall not read
Because of the hills that hang
In the east, the shreds of thought and
Hopes that hang in my head.

I think, as I do now,
What do you think of islands
Who have made the formative journey
From antarctic to arctic —
Have laid yourself in the breech
Of this time's gun, to be fired
Into God knows what target?
In all that violent process
You follow the arc of islands.
The seas are shaping something.

In the bus rounding the river
Which the English think looks English
(Not reading between the willows)
I gaze through the jolting window,
Never expecting a symbol
To join our thought or reclaim
The undeniable oceans
That freeze or flame between us;
But you were the pine in the park,
The toughest, that we admired,
But could not establish the name.

And stopping between the colleges
Where over the mounded foliage
Of chestnuts, the six miles off
Hills shoulder the sun,
I wonder if half our worries
Were nineteenth-century Gothic:
These were the stones laid on us:
Did rebel imagination
Serve us no better than Samson's
Wrench, raving the roof down,
For building the City of God?

I did not expect a symbol,
Resigned to no sign given;
But the clock has stopped in the tower,
The ivy is stripped from the walls.
I have only to walk to work.
There is neither time nor money
For putting up sham pavilions;
Only the night's work
For me, battle or boredom
For you. O there will be poets
And there will be wars, and work,
And a child. You will return.

You wanted thoughts like the Arrow
River, and luminous
But never cold; you will have them.
'There is only hope for people
'Who live upon islands' — (no poet
Could mean just that, but something
Was in his mind at the time.)
All I can add in our case
Is, we do not choose our islands,
But mountains are magnets where
Our fathers sailed in under,
Heroes or hangdog exiles
Or (it doesn't matter) marooned.

The ivy is swept and burned
And the sallow clock has stopped
That would never keep good time.
One generation of exiles,
Two more of amphibious hauntings
Of beaches, and now this other
We needed to keep so badly.
O I could go down to harbours
And mourn with a hundred years
Of hunger what slips away there,
If that were not fearing the future.
Any day you may return.

RITE OF SPRING

Cold, limp with winter burial,
And mouldy with excessive rain,
My optimism shows no root
Now that I dig it up again.

Too easily the spade goes in,
Too heavily the spade heaves out;
A weekly tenant of the swamp,
I till in jest and plant in doubt.

I neither, between famous seas,
Dandle my idylls, island-graced,
Nor angrily enjoy a land
Not unequivocally waste.

Willow and lilac split the bud
And seagulls bray behind the plough:
This corm of courage shows no root,
The gilt is off that Golden Bough.

IN SUMMER SHEETED UNDER

In summer sheeted under
Acres of warm iron
We who drained our estate
Sleep in a wind, drying

The skin of our days,
Sucking our need of water
From private tanks, tapping
The secret strata.

Now is the confident season
For all exotic growth,
Fleshy of limb and leaf
Towards the blunted south.

Our clay is crusted, our
Tar sweats and shimmers;
Windows stand wide open
The desert of summer's

Pride, pride of our time
In a little dry dust;
Men but not as trees, walking
Fast, wordless. In a mist.

PANTOUM OF WAR IN THE PACIFIC

. . . if th' assassination
Could trammel up the consequence, and catch
With his surcease, success; that but this blow
Might be the be-all and the end-all . . . here,
But here, upon this bank and shoal of time . . .
— *Macbeth*

The scale was blown up early in the piece.
To calculate what constitutes a thrill
Is harder than success from his surcease —
The casualties were few, the damage nil.

To calculate what constitutes a thrill
Hits home between the dreadful and the dread.
The casualties were few, the damage nil;
Numbers adjust the size of tears we shed.

Hits home between the dreadful and the dread
The atoll razed, the island changing hands.
Numbers adjust the size of tears we shed;
Nerves are the faculty that understands.

The atoll razed, the island changing hands,
With what explosions and what whisperings,
Nerves are the faculty that understands.
Daily death's rumour towers on sturdier wings.

With what explosions and what whisperings
Are vital points for any public statement;
Daily death's rumour towers on sturdier wings
Than life's canard content with fear's abatement.

Are vital points for any public statement
A frank design for death in true proportion?
Than life's canard content with fear's abatement
Nothing's more liable to plain distortion.

A frank design for death in true proportion
Is harder than success from his surcease —
Nothing's more liable to plain distortion.
The scale was blown up early in the piece.

LANDFALL IN UNKNOWN SEAS

*The 300th Anniversary of the Discovery of New Zealand
by Abel Tasman, 13 December, 1642*

I

Simply by sailing in a new direction
You could enlarge the world.
                              You picked your captain,
Keen on discoveries, tough enough to make them,
Whatever vessels could be spared from other
More urgent service for a year's adventure;
Took stock of the more probable conjectures
About the Unknown to be traversed, all
Guesses at golden coasts and tales of monsters
To be digested into plain instructions
For likely and unlikely situations.

All this resolved and done, you launched the whole
On a fine morning, the best time of year,
Skies widening and the oceanic furies
Subdued by summer illumination; time
To go and to be gazed at going
On a fine morning, in the Name of God
Into the nameless waters of the world.

O you had estimated all the chances
Of business in those waters, the world's waters
Yet unexploited.
                    But more than the sea-empire's

Cannon, the dogs of bronze and iron barking
From Timor to the Straits, backed up the challenge.
Between you and the South an older enmity
Lodged in the searching mind, that would not tolerate
So huge a hegemony of ignorance.
There, where your Indies had already sprinkled
Their tribes like ocean rains, you aimed your voyage;
Like them invoked your God, gave seas to history
And islands to new hazardous tomorrows.

II

Suddenly exhilaration
Went off like a gun, the whole
Horizon, the long chase done,
Hove to. There was the seascape
Crammed with coast, surprising
As new lands will, the sailor
Moving on the face of the waters,
Watching the earth take shape
Round the unearthly summits, brighter
Than its emerging colour.

Yet this, no far fool's errand,
Was less than the heart desired,
In its old Indian dream
The glittering gulfs ascending
Past palaces and mountains
Making one architecture.
Here the uplifted structure,
Peak and pillar of cloud —
O splendour of desolation — reared
Tall from the pit of the swell,
With a shadow, a finger of wind, forbade
Hopes of a lucky landing.

Always to islanders danger
Is what comes over the sea;

Over the yellow sands and the clear
Shallows, the dull filament
Flickers, the blood of strangers:
Death discovered the Sailor
O in a flash, in a flat calm,
A clash of boats in the bay
And the day marred with murder.
The dead required no further
Warning to keep their distance;
The rest, noting the failure,
Pushed on with a reconnaissance
To the north; and sailed away.

III

Well, home is the Sailor, and that is a chapter
In a schoolbook, a relevant yesterday
We thought we knew all about, being much apter
        To profit, sure of our ground,
No murderers mooring in our Golden Bay.

But now there are no more islands to be found
And the eye scans risky horizons of its own
In unsettled weather, and murmurs of the drowned
        Haunt their familiar beaches —
Who navigates us towards what unknown

But not improbable provinces? Who reaches
A future down for us from the high shelf
Of spiritual daring? Not those speeches
        Pinning on the Past like a decoration
For merit that congratulates itself,

O not the self-important celebration
Or most painstaking history, can release
The current of a discoverer's elation
        And silence the voices saying,
'Here is the world's end where wonders cease'.

Only by a more faithful memory, laying
On him the half-light of a diffident glory,
The Sailor lives, and stands beside us, paying
        Out into our time's wave
The stain of blood that writes an island story.

ATTITUDES FOR A NEW ZEALAND POET

I   THAT PART OF YOU THE WORLD OFFENDED SO

That part of you the world offended so
Has atrophied, or else your strategy
Has changed, or else you have so much to do,
The simplest way is seeming to agree.

The falling cities, bones, the brutal sky
And waste land botany do not recur.
Now, it is not an easy question why
You were ashamed that things were as they were.

Come world, poor Tom-world, and let us reason
Together, settle down and take our time:
We shall have bomber and bud in the same season,
Music and malice both in the one rhyme,

Thunder and tears; committed at this stage
Neither to horror nor a horrible age.

II   WORLD, UP TO NOW WE'VE HEARD YOUR
HUNGERS WAIL

World, up to now we've heard your hungers wail
No more than mock alerts; a South Seas moon
Unspeckled by our deaths can safely sail,
Escorted by our Never past our Soon.

The great sad duchess by a trick saw pass
Shapes of her husband and her children dead;
But farther off, darker than in a glass,
The natural body of our grief is read.

Men of our islands and our blood returning
Broken or whole, can still be reticent;
They do not wear that face we are discerning
As in a mirror momentarily lent,

A glitter that might be pride, an ashy glow
That could be pity, if the shapes would show.

III   THE SKELETON OF THE GREAT MOA IN THE
        CANTERBURY MUSEUM, CHRISTCHURCH

The skeleton of the moa on iron crutches
Broods over no great waste; a private swamp
Was where this tree grew feathers once, that hatches
Its dusty clutch, and guards them from the damp.

Interesting failure to adapt on islands,
Taller but not more fallen than I, who come
Bone to his bone, peculiarly New Zealand's.
The eyes of children flicker round this tomb

Under the skylights, wonder at the huge egg
Found in a thousand pieces, pieced together
But with less patience than the bones that dug
In time deep shelter against ocean weather:

Not I, some child, born in a marvellous year,
Will learn the trick of standing upright here.

JACK WITHOUT MAGIC, 1946

JACK WITHOUT MAGIC

Cleverer than ever you busy brain,
Nature you dread, and next to nature, art:
Jack without magic springs his traps in vain
Against these giants and genii of the heart.

DIMENSIONAL

The oil the blue
Peculiar gleam
Is on, not through
The beer-brown stream;

Flat viscous flow,
Vein of the valley;
The sun should know
How hotly shallow

That mirror skin
That sliding shape
Whose sandflies sing
The never deep;

Whose gusty flies
In a windless air
Repeat the song
In the earth's ear:

Hot and thin, and
Hot and shallow

Shakes the sand
And looks the yellow

Glimmering stone
Under the stream;

We have seen
How these become

Thin and hot,
A different shape

The oil the blue
The never deep.

Picton, 1938

CHILDREN, SWIMMERS

Children, swimmers, the whole brilliant harbour
Coveting the young bodies, how far drowned
Under the wrack-curdled tide of my mind
You are, and you fellow-swimmer deeper

Than all since I, envying every bead of the sea
Jewelling your skin, its passionate regard shining,
Coveted barely with a look, complaining
With a gooseflesh my numb thought in the warm day:

And saw the days pass, and upon the shrunken
Soot-sprinkled pool-green harbour the days pass:
Oh but how under sea glitters no less
Your flesh against time's fathoms, and not sunken

Ever, astonishes with a breath this drowned
Valley where tides are lost and love's dead found.

PARADISE REVISITED

Milton made Eve his blonde, but she is dark
And dark is Eden where her tree ascends;
And yet she shines; no shy deer in God's park,
She's formidable. The fruit between her hands

Is moon to her deliberate earth; the cold
Smooth yellow rind of moon or fruit invites
Tongue, or on branch alight allures handhold.
Temptress, to darken her delights

Offers her apple with one withering leaf,
Ripeness and death in hand; imparts that knowledge,
Yet lovingly lets in the thief
Of innocence: moon-sodden foliage

Parted, lays her big limbs unshadowed bare
To the white clamberer's prehensile stare.

SELF-PORTRAIT

The wistful camera caught this four-year-old
But could not stare him into wistfulness;
He holds the toy that he is given to hold:
A passionate failure or a staled success

Look back into their likeness while I look
With pity not self-pity at the plain
Mechanical image that I first mistook
For my own image; there, timid or vain,

Semblance of my own eyes my eyes discern
Casting on mine as I cast back on these
Regard not self-regard: till the toy turn
Into a lover clasped, into wide seas,

The salt or visionary wave, and the days heap
Sorrow upon sorrow for all he could not keep.

THE WAKING BIRD REFUTES

Rain's unassuaging fountains multiply
In air on earth and leaf. The Flood began
This way, listened to at windows by
The sleepless: one wept, one revolved a plan,

One died and rose again, one felt
That colder breath blow from the poles of lips
At love's meridian. This way now the spoilt
Firmament of the blood dissolves and drops;

The bright waste repossessive element
Beats barely audible, one sound imposing
Silence upon silence. This way I went
To pull our histories down, down, heavens accusing

Of rainbowed guile, whose penal rains descend.
The waking bird refutes: world will not end.

UNHURT, THERE IS NO HELP

When was it first they called each other mine?
Not in Donne's day: by then their love had grown
Or shrunk from Phoenix into spider, sign
Of sinner turned addict. Love, be your own

And stay the far side of that Tree
Whose seed struck earth between us; give again
A bite of apple; do not mind if He
Is somewhere in the garden, or that pain

Is frost or blight and the leaf blackens.
That is your birthright and redeeming sin.
Unhurt, there is no help for her who wakens
Puzzled, her sole power gone, in the obscene

Daffodil bed where the decrepit knees
Promised speech from heaven, and could barely please.

DUNEDIN

for James K. Baxter

Is it window or mirror the enormous
Deforming glass propped on horizons here?
What did we see? Some town pinched in a pass
Across which stares perpetual startled sheer
Vacuous day, the kind blind wilderness,
Space put behind bars, face pushed too near:

Painfully upright among lost hills
Bowed under cloud, made fast to the shocked ships
Locked in an eddy, dwelling. There, none wills
Redress or dreams it, or pondering some lapse
Out of a dream strays back into that town

A mirage of the cracked antarctic stole,
Or stumbles on the original dazed stone
Pitched out of Scotland to the opposite Pole.

TO D.G. OVERSEAS

Little at present, but to promise you
This morning, the still island, waking wholly
Like Adam from the bride-sleep, all things new;
Not a shout yet, or plane, these few
Bees out on summer Sunday morning early
Play bombers over parks and domes of bloom;
The Port Hills fallen in canvas folds that soon
The winking windscreen spangles. Home
Huddled like this would wake and day begin
Hardly noticing that you had come in.

1942

DARKNESS, PATIENCE

Darkness, patience at the root of the tree;
One bloom exhausted drops, or a lopped hand.
So my precocious legend, flowered and fallen,
Winter has whipped that colour from the land.
Darkness, patience in the blood that hides
Its unborn springs, runs colder but not sullen.

AT DEAD LOW WATER, 1949

AT DEAD LOW WATER

I

At dead low water, smell of harbour bottom,
Sump of opulent tides; in foul chinks twirl
Weed and whorl of silt recoiling, clouding
The wan harbour sighing on all its beaches.

The boat was not deliberately abandoned
But tied here and forgotten, left afloat
Freakishly, bobbing where the summers foundered,
Jarring each wave the jetty's tettered limbs;

Worm carves wave polishes original shapes,
Bolt and knot give way, gaps in the decking
Turn up again, driftwood on other sands.
All drifts till fire or burial.

Life, trapped, remembers in the rancid shallows
What crept before the enormous strides of love
When the word alone was, and the waters:
Goes back to the beginning, the whole terror

Of time and patience. Bolt and strake are frilled
With the shrimp's forest, all green-bearded timbers.
Salt rocky chink, nude silted cleft give off
Birth smell, death smell. Mute ages tread the womb.

II

Nervous quiet not calm possesses
Sea water here, the wave turns wary
Finding itself so far inland.

The father with the child came down
First thing one morning, before any
Dreamt of visiting the beach; it was

Daylight but grey, midsummer; they
Crossed high-water mark, dry-shod,
Derelict shells, weed crisped or rotting,

Down to the spongy rim, slowly
Without fear, stepping hand in hand
Within an inch of the harmless sea

Pure, unfractured, many miles,
Still steel water sheathed between
Once violent hills, volcanic shapes.

O memory, child, what entered at the
Eye, ecstasy, air or water?
What at the mouth? But carefully

Morning by morning incorruption
Puts on corruption; nervously
Wave creeps in and lingers over

Tideswept heaps where the fly breeds:
Memory flows where all is tainted,
Death with life and life with death.

Twenty years. A child returned
Discerns in quicksand his own footprint
Brimming and fading, vanishing.

III

Failed at the one flood we do not count
On miracles again, and you may say
We die from now; while each amazed migrant
Waves back, and cannot tear his eyes away

From his own image, the weeping threatening
Accusing thing, and knows death does not rid
Him even of the deformed sunk sifted thing,
Memory's residue; because the dead,

Father and child, still walk the water's edge:
A kindness, an inconsequent pastime, froze
In time's tormented rock, became an age
When tropics shifted, buried rivers rose,

Meaningless but for individual pain
No death, no birth relieves or lunar pulses drown.

Governor's Bay, December 1944

TOMB OF AN ANCESTOR

I   IN MEMORIAM, R.L.M.G.

The oldest of us burst into tears and cried
Let me go home, but she stayed, watching
At her staircase window ship after ship ride
Like birds her grieving sunsets; there sat stitching

Grandchildren's things. She died by the same sea.
High over it she led us in the steepening heat
To the yellow grave; her clay
Chose that way home: dismissed, our feet

Were seen to have stopped and turned again down hill;
The street fell like an ink-blue river
In the heat to the bay, the basking ships, this Isle
Of her oblivion, our broad day. Heaped over

So lightly, she stretched like time behind us, or
Graven in cloud, our farthest ancestor.

II   TO FANNY ROSE MAY

Great-aunt, surviving of that generation
Whose blood sweetens the embittered seas between
Fabulous old England and these innovations
My mountainous islands: in the bright sad scene

I praise with you your voyage, and hers who sleeps
A sister folded in the hill cemetery,
Sacrifice or seed lodged on those slopes
That seem barbaric, by the unworshipped sea

Toward which she would shade her eyes. I know the fires
That forged the harbour and the heights glow still,
A million years old memory, but there's
Neither memory nor world here but that hill

Where struck your voyaging sister seed, from whom
I grow, and this praise flows, this blood, this name.

FOUR DESCRIPTIONS AND A PICTURE

I   GENESIS

Original sea, no breath or bird, your eyes
Nourished their unborn sun; upon the face
Of waters wary of love I moved: I praise
The evening and the morning. Now your voice

Made birds of the dumb salt, I heard
Aeonial Phoenix and interpreted,
'Be fire in me, be death and birth'; the third
Day pain was made, we saw that it was good,

Walking with difficulty, speech failing,
On the hill passing the stone pillar, man
And woman sole on earth, erect or falling,
Compelling, pitying. Trumpets the next dawn

Sounded above the levelled flood: we came
To the Garden, giving each beast and tree a name.

II   WITH HOW MAD STEPS

Nightwatchman in some crater of the moon —
No, not that lunatic
But the dumb satellite itself, my tune
The cold sphere's silence; and I stick

(Abiding, law-abiding) to that orbit
Fire once described, tossed into space to cool
From my earth's body; a gyrating habit.
What if she watches? She'll

Mask with the mirror of her tides those shores
Her flesh makes in the heavens, and even
While dawn destroys me her young foliage stirs;
Neither is mathematical space forgiven

My dear earth's distance, though her heart descry
With how mad steps, her moon, I climb the sky.

III   SHE SITS WITH HER TWO CHILDREN

She sits with her two children in the holy evening,
You find your way there over the bare mountains,
Her mirror's landscape mild, the beasts deceiving
With heart's trick sword and cloak. Her rigid fountains

Timeless their shining seed to time let fall
Where the root screams for death. She has spread a table
For the foretold prince who will
Strike blind her mirror with a kiss, the bubble —

Her high blood's iridescent sphere — send down
In a mist, her mortal dew, naked deliver
Her from her cage of waters. There alone
With her two children the goldhaired and the clever

She waits for the armed angel, bird or breath
Descending, out of the mirror leaning, death.

IV   THEN IF THIS DIES

Then if this dies, by so much we die too,
Blood has been shed before
And when the heart was dry the brain would go;
But this one beats, and stings his nerve the more

Because death finds him in a waiting torment
Lancing a straw hope against that steel
Night's disappointment
(Their starved lips in the room); the fall

Of leaf, or house that glacier groaning
At frightful pressures, never was her step
(Listening till morning):
For so we die, and do not stop

Loving or dying, so we wait
Indoors; death has not finished with us yet.

The door stood wide, she stood
Between those pillars of the sea:
She leaned against the evening light,
Mountains no taller than her knee,
The first star at her breast, her eyes
Turned where the top of heaven should be.

All darkens but her image there.
What was the god's disguise? — the far
Pacific dims, she is alone
Where no more sea shall be, or mar
Her gaze with tears, nor blood defile
The virgin mother of a star.

OLD HAND OF THE SEA

Old hand of the sea feeling
Blind in sunlight for the salt-veined beaches
O setting on a tide my bearded boat a-sailing
Easy as the bird's breast that barely touches

Immemorial deeps of death:
Here, now, my harbour, child's play pool,
Sifters of sunk bright treasure, breaker of earth,
Is monster and lover of the gazing soul.

Horizons bloomed here on the globes of eyes,
Here grieving fog fastened those lids with tears
Disfiguring, transfiguring; holidays
Nested like bird or girl. All disappears

But the salt searching hand. O sightless tides
What blossom blows to you from spring hillsides?

EDEN GATE

The paper boat sank to the bottom of the garden
The train steamed in at the white wicked gate,
The old wind wished in the hedge, the sodden
Sack loved the yellow shoot;

And scampering children woke the world
Singing Happy Doomsday over all the green willows
That sprang like panic from the crotch of the cold
Sappy earth, and away in the withered hollows

A hand no warmer than a cloud rummaged
At the river's roots: up there in the sky
God's one blue eye looked down on the damaged
Boy tied by the string of a toy

And saw him off at the gate and the train
All over again.

MUSIC FOR WORDS

To Douglas Lilburn

No ancient singing dancing infancy
Made luminous, made wise our island earth;
No tongue is suddenly sweet, no foot steps free,
The sneer at natural joy will pass for mirth.

If on the street a rhythmic speech is heard
Ears prick, heads turn towards the foreign clown
Whose musical greeting's like a waking bird:
They fear great Pan will bankrupt half the town.

A whip for these dead heels to make them dance!
Once I had nothing better to suggest,
As if blood could be got out of the dry bones:

But since you sang my words I count on most
Music, and a heroic eloquence
To remake man out of this chattering dust.

LILI KRAUS PLAYING AT CHRISTCHURCH

A poem for Lili Kraus —
But the word could not imitate the winged
Instrument, or so build with hands the house
Not made with hands, although it longed

For breath and bone like this, the sound
Made flesh to dance and die; a music blown
To unburn Troy on the sea-deafened ground.
You do not dance alone

Or hold no hand, here on the beautiful
Coast where seas and mountains dazzling turn
Their face of thirst: the dull
Heart flames, the Wanderer's forlorn

And listless 'Where?' is answered, as he hears
Love like a bird sing in her tower of tears.

July 1946

A SONATA OF SCHUBERT

You move to the piano. What is it we know?
You have taught your hands to die;
All that we have to and most fear to do
Now to be done, sufficingly,

If hands could call the lapsed soul again
With music's trumpet-silences to witness
The mortal marvel of its joy and pain.
It is the falling brightness

From keen unusual skies, omen of birds,
Day breaking at the beach of sacrifice.
We are strange, strange to ourselves. Who is it applauds
His own transfiguring? Who plays?

Not you, not we — this, we had never dreamt,
These hands between us and the heavens' contempt.

March 1947

A LEAF

The puzzle presented by any kind of a leaf,
One among millions to smudge your airy sceneries
Or among millions one your window tickler
Gust upon gust agitates, a trifle sharp
Enough to murder sleep:

Shape of a leaf, shine of a leaf,
Shade of a leaf yellow among yellow leaves of
The prophet Micah with a slip of perished silk
Marks nothing, still is a character, a syllable
Made flesh before the word:

Bud of a leaf, blade of a leaf
Given a strange twist, given for something to do
With deadly baffled fingers happy to squeeze
Blood from a conundrum: insoluble but endlessly
Amusing in the attempt.

TO FORGET SELF AND ALL

To forget self and all, forget foremost
This whimpering second unlicked self my country,
To go like nobody's fool an ungulled ghost
By adorned midnight and the pitch of noon
Commanding at large everywhere his entry,
Unimaginable waterchinks, granular dark of a stone?
Why that'd be freedom heyday, hey
For freedom that'd be the day
And as good a dream as any to be damned for.

Then to patch it up with self and all and all
This tousled sunny-mouthed sandy-legged coast,
These painted and these rusted streets,
This heart so supple and small,
Blinding mountain, deafening river
And smooth anxious sheets,
And go like a sober lover like nobody's ghost?
Why that'd be freedom heyday, hey
Freedom! That'd be the day
And as good a dream as any to be damned to.

To sink both self and all why sink the whole
Phenomenal enterprise, colours shapes and sizes
Low like Lucifer's bolt from the cockshied roost
Of groundless paradise: peeled gold gull
Whom the cracked verb of his thoughts
Blew down blew up mid-air, where the sea's gorge rises,
The burning brain's nine feathering fathom doused
And prints with bubbles one grand row of noughts?
Why that'd be freedom heyday, hey
For freedom, that'd be the day
And as good a dream as any to be damned by.

IDYLLS IN COLOUR FILM

I   CRISTOBAL

Top to bottom of a skin white wall
Some thin vine blossom bleeds, the sun
Indolently erodes the sill.
Blood can run cold in this hot town.

And the blue sky bends a very smooth look
And the water keeps malignant calm
And the itchy mouth the Canal has makes
Lips to compress their ocean's arm.

Fat with colour the day commands
Holstered, blazing boss of the street.
Time daren't stir, nor the four winds.
Death is detained, but won't be late.

Cool off at El Tropico; fans,
Cans, fans and a glassful which
Can't go bad like the barrow man's
Bag of oranges while you watch.

Polyglot, polychrome droop or blow
Lush hybrids of the dollar shallows.
Nylon blooms and rags in a row,
Negress purples, negress yellows

Shame without strutting step or breast
Pale casual trash two hours ashore;
From bodily darkness have digressed
By a flowery shift of skins, no more.

Now continents and oceans lie
Farther than planets, and the scarlet
Or bruise-blue petals kiss your knee,
Romancing in an isthmian twilight

Of temperate islands.
                        The Zone Troops
Strike MacArthurian attitudes.
Avid the traveller slums the shops,
Tickling a vein which no blood leads

That street where one was knifed last night.
Home and aboard is where to be,
With a mast-high moon, eyes crackling bright.
The Caribbean's the next sea.

II   CURACAO

The slimed embrasures of old fortress walls
Green lower-lipped outside Saint Anna Bay
Cannot articulate: this hoarse wind smells
Of oil; two hundred tankers night and day

Hod El Dorado past the Bridge of Boats
Up the foul stream and down. The Dutch façades
Cold and small as coral are the sights
Most photographed: but memory knows no aids

One mile from Willemstad (past midnight, that
Refiner's fire across the basin mimes
Hell but fools nobody) while we set foot
Again on the low desolate slope whose name's

Nothing and nowhere: fingering the leaf-shuttered
Inconsequence of streets. For the wind here's
Close and vigilant, misses no flitted
Grain or leaf, watches each step, cares

For every stone in Hoogstraat.
                              Have we lived
Anywhere if not here, walking alone
Through dreams or deaths awake, having arrived
One hour ago, by morning to be gone?

ELEGY ON MY FATHER

Tremayne Curnow, of Canterbury, New Zealand, 1880–1949

Spring in his death abounds among the lily islands,
There to bathe him for the grave antipodean snows
Fall floodlong, rivermouths all in bloom, and those
Fragile church timbers quiver

By the bourne of his burial where robed he goes
No journey at all. One sheet's enough to cover
My end of the world and his, and the same silence.

While in Paddington autumn is air-borne, earth-given,
Day's nimbus nearer staring, colder smoulders;
Breath of a death not my own bewilders
Dead calm with breathless choirs
O bird-creation singing where the world moulders!
God's poor, the crutched and stunted spires
Thumb heavenward humorously under the unriven

Marble November has nailed across their sky:
Up there, dank ceiling is the dazzling floor
All souls inhabit, the lilied seas, no shore
My tear-smudged map mislimned.
When did a wind of the extreme South before
Mix autumn, spring and death? False maps are dimmed,
Lovingly they mock each other, image and eye.

The ends of the earth are folded in his grave
In sound of the Pacific and the hills he tramped singing,
God knows romantically or by what love bringing
Wine from a clay creek-bed,
Good bread; or by what glance the inane skies ringing
Lucidly round; or by what shuffle or tread
Warning the dirt of miracles. Still that nave

He knelt in puts off its poor planks, looms loftier
Lonelier than Losinga's that spells in stone
The Undivided Name. *Oh quickening bone*
Of the Mass-priest under grass
Green in my absent spring, sweet relic atone
To our earth's Lord for the pride of all our voyages,
That the salt winds which scattered us blow softer.

London, November 1949

WHEN THE HULK OF THE WORLD

When the hulk of the world whirls again between
Us for the ships shift me where your dusk is dawn
    My skyblue side of the globe,
Where the mooncast squid's eye of a downcast ocean
Goggles till it gets me in the beam of its brine —
    Oh then, sweet claustrophobe
I leave among the lost leaves of a London wood
(So dark, we missed the middle of our road)
    Can spring condone, redeem
One treachery of departure from that life,
Shiftless to fetch this love?
    Seas will be seas, the same;
Thick as our blood may flood, our opposite isles
Chase each other round till the quiet poles
    Crack, and the six days top
Totter, but catch us neither sight nor hold;
Place will be place, limbs may not fold
    Their natural death in dreams.
I pray, pray for me on some spring-wet pavement
Where halts the heartprint of our salt bereavement,
    Pray over many times,
Forgive him the seas forgive him the spring leaf,
All bloom ungathered perishable as grief,
    For the hulk of the world's between
And I go as a ghost, one flesh I and the wind
That lifts us both so lightly, but so bound
    Never to be ghost alone.

THE EYE IS MORE OR LESS
SATISFIED WITH SEEING

Wholehearted he can't move
   From where he is, nor love

Wholehearted that place,
   Indigene janus-face,

Half mocking half,
   Neither caring to laugh.

Does true or false sun rise?
   Do both half eyes tell lies?

Cradle or grave, which view's
   The actual of the two?

Half eyes foretell, forget
   Sunrise, sunset,

Or closed a fraction's while
   Half eyes half smile

Upon light the spider lid
   Snares, holds hid

And holds him whole (between
   The split scarves of that scene)

Brimming astride a pulse
   Of moon-described eyeball's

Immobile plenitude —
   Flower of the slight stemmed flood.

Snap open! He's all eyes, wary,
   Darting both ways one query,

Whether the moonbeam glanced
   Upon half to whole enhanced,

Or wholly the soul's error
   And confederate mirror.

IN MEMORY OF DYLAN THOMAS

*And the Lord God formed man of the dust of the
ground, and breathed into his nostrils the breath of
life; and man became a living soul.*

Never a talking but a telling breath
Fanned fire from clay upright to the tip of his tongue,
Who burning to tell told all the days of his death
It was the ghost alive in a beast's lung
Panting for-ever out.
Now the five gates are shut,
The grassy fingers sheathed in enough dust,
And the last work, at most, is what all must.

He hardly knew what struck him the first spark
Bursting the bolts of sense upon the frame
Of things. It was light outraging the pure dark.
It was the ghost buried alive in time,
Purse-lipped for pain,
That blew upon his brain
The iridescent sweaty swarms that rose
Winged imagos, out of their wormy throes.

Adam and Eve behind the village bethel
Played snakes and ladders. Bibles were hot to touch;
He laid his open on the cool of a sill, the wrath all
Feared he fondled; fruit-in-hand, found such
Were all men's bedfellows.
And he could never close

Genesis for appleblossom's joy, our tripping
First girl and boy in plucking time caught napping.

Self-scrutineer, with what pierced eyes he pored,
Live coals upon the body's private inches.
Shame in the ghost rebuffed what flesh adored,
But the game beast on a griddle heaved its haunches:
Sinful, infinitely worth
Saving, the beasts of earth
At the end of their tether either way, that fled
Between the matin-bell and midnight bed.

And he said, What hast thou done? the voice of thy
brother's blood crieth unto me from the ground.

A town boy, he trod
The earth beneath the pavements
And knew stones could bleed.
Storming bereavements
Inflamed his eyes. He was afraid

With the common fear that time
Of a blitzing sickness,
But under blood and blame
Exclaimed, so blazed his darkness
Genesis' thunderbolt shot home.

Irrational good, caged
In Faith's condemned cell, burning
Its own breast unassuaged —
Crybaby crying the morning
Stars out while Creation raged.

And out of the ground the Lord God formed every
beast of the field, and every fowl of the air; and
brought them unto Adam to see what he would call
them; and whatsoever Adam called every living
creature, that was the name thereof.

Laugharne village peters out an inch from the fishy bay
Whose rackless tides lightly incuriously rap their twice-a-day
Reminders to hewn human stone deaf as cockle shells
That a lifeless landscape suckles, fills and flushes the salt wells,
And the moon is a spirit.
                         By day by dead pearl calm
He valued the mere view of it the bare sea-moulded arm
Relaxed about slack water. Southward the ship shape
Of the shade of an isle is Lundy. Some lounging cape
Condescends to the vanishing west; a few miles that way brings
You, map-witted, to Pendine Sands.
                                    Mere living things
Crackle their moments out over the breath-heavy green
Foreshorelands, glimmers of Godhead not unseen
But often to crawl, creep, scamper, flit or fly,
Starting under his feet in the track of his eye
Who named them, with praise again as Adam unfallen had,
Praise that never to Adam fallen the Maker forbade.
Named the heron son of Zebedee fishing his moody shoal.
Named the congregation of crabs, dabs, waterbirds, the owl
So fell to fur, the ranger fox outsnapping a winter's cold.
Named, who never could have told
The tally of his heart's household.

A window shalt thou make to the ark, and in a cubit
shalt thou finish it above: and the door of the ark
shalt thou set in the side thereof; with lower, second,
and third storeys shalt thou make it.

A stack of whitewashed stone
Cramped square upon a lap of rock
And butted endwise to a bushy bluff,
One chink of the foreshore there,

The house — locally known
As Boathouse — house enough
Or Ark at flood-time fit to bear
Pigeon-postman Noah and all his stock.

And the Lord smelled a sweet savour: and the Lord
said in his heart, I will not again curse the ground
any more for man's sake; for the imagination of
man's heart is evil from his youth: neither will I
again smite any more every thing living, as I have
done.

Sir John's Hill. Bramble and scrubby growth
Humped not much higher than chimney-puff.
By tide-scurf, dead weed, up and over the path
Ramble, far-fetching scholar, the brief rough

Prose of a broken landscape, summoning how
On this earth, out of all rare wringers
Of hands and hearts one here saw heaven's bent brow
Pitifully judging birds and singers.

'Ware the hawk, 'ware the hill,
Claw clenched for the trilling throat,
The shadow, the shudder, the kill,
Feathers afloat —

But in the map of mercy among a city's
Dying millions he fell,
Who chose of heaven's thousand thousand pities
The sparrow's one, and all.

KEEP IN A COOL PLACE

A bee in a bloom on the long hand of a floral
Clock can't possibly tell the right time
And if it could whatever would the poor bee do with it
In insufferably hot weather like this?

Everything white looks washed, at the correct distance
And may be the correct distance. You could eat

Our biggest ship sweet as sugar and space can make her.
Every body's just unwrapped, one scrap of a shaving

Left for luck or the look, the maker's seal intact,
Glad to be genuine! The glassy seaside's
Exact to the last detail, tick of a tide,
Fluke of the wind, slant of a sail. The swimmers

On lawns and the athletes in cosy white beds have visitors
And more flowers. Poor bee! He can make up time
At frantic no speed, whether tick or tock,
Hour or minute hand's immaterial. That's

Exactly how it is now. It is. It is
Summer all over the striped humming-top of the morning
And what lovely balloons, prayer-filled (going up!) to fluke
For once and for all the right time, the correct distance.

TO INTRODUCE THE LANDSCAPE

To introduce the landscape to the language
Here on the spot, say that it can't be done
By kindness or mirrors or by talking slang
With a coast accent. Sputter your pieces one

By one like wet matches you scrape and drop:
No self-staled poet can hold a candle to
The light he stares by. Life is the wrong shop
For pictures, you say, having all points and no view.

Ponderous pine wagging his wind-sopped brushes
Daubs Latin skies upon Chinese lagoons.
What tides leak through the mangroves and the rushes
Or lofted, wash long needles and large cones?

And where, from here, do you go? Out with the tide
You won't, without some word that will have lied.

JACK-IN-THE-BOAT

is always ready to row across the bath or lake. Wind up the
motor, and watch him dip his blades like a true oarsman —
in, out, in, out — with never-tiring enthusiasm.
                          — Legend on a toy-maker's package

Children, children, come and look
Through the crack in the corner of the middle of the world
At the clockwork man in a cardboard house.
He's crying, children, crying.
    He's not true, really.

Once he was new like you, you see
Through the crack in the corner of the middle of the night,
The bright blue man on the wind-up sea,
Oh, he went so beautifully.
    He's not true, really.

O cruel was the pleasure-land they never should have painted
On the front and the back, the funny brand of weather,
For the crack in the corner of the middle of the picture
Let the colours leak away.
    He's not true, really.

One at a time, children, come and look
Through the crack in the corner of the middle of the day
At Jack-in-the-Boat where the light leaves float.
He's dying of a broken spring.
    He's not true, really.

MEMENTOS OF AN OCCASION

Wallace Stevens, 1879–1955

I

Dead but to the world, Stevens, do you find
The anecdotes lucid there, compared with these?

And what comparisons with your style when crossing
Composedly the blue thresholds to sit down
Oceans away (because all airs bore alike
And Indian-wise an alien offshore fragrance) —
Or mulch with moist real hands the seedy words
To bear in season as fresh-cut coxcomb blooms
As anyone else's green and god-sown country
Whose natives, planting and watering botany books,
Had their disappointments?

              Can they be less alien
Or more at home, the breath-stopped kiss-shaped nomenclatures
Down where the dead are?
              If we have all met somewhere
Elsewhere before?

II

          A well-set-up shade passed
Forth between ranting sun and rabble retina,
Announcing a prim masque, a conducted illusion
Out of worse nothing.

            It was not quite as if
The snake, uniquely accomplished could slip in and
Out of the time-worn pelt experience till
Crackle! and lastly dry scurf popping
Nipped up thin air, dumbfounded all as-ifs —

129

III

Let that have been as it may, you are the type
Should manage a vaporous shift of habitat
To where, if any can raise a squeak yours may be
Intelligible, as ghostliest counsel goes,
As poems, the ponderable these, are eligible,

IV

Capable to detect where reality was not
And scrupulous what to put in place of it.

SPECTACULAR BLOSSOM

Mock up again, summer, the sooty altars
Between the sweltering tides and the tin gardens,
All the colours of the stained bow windows.
Quick, she'll be dead on time, the single
Actress shuffling red petals to this music,
Percussive light! So many suns she harbours
And keeps them jigging, her puppet suns,
All over the dead hot calm impure
Blood noon tide of the breathless bay.

Are the victims always so beautiful?

Pearls pluck at her, she has tossed her girls
Breast-flowers for keepsakes now she is going
For ever and astray. I see her feet
Slip into the perfect fit the shallows make her
Purposefully, sure as she is the sea
Levels its lucent ruins underfoot
That were sharp dead white shells, that will be sands,
The shallows kiss like knives.

Always for this
They are chosen for their beauty.

Wristiest slaughterman December smooths
The temple bones and parts the grey-blown brows
With humid fingers. It is an ageless wind
That loves with knives, it knows our need, it flows
Justly, simply as water greets the blood,
And woody tumours burst in scarlet spray.
An old man's blood spills bright as a girl's
On beaches where the knees of light crash down.
These dying ejaculate their bloom.

Can anyone choose
And call it beauty? — The victims
Are always beautiful.

EVIDENCES OF RECENT FLOOD

> *Adam and Eve and Pinch Me*
> *Went down to the river to bathe,*
> *Adam and Eve were drowned,*
> *And who do you think was saved?*

I   LOGBOOK FOUND ON ARARAT

Only one night the
                    squall made a great show,
thunderclaps fit to burst,
                    mightily flapped
linens and lightnings,
                    heaven's menagerie leapt
loose upon decks
                    and the herd snarled below.

Calm yawned by dawn
                              assuaged our seafaring
staring by some land's lamp
                              outlimbed, so gloomy,
less than it loomed a
                              withering gulf could show me,
but snuffed-out beacons
                              uncaring, uncuring:

blindalleyed seaways,
                              suburban promontories.
Dogging a dumb spark,
                              diamond in the spine
(dead by my reckoning
                              both the red and the green),
my only ship shaped home
                              lonelier than seas

pattering at the prow
                              between pouring deeps:
fearfully at flood-peak
                              unfathomed my ark
the dove-watch kept
                              in cages of wickerwork,
bickering and bloody
                              the beaks and claw-tips:

no not fair-feathered
                              upon the first isles
these cage-birds thwarted
                              at each other's throats;
though landward upon a lipping
                              liquor she floats
and flood no more now
                              than upon sands prevails.

Groping for moorings
                              the grave side of dawn
God! horrorstruck we see

                  from what hoodwinking hidden
wrecks gasped the rescued
                    grew some certainty
love soiled some shore yet
                    Oh some sheer crown

of the earth rage overlooked
                    I look-out stared
at mirrorstricken my own
                    land manfully back:
all I steered mists to gain by
                    drowning, luck
or the All-Duplicity on
                    high had spared:

the cocks crescent
                    upon crags and sills
the seed surgent in
                    brine-sodden furrows
the girl congealed in smiling
                    salt, all sorrows
shambling, All-Shallows
                    in a slough of souls.

None here could drown
                    though thou God jerk the bells
unfathomable steeplejacked
                    rungs below:
mockers when thy rains wreathed,
                    ripe mockers now,
the obsolete polyp
                    sobbing in their skulls:

and their lame talk pursues
                    prediluvian lines
and all weather or never
                    is thy Name's news spoken
and those mortal talons
                    of the dove not mistaken

and thy deluge a dribble

                    whose drunken ebb sucks

bald an earth born to us

                    of shipwreck, hooked

by the gills on Ararat,

                    grounded for our pains.

II   A CHANGELING

Once where the leaky

                    islands and the lame

swimmers ducked

                    and draked between earshots

of stars and oceans

                    there plummeted a fulgent

freak with unwebbed

                    fingers, a girl kind of

fish whose fire and

                    water works and bellied

moon waxing in the summer

                    seascape bared

(with her light like ashes

                    of a god absconded)

our home hill-toppled town

                    grown cold as wishes.

Lithe she unlocked

                    the circuit of the harbour

tickled she fore and aft

                    the daft old sulking

bottoms, with her tail tipped

                    many a green

mooring-chain, diving in a

                    weedy boy's skull

her small bell sang.

                    Such miracles of the lovers

and fishes followed her

                    that sodden straw

sparked, sat up and glared like some
                                      god-bonfired navy
most classically scuttled, glory's
                              dredges dismasted.

Swim! spied our laddery
                        town from all its rungs;
corks, bladders and the last
                              breath beat the surges;
till her sunken silver
                    filleted in the main
of mankind wilted
                  on the bright tide's verge.
Hooked and played
                  and laid upon the sands
loose she lay
            under the yellow lupin.
Cold fell the quiet coast,
                          midnight looming
and the midnight ebb
                    and when it struck she rose

up lightly, her stains
                      were silken, she shook out
her hair in the teeth of the
                              tide's thunder so
idly that the moon
                  sank without a cry
nor dared we more than dumbly
                              trail her tiny
mortal steps deep down
                      to the town train.
Listen! those whistles
                      down our line to the grave.
Listen! those bells
                  to toll the changeling home
ding at the ebb, ocean,
                      dong at the flood.

Sob, shabby islands
                in your dull weeds doting
on a fleeting fable
                a feather in the sun.
All your white horse
                wishes would not wash
one white shell from the
                wave the changeling swam.
She's home and dry
                and high among the ladders
as plain as daylight that's
                back like an old debt,
drowned swimmers in her eyes
                and stars, and oceans,
her comb and her glass
                and her ticket in her hand.

HE CRACKED A WORD

He cracked a word to get at the inside
Of the inside, then the whole paper bag full
The man said were ripe and good.
The shrunken kernels
Like black tongues in dead mouths derided
The sillinesses of song and wagging wisdom:
These made a small dumb pile, the hopping shells
Froze to the floor, and those made patterns
Half-witted cameras glared at, finding as usual
Huge meterorites in mouseland.
What barefaced robbery!
He sat, sat, sat mechanically adding
To the small dumb pile, to the patterns on the floor,
Conscious of nothing but memories, wishes
And a faint but unmistakable pricking of the thumbs,
The beginnings of his joy.

A SMALL ROOM WITH LARGE WINDOWS, 1962

A SMALL ROOM WITH LARGE WINDOWS

I

What it would look like if really there were only
One point of the compass not known illusory,
All other quarters proving nothing but quaint
Obsolete expressions of true north (would it be?),
And seeds, birds, children, loves and thoughts bore down
The unwinding abiding beam from birth
To death! What a plan!
                        Or parabola.
You describe yours, I mine, simple as that,
With a pop and a puff of nonchalant stars up top,
Then down, dutiful dead stick, down
(True north all the way nevertheless).

One way to save space and a world of trouble.

A word on arrival, a word on departure.
A passage of proud verse, rightly construed.
An unerring pen to edit the ensuing silences
(That's more like it).

II

              Seven ageing pine trees hide
Their heads in air but, planted on bare knees,
Supplicate wind and tide. See if you can
See it (if this is it), half earth, half heaven,
Half land, half water, what you call a view
Strung out between the windows and the tree trunks;
Below sills a world moist with new making where
The mangrove race number their cheated floods.
Now in a field azure rapidly folding
Swells a cloud sable, a bad bitching squall
Thrashes the old pines, has them twitching
Root and branch, rumouring a Götterdämmerung.
Foreknowledge infects them to the heart.
                              Comfortable
To creak in tune, comfortable to damn
Slime-suckled mangrove for its muddy truckling
With time and tide, knotted to the vein it leeches.

III

In the interim, how the children should be educated,
Pending a decision, a question much debated
In our island realms. It being, as it is,
Out of the question merely to recognize
The whole three hundred and sixty degrees,
Which prudence if not propriety forbids,
It is necessary to avail oneself of aids
Like the Bible, or no Bible, free swimming tuition,
Art, sex, no sex and so on. Not to direct
So much as to normalize personality, protect
From all hazards of climate, parentage, diet,
Whatever it is exists. While, on the quiet,
It is understood there is a judgement preparing
Which finds the compass totally without bearing
And the present course correct beyond a doubt,
There being two points precisely, one in, one out.

IV

A kingfisher's naked arc alight
Upon a dead stick in the mud
A scarlet geranium wild on a wet bank
A man stepping it out in the near distance
With a dog and a bag
                              on a spit of shell
On a wire in a mist
                              a gannet impacting
Explode a dozen diverse dullnesses
Like a burst of accurate fire.

AN OPPRESSIVE CLIMATE,
A POPULOUS NEIGHBOURHOOD

I

I look from this back window straight across
To that back window and there see standing
In the through-current rippling his white vest and briefs
A grey-headed man who turns, retreats, returns
(For the coolness, no doubt, of linoleum to the naked sole)

And looks from that back window straight across
To this back window and there sees standing
In the through-current naked but for my white briefs
A brown-headed man. Put it that we note and respect
Each other's individuality, he is not chagrined

Because I am content with briefs and reject the vest,
Nor is my own free spirit offended because he
Cannot comfortably acquiesce. This inspection complete,
I too turn from the rear and pad the apartment through
(For the coolness, truly, of linoleum to the naked sole)

To the street-front window and there see a brown-thighed girl
Crotched on a ground-floor sill. One up and to the right
A blue nightgown bodilessly gets out of bed
And passes from view. A boy rearranges his pillow.
I pan to the flight above, a hand shifts a pot-plant

From the sill, one hand, the perfection of anonymity.
What we cherish is our own business, this hand innocently
Withdraws its treasure. Put it simply that the owner may be stripped
Naked for the heat and has nothing to hide but himself.
Satisfied, I put no impertinent question to myself

Concerning these comparisons, least of all any literary question.
Hell, let's face it, is horribly hot and overcrowded,
But where else do you find the niceties of neighbourly regard
More observed and the mitigable nuisance of neighbourly love
Better understood than in this City we have been building so long?

II

A dog howls all morning Saturday.
His inhuman frequencies
Touch like sad art with its astonishing
Human unlikenesses.

Somebody tied the poor dog up
In the hinder-precinct of some brownstone,
And shut the door and the garden gate
And went out, and left him alone.

Thickly in this thick heat the dog
Ululates, convoking the neighbours, say,
500 to 600 East 84th and 85th streets,
To tell of some too far away

Catastrophe, some canine Cathay
Scourged by earthquake or famine —
Some disaster in Canis Major our myopic
Instruments cannot examine.

Dog, dog, I'm tied up too.
Be my guest, my metaphor.
Be Fool to my Lear till the neighbours hear
And maybe open the door.

The dog howls. It's a dog howling.
If it warbled, it would be a bird.
If we don't make ourselves intelligible,
We make ourselves heard.

Dog, dog, they will come and untie you.
You shall have a pat and a bone,
And a run with the Gracie Square dogs
To whom you are personally known.

My telephone doesn't ring of itself —
That calls for the human hand.
Dog, dog, all it takes is patience,
Which dogs don't understand.

New York, July 1961

ON THE TOUR

Verwoerd be our Vatchwoerd!

OR

GOD AMEND NEW ZEALAND

A timely little Poem for all Ages and Races, suitable for Recitation or Singing at Rugby Reunions, Church Socials (leading Denominations), R.S.A. Smoke-concerts, Hangis, Tangis, etc. etc. etc.

By ALLEN CURNOW

DEDICATED

in sincere if astonished Admiration of his exemplary Devotion to the Rugby Broederbond, unswayed by popular Clamour, undaunted by seditious Conspiracy among the nation's Religious Leaders, Catholic and Protestant, and unswerving before the Racial Intolerance of the Maori People

to T.H. Pearce Esq.

Manager of the 1960 All White Rugby Team

ON THE TOUR

Air: *On the Ball*

Oh, some talk of Colour and some talk of Christ
    And the Bullets and Whips of the Boer:
What have these got to do with the Glory in view
    For our Tom's gallant Team on the Tour?

On the Tour, on the Tour, on the Tour,
You can play if you're racially pure.
All Whites together, we're Birds of that Feather,
That's how we got picked for the Tour.

Let political Thought never sully our Sport,
    Let us play on that purified Plane —
Where Verwoerd's Police and their Guns keep the Peace,
    While they join in our Rugby Refrain:

On the Tour, on the Tour, on the Tour,
For God's sake, let's keep the Game pure!
We can't win a Test if we're under Arrest,
So our Policy's plain for the Tour!

If there's Blood on the Hand we shall shake as we land,
    Soft Speeches will soap it away.
We'll be deaf to the Wails of the Nameless in Gaols,
    Where the White Fury battens its Prey:

On the Tour, on the Tour, on the Tour,
We're on Side with the 'Bok and the Boer.
While each poor censored Rag dribbles Lies through its Gag,
Their Press won't lack Space for the Tour!

Jones, Bremner and Watt, Clarke, Nesbit — the Lot —
    How gladly they'll welcome us there!
Not a Word of the Blacks who were shot in their Tracks.
    That wouldn't be friendly, or fair.

On the Tour, on the Tour, on the Tour,
White Bullies will rest more secure.
And the World will take Note that we each cast a Vote
For Verwoerd, when picked for the Tour.

The Blood that was shed by the brave Maori Dead
    Was the same simple Hue as our Own.
But we're raising the Bar, like the Sportsmen we are,
    When it suits us to go it alone.

On the Tour, on the Tour, on the Tour,
We'll endure what we have to endure.
We'll mind our white Manners like true Afrikaaners —
What else can we do, on the Tour?

In Scrum or in Line-out, whenever we dine out,
 We'll breathe not a Word that offends:
It would upset our Host if we called for a Toast
 To our absent brown-pigmented Friends!

On the Tour, on the Tour, on the Tour,
We'll be watching our Step, to be sure.
We've got Consciences — true, but it just wouldn't do
To take them abroad on the Tour!

Let Nash count the Votes and let Hogg count the Cash,
 We'll count every Point that we score.
We'll not count the Dead or the wounded who fled —
 It's not That they selected us for!

On the Tour, on the Tour, on the Tour,
It's the Game's irresistible Lure!
At old Stellenbosch we shall get a Brain Wash,
Which is just what we need on the Tour.

Oh, we're Whineray's Whites, and we champion the Rights
 Of Rugby to trample rough-shod
Upon Conscience and Creed, while it follows the Lead
 Of a double damned Dutch Reformed God.

On the Tour, on the Tour, on the Tour,
Apartheid's the Truth for the Tour:
We're picking no Quarrels with colour-blind Morals,
When we talk Double Dutch on the Tour!

CAPITOLINE SPRING

I

Spring thunder thumps on Friendship Heights
and claps the young sprigs to attention,
stiff with budding the new-born green.
Momentarily the rain dark day
divides to let the lightnings down,
perfectly harmless! nobody's hand is
in it, but visibly, audibly spring
changes the weather, changes nothing
in the imperturbable traffic lanes.

The matrix cracked, the god still born,
white Lincoln stares from his stone seat.
He judges none. And, to judge rightly,
it was not just to sculpt him so.

II

Spring thunder thumps in the white wrist
and the dark wrist across the tables.
What obsolete engine speeds the pulse?
The drugstore's gaudy *hortus siccus*
(whose shy voluptuaries linger
over the paperbacks) expresses
those old mythologies deformed,
these pastorals!
Murdered or murderous shepherdesses
unseasonably naked lie,
such uncouth heats and chills as hell
and analysts' names are made on.
What pure economy of means
mounted those grave grey marble breasts upon
The Sexual Responsibility of Woman,
twice cleansed, by chisel and by camera,
cold adumbration! for the freshman libertine

the severities of grammar, the selected passage,
lastly the Masters, with what gust remains.

Lincoln stares at Washington's blunt needle,
the seated Zeus, the hyperbolic obelisk
erect the stone gaze blinds itself upon.
Somewhere in air between an immense grandeur
cracks, and of that inaudible dissolution
the slow detritus invisibly dusts
the cherry blooms, the lovers' cheeks,
the lenses of the cameras and binoculars.

The still born god! It is not quite
or simply the fact of being turned to stone.
It was not just to sculpt them so.

III

Spring thunder thumps in the delicate wafer
the dogwood ministers, the dog's
blood, the squirrel's erectile plume
twitching, as boys' knees in the Zebra Room
touching the knees of girls, whinneying.
Some power attends the column and the statue,
or the momentum in dead power still rolls
far and unfelt as a galactic shift,
imperturbable recession.
                              Those most massive,
most incontrovertible images of the gods!
Who could have modelled them but those
had long since despaired of belief in them,
whose hands at the thought of them shook no longer?

IV

Toynbee's large tired head, the microphone
hung round the neck, protests the immensity
of knowledge, the uncontrollable pullulation

of texts, calls on the All-in-One.
From Lisner Auditorium let our cry
come unto thee, from 21st at H Street,
hear us, ineffable Synthesis, we beseech thee!
And faintly trusts the larger hope.

Spring thunder thumps. Whatever shapes our ends
or ends those shapes assume, here on the Heights
the inordinate god in the unprotesting leaf,
the knees, the wrists, thunders, renews,
rough-hews his exits.
                              The untrustworthy
blood that denied him is the rock.

The empty sepulchre is plugged with stones
only the patience of huge fears, huge failures
could cut so snugly, polish so eloquently.

It was not just to sculpt them so.

[*Unpublished, Washington, 1961*]

VISIBILITY ALMOST NIL

Necessity, now that [the] evening fog advances
Upon San Francisco & occupies the chalky suburb,
Gropes for the mind through metaphor. This image is
Physically present, & must do.

Fog's predictable, regular in its habits.
It is not, as I come to understand, necessity.
Come to that, the fog is not even necessary.

No clash of toothy bolts, no abrupt agony,
Made of ubiquitous vapours a necessity of fog,
From choice upon choice, from scrupulous agonies.

Necessity's over & over cancelled freedoms blind
Fierily not foggily & then how does it grope on this
That advances upon & occupies San Francisco?

Because, like a man whose choices come to some end
In departure from this city to which the fog cleaves,
I find here a minor figurative subtlety.

Cancelling hilltop by hilltop the chalky suburb,
Fog cancels choice upon choice till a single this sole block
Between Edna & Detroit on Monterey Boulevard

Is left upon which vision may dwell at all
Scrupulously as to the angle and the observed fact.
Fog is not necessity, no, but the fog exhibits

Necessity reversed, such as travellers may verify
From any airport. This cloud of innumerable choices
That cease to be choices, being innumerable,

Obliterates all but the lineaments of a destination,
A dwelling, an embrace, a bed, an embodiment
Of death to be lived and the shadow (at least) of necessity.

[*Unpublished, San Francisco, 17 August 1961*]

VETERANS DAY IN THE METROPOLITAN MUSEUM OF ART

> Penetrators are permitted into the museomound free. . . .
> — James Joyce. *Finnegan's Wake.*

I met a traveller (in a sense) who said:

Ozymandias didn't actually appear
in person.
Gossip drily posited a chill. Still
It was heartening to see such a turn-out of the junior

148

Colossi, the cadet branch, how they did the honours.
Nobody could have said, had it occurred to him,
Antiquity did itself less than proud, or us
For that matter, on the occasion of this visit.

So many others were unavoidably present.

Artemis queen of tumbledown heaven, for one,
Not indeed with *wishèd sight*, as the old song says,
Nor state much congruous with her *wonted manner*.
Yet blessed us by proxy of some tons of marble
Voluted, fluted, uncouthly topped and tailed,
Out of her famed trans-hellespontine dump.
Time, the old dealer, buried it like a dog,
The genuine glory that was, et cetera,
And nosed it up again. Great goddess!
Whoever saw such a lopped column as now
Hung dead in the middle of the gallery, magnifying
Imprecisely nothing?
                              Long-winded speeches
From bronze age middens, mumbled in stone. Meanwhile
The museum cafeteria fed the hungry,
A rumpus of nymphets contributed *confused noise*
Appropriate to the scene and swelling act.

The Cypriote votaries came colossally
With cups and doves, — votary to votary,
Male and female greeted we them, they us, —
Whose limestone lips didn't part from ingrained habit
Formed before they were, these three thousand years,
The hereditary fine unscornful smile:
Unparted, unpouted, unrecalcitrant,
Never mind what a blank eyeball might betray
Had sculptors played with shifty looks, been silly
Enough to think those mattered.

                              Their good taste,
Correcting our bad manners, sublimating
Our gross pygmalionism, translated us

A little above ourselves; our faces wore
The impressive moment's momentary impression,
Almost the fine smile itself! our selves
Confronting ourselves, an antique frame of mind.
We omitted to tell our hard luck stories even
To our selves, to bother ourselves with any luck
But that insinuating longevity of their stone,
Softly as it stood, hard by any comparison.
Strictly, an impossible situation
For all present. Why couldn't somebody somehow
Do something, drastic as a bullet, a coronary,
A low word at the top of his voice?
Jejune crux. Juvenile expostulation.

There are many, and other mansions. Step this way.

Another thousand years, another gallery, —
Immensely familiar, *in form and manner*
Like the king that's dead, — blown up in marble, Constantine!
What's become of that garrison of geese,
Those legions lost in Asia, since we mugged
[Our Roman History. Dull texts on shiny paper.]

That's Caracalla to the life, you'd pick it
By the cantilevered scowl alone with its sex.

Art there, Truepenny?

                    The votaries withdrew,
As, going, we came to ourselves.

[*Unpublished, New York, 1966*]

TREES, EFFIGIES, MOVING OBJECTS, 1972

I   LONE KAURI ROAD

The first time I looked seaward, westward
it was looking back yellowly,
a dulling incandescence of the eye of day.
It was looking back over its raising hand.
Everything was backing away.

Read for a bit. It squinted between the lines.
Pages were backing away.
Print was busy with what print does,
trees with what trees do that time of day,
sun with what sun does, the sea
with one voice only, its own,
spoke no other language than that one.

There wasn't any track from which to hang
the black transparency that was travelling
south-away to the cold pole. It was cloud
browed over the yellow cornea which I called
an eyeball for want of another notion,
cloud above an ocean. It leaked.

Baldachin, black umbrella, bucket with a hole,
drizzled horizon, sleazy drape,
it hardly mattered which, or as much
what cometing bitchcraft, rocketed shitbags,
charred cherubim pocked and pitted the iceface
of space in time, the black traveller.
Everything was backing away.

The next time I looked seaward,
it was looking sooted red, a bloodshot cornea
browed with a shade that could be simulated
if the paint were thick enough, and audible,
to blow the coned noses of the young kauri,

the kettle spout sweating,
the hound snoring at my feet,
the taste of tobacco, the tacky fingers
on the pen, the paper from whose plane
the last time I looked seaward
would it be a mile, as the dust flies,
down the dulling valley, westward?
everything was backing away.

II FRIENDSHIP HEIGHTS

By night by fishes' light
I am absently walking in another summer,
a stranger here myself. The streetlamps
and the headlamps hang and swim in waves
greened round, quite extraordinarily like
a fish-tank forest. Presently I shall see
deep avenues there, extraordinarily like
a neighbourhood called Friendship, another time.

On the sidewalk an iron receptacle
NOT FOR THE DEPOSIT OF MAIL.
This other one is the right one
FOR U.S. MAIL, the hollow lovers' tree
black as a thought of the world inside.

Receptacle, receive me, receive me.

Each cave is calm as if no traffic stormed,
the six-lane fugue is lost on the deaf leaf.
Cave, storm, fugue, forest could be very like
a neighbourhood called Friendship: only semblances
are lost on the black hollow iron tree
and the deaf leaf gurgles to itself by night
by fishes' light. Another semblance might
be absently walking, in another summer,

extraordinarily like the goodness, say, of God,
something scented *and weeping in the evening dew.*

The zoo closes,
the horned owl dozes,
his dinner is done
and the bunnies are dead,
the green runs red,
see how they run
underneath the water where the sharks do fly
my, oh my!
underneath the water where the sharks do fly.

III   AN UPPER ROOM

Where is the world? Upstairs.
At the end of the corridor. The last room.
I have drawn the curtains back, under the window
I am waiting for my students, my sixty-first
year is high cloud that alters as it filters
the sun, good light while it lasts, for reading.
I can hear them growing up the stairs.

Goosey goosey gander
Whither do you wander?

Our book is open. Volcanic islets visit
over the top of the tide which is full, and full
of dead men's images, pouring into the room
Through the dear might of Him that walk'd the waves.
(Could you do that? Keep clear of the margins.
Here my line starts and it finishes *here*,
no later than the light lasts.)

We speak only
to each other but as if a third were present,
the thing we say.

Smaller than thought can think
the hours between us shrink,
books wink, volcanic islets sink
below that brink,
black margin, blind white ink.

There I found an old man
Who wouldn't say his prayers.

Dead bunnies. Blinded teddy bears.

IV   AGENDA

A man who has never visited the Uffizi
isn't educated. English remark.

Be a playboy at 35. South British Insurance.
Picture of man fishing, from boat, with bottle.

Enjoy sex and stop breeding. Message to the age
from the Doctors Kronhausen, on waking.

V   DO IT YOURSELF

Make it what height you like, the
sky will not fall nor will the dead
president rise because of his

O
B
E
L
I
S
K
5
5
5
f
t
.

nor is it any wonder that it is
one measured mile down river to the

       P   I

   A   T

 C   O   L

one measured mile up river to the

     L I N C

     M   O

       E   L

     M   N

   O R I A L I

  N C O L N M E

 M O R I A L I N

With a few simple tools the handyman
can erect his thought upon Waiheke, volcanic islet,
lat. 37S long. 175E for the time being.

Read the instructions carefully.

VI   NAMES ARE NEWS

A wood god botherer stands
not fifty feet from his own
door, calls trees by name.

Speak up we can't hear you.

Metrosideros robusta,
the northern rata. Usually
commencing life as an epiphyte
becomes a tall, massive tree
60 to 100 feet high.

Louder please.

Flowers are broad, dense,
terminal, many-flowered cymes,
dark scarlet.

What?

Dark scarlet.
Don't lean that weight! I call.
Shall I make you feel the full
rigour of a description?

Close!

For godsake no.

Closer.

Lord, I am small.
I break easily. I call
red cumulus green bubbled
cloud with a bloody curd,
not flowers, not cymes.
How fast do I have to talk?

Talk.

Seed vessels fly
forty thousand feet high
jetting towards a dark
destination up, up!
Funny how the sexual jets
grumbling aloft resemble
cymes, dark scarlet.
Can a machine do more?
Tall, massive clouds,
thunderheaded trees,
don't commence life that way.
Green pod, sky boring jet
nevertheless resemble.

Birds whistle and shit.

Lord,
I cannot compel you,
I implore you, by the dust
of a rigorous description
cracked by its own rigour,
lean easier, for the sake
of a chance resemblance.

Dark stays. Light goes.

Dark scarlet, inhuman,
silent in the fly-simmering
January sunlight
suffers no disguise,
description, resemblance.
A wood god botherer darkens
a moment his own doorstep,
enters, writes quickly,
adds a postscript.

The *New Zealand Herald* comes
late here, with the milk.
That was last week, the
pathologist's evidence
described the dead brother's
body, the burned-out farmstead,
what fat was burned away,
what skin, what battering the
skull *sustained* before the
Fire. And the oil-feed.
And the living brother by the rigour
of a description *stood*
erect, and the Court covered its
embarrassment, and ours, by the
rigour that was its only
rigour, of a description.

Flowers are broad, dense,
terminal

Louder please.

Jetting towards a dark
destination up, up!
It's a long long fall and a crack like doom
between the martinis and the satchels
up there and the dark down here.
Far too many flies, birds, worms, to begin with,
and that's not the end.

No.

VII   A FAMILY MATTER

Adam was no fool. He knew that at his age
a man must plan for his retirement. Or else.
He saw no better way than back to the bush.

An image in disrepair could study itself
in a pool, or such distraction from itself
as a bird flashing a scale upon his ear.

There was Cain to take over the business. There were signs.
Light no fires. Discharge no firearms.
Ten acre block for sale. Your private kingdom.

Lianes noosed harmlessly, the water ran
down above and below the road ran down
primevally babbling. Close to the foot

of a young totara, *Podocarpus hallii*,
Adam stumbled, and very nearly fell
over an old survey peg, half rotted.

If it blew like the wrath of God it was all blown over
ages ago, the angel hooked it, having lashed
round with a sword in a flaming bad temper.

Regeneration, conservation, were words
with which he comforted his mind, if angels,
vandals, vermin, got muddled in his mind.

Cain used to come over at the week-ends
and bring the children, who loved it.
Something must be done with it when the old man went.

VIII   THE KITCHEN CUPBOARD

Sun, moon, and tides.
With the compliments of the *New Zealand Herald*
and Donaghy's Industries Limited makers
of the finest cordage since 1876.
Look on the inside of the cupboard door,
the middle one, on the left of the sink-bench.

All the bays are empty, a quick-drying wind
from the south-west browns the grey silt
the ebb-tide printed sexily, opulently,
making Nature's art nouveau, little as it matters
to mudlarking crabs and the morning's blue heron.

Olive, olive-budded, mangroves wait for the turn,
little as it means, to call that waiting.

A green car follows a blue car passing a brown car
on the Shore Road beyond the mangroves which wait
no more than the tide does because nothing waits.
Everything happens at once. It is enough.

That is not to say there is nothing to cry about,
only that the poetry of tears is a dead cuckoo.

The middle one, on the left of the sink-bench.
I stuck it on with sellotape. Not quite straight.

IX   A DEAD LAMB

Never turn your back on the sea.
The mumble of the fall of time is continuous.

A billion billion broken waves deliver
a coloured glass globe at your feet, intact.

You say it is a Japanese fisherman's float.
It is a Japanese fisherman's float.

A king tide, a five o'clock low, is perfect
for picking mussels, picking at your ankle-bones.

The wind snaps at the yellow-scummed sea-froth,
so that an evanescence of irised bubbles occurs.

Simply, silverly the waves walk towards you.
A ship has changed position on the horizon.

The dog lifts a leg against a grass-clump
on a dune, for the count of three, wetting the sand.

There is standing room and much to be thankful for
in the present. Look, a dead lamb on the beach.

X   A FRAMED PHOTOGRAPH

The renaissance was six months old.
All the Kennedys were living at that time.
Jackie was hanging pictures in the White House.
I figured he could use the experience, Jack hornered,
when he starts in legal practice, naming Bobby
for Attorney-General.

Act one, scene one,
of the bloody melodrama. Everyone listened
while everyone read his poems. BANG! BANG!
and we cried all the way to My Lai.

To be silverly framed,
stood on the Bechstein, dusted daily
by the Jamaican girl whose eyes refuse them,
seeing alien Friendship one prolonged avenue
infinitely dusted, is a destiny which simply,
silverly they walk towards, towards my chair,
what jaunty pair
smiling the air
that flutters their trousers on Capitol Hill?
Why, Hiroshima Harry and the dandy Dean,
dust free. Heavenly muse!
fresh up your drink and sing.

What, exactly,
did he do at the Pentagon? He guessed he was
a deputy assistant secretary of defence,
a political appointment, modestly confided.
Hospitably home at cocktail time he took
one careful gin and tonic, excused himself
to mind State papers.

Dust the Bechstein, Anna.
Dust the megagothic national cathedral.
Dust destiny.

Fresh up. There is plenty of ice.

Receptacle, receive me.

Things are things carried
away by the wind like this
big empty carton which
bumps as it skids as it
arse-over-kites over
anything else that's loose
dust, for instance, while
    all the little angels
    ascend up ascend up
things are things emptied
on the tip of the wind
arsey-versey vortically
big print for instance
APPLE JUICE nothing in the
world ever catches its
carton again where the
wind went ƎƆIUႱ Ǝ⅃ԀԀⱯ
loose as the dust or the
water or the road or the
blood in your heels while
    all the little angels
    ascend up on high
    all the little

God!
That was close, that bus
bloody nearly bowled the
both of them the dog with his
hindleg hiked and
APPLE JUICE bumped off the
wind's big boot
        angels
    ascend up
hang on there
as long as you can
you and your dog before the
wind skins the water off the

road and the road off the
face of the earth

                on high
      which end up?
      Arse end up
full beam by daylight
this funeral goes grinning, a
lively clip, a tail wind, the
grave waiting
hang on to your hands
anything can happen
once where the wind went
fingers you feel to be
nailed so securely
can come loose too
hold on to your ears and
run dog run while
simply, silverly
they walk in the wind that is
rippling their trousers
Hiroshima Harry and the
dandy Dean
dust free dusted while
      all the little angels
      ascend up ascend up
with
Plato in the middle
holding out his diddle in the
way souls piddle from a
very great height and
dead against the wind,
dead against the wind.

XII   MAGNIFICAT

Who hasn't sighted Mary
        as he hung hot-paced
by the skin of the humped highway
        south from Waikanae
three hundred feet above the
        only life-sized ocean?
Tell me, mother of mysteries,
        how long is time?

Twelve electric bulbs
        halo Mary's head,
a glory made visible
        six feet in diameter,
two hundred and forty-five feet
        of solid hill beneath.
Tell me, mother of the empty grave,
        how high is heaven?

Mary's blessed face
        is six-and-a-half feet long,
her nose eighteen inches,
        her hands the same.
Conceived on such a scale,
        tell me, Dolorosa,
how sharp should a thorn be?
        how quick is death?

Mary's frame is timbered
        of two-by-four,
lapped with scrim and plastered
        three inches thick.
Westward of Kapiti
        the sun is overturned.
Tell me, Star of the Sea,
        what is darkness made of?

Mary has a manhole
          in the back of her head.
How else could a man get down there
          for maintenance, etc?
Mary is forty-seven feet,
          and that's not tall.
Tell me, by the Bread in your belly,
          how big is God?

I AM THE IMMACULATE
          CONCEPTION says
Mary's proud pedestal.
          Her lips concur.
Masterful giantess,
          don't misconceive me,
tell me, mother of the Way,
          where is the world?

XIII   A FOUR LETTER WORD

I

A wood god bothering cantor
rolls out his call. He names

tanekaha, kaiwaka, taraire.
Mispronounced, any of these

can strike dead and dumb. Well spoken,
they are a noise neither of the writhing root

nor glabrous leaf nor staring flower,
all that can unspeakably supervene.

II

Tane mahuta is a very big tree,
because of the signboards at the roadside.

Tired trunk, punky at the heart,
disyllabic Tane is too venerable

for words. True, that at a given sign
they stop their cars and walk no distance

to have seen, to have found themselves,
as advertised, in the absence of the god,

to have decently exposed some inches of film
in honour of his great girth.

Strike him with lightning!
the old aboreal bore.

Cut him up for signboards. Just look at that,
such longevity, such bulk, such lumbering tonnage.

III

Titans were titanic in the old days
before the defoliant Thunderer.

The children had no fathers then, as now.
No nativity ode for Tane. At his namegiving

nobody had the time, having time only
short of an unspeakable supervention

to blurt him, Logos begotten of log,
the disyllable, as he came.

IV

In the technologies nothing can be done
without a divine sub-contract:

this one for the felling, the hollowing,
prone canoe, erected post;

Tane demiurgos,
lord of an obsolete skill:

not to keep an old man ticking
with a dead boy's heart

(cut while warm, after the crash,
pray for this tissue not to be rejected);

an instance now, look at it like that,
of what can unspeakably supervene,

ever since like cats in the dead of night
the first heaven and the first earth

coupled and begot,
and the theogonies littered the place

with the lordliest imaginable
stumps. That's life. That's fear

of this unspeakable that smashed the mouth
open, stamped on the balls and

ripped from the tongue's root, womb syllabled,
Tane, Tane mahuta.

XIV   BOURDON

Spring thunder thumps on Friendship,
    high hands divide, collide,
let lightning down and wet the town,
    blinding the riverside
where Lincoln stares but never sees
what Washington is up to.
That cloud-cuffed shaft, those stony knees,
heaven's thunderstruck antipodes
    discover, arse-end up too.

The matrix cracks, the god still born
    stares his measured mile,
marble trousered, marble browed,
    throned in classical style.
Stone eyelids grind, a stony throat
    chokes with cherry bloom.
The matrix cracks again, again!
Sifting riverwards in the rain
a slow detritus dusts the brain
    under a sunless dome.

Thunder is a bluejay cock and a hen
    and a roll of the wrists,
the gods alone are solid stone
    dressed like beasts.
Rain courses down the stone, the stairs,
    and the knees that wear
stone still, a stony gaze is
snug as a bullet, smooth as phrases,
    the well plugged sepulchre.

XV   A HOT TIME

They were doing their thing in the burning fiery furnace,
you couldn't hear the flute, harp, sackbut, psaltery
and all kinds of music for the silence of the flames.
Everything was very quiet in the heart of the furnace.

The wine was red, the acrylic was vermilion,
the pictures on the walls were hanging by their nails.
The needle was a diamond paddling in the bloodstream
issuing from the heart of the silence of the furnace,

streaming where it paddled in the stream that it was,
homing on the centre never to be punctured.
All the holy children were dancing on the needle
doing nothing but their thing in the burning fiery furnace,

Shadrach and Shakeback and Meshach and Sheshach
and Abednego and gay to bed we go along and upwards
of a hundred holy children in the burning fiery furnace.
It was dead still and silent at the centre of the disc.

There was the golden image, balls to the golden image,
balls to Nebuchadnezzar the king who set it up.
Not a note was audible over the silence of the flames,
of the psaltery and the dulcimer and all kinds of music.

Came the holy cold of morning, with all kinds of music
raking out the furnace, when their thing was done,
and which child broke silence, squeaking from the ashes,
issuing from the music of the flute, harp, etc.,

Shadrach or Shakeback or Meshach or Sheshach.
or gay to bed we go along with Abednego or whom?
growing up the stone stair, issuing from the music,
sucking on a diamond like an apricot stone, saying

There I found an old man who wouldn't say his prayers,
I took him by the sackbut and threw him down the stairs,
I adore Doctor Logos, but Yeats is so mysterious,
because he doesn't communicate *like Shakespeare does to me.*

XVI   THERE IS A PLEASURE IN THE PATHLESS WOODS

When the green grenade explodes, does the kauri
experience an orgasm of the spent cone?
What is the king fern doing with its hairy knuckles?
Wildling and epiphyte, do they have problems too?
There's a reason for the spastic elbow of this taraire.
Look hard at nature. It is in the nature
of things to look, and look back, harder.
Botany is panic of another description.

XVII   LONE KAURI ROAD

Too many splashes, too many gashes,
too big and too many holes in the west wall:
one by one the rectangles blazed and blacked where the
sun fell out of its frame, the time of the day
hung round at a loose end, lopsided.

It was getting desperate, even a fool could see,
it was feverish work, impossible to plug them all.
Even a fool, seeing the first mountain fall
out not into the sea or the smoking west but into
the places where these had been, could see the spider
brushed up, dusted, shovelled into the stove, and
how fast his legs moved, without the least surprise.

171

A tui clucked, shat, whistled thrice.
My gaze was directed where the branch had been.
An engine fell mute into the shadow of the valley
where the shadow had been.

XVIII   ANY TIME NOW

Extraordinary things happen every day
in our street only this morning
the ground opened at my feet
without warning
unless it was a cloud in the south
balled like a swelling in the mouth.

And the air was fresh, being winter
time when the ground broke
disclosing a billion bodies burning
under a thin smoke.
Was it then that I saw in my walk
an eggshell, a capsicum stalk?

Such details are always so terribly
(if that is the word) distinct
as grit under the eyelid, like today
when the ground blinked,
disclosing what never should be seen.
Walking is a pleasure, I mean.

Fortunately there was not very much
traffic and no kiddies playing,
couldn't have picked a better day for it
I was just saying
when the ground closed over the sky
hollow as the ground was high.

AN ABOMINABLE TEMPER, 1973

TO THE READER

Look for my fingerprints.
Good luck to you. I wore
no gloves when I burgled
your house and made off with
as much as I could carry,
a precious little. Now
I give myself up, what's in it
for you? All yours,

little as you knew or stared
or dreamt, the night I stole
in my stockinged face and feet,
shit-scared you'd wake and catch me,
when I whipped your skinny wallet,
your ten-dollar watch, pearls
of more pearliness than price.
You missed them, did you?

All losses are loss,
life itself the most trifling
some experts testify.
Hardly less precious, then,
to get your own back now,
a little, a little the worse
for wear, a restitution.
It's that, or nothing.

A WINDOW FRAME

I

This paper is eleven and three-quarter
inches long, eight and one-quarter inches
wide, this table four feet five inches long,
thirty-two inches wide, this room

twelve feet square, this house one
thousand square feet, this window encloses
two leafless peach branches on which I count
fifty twigs and then give up, one mile

away the morning sunlight whitens or darkens
what I take to be the walls of houses
and the roofs along a long ridge of the land.
I should be used to it by now, the refusal

to move an inch closer, an inch to the right
or left or (so long as I look) to dismantle
the hallucination of fact, the refusal even
to speak, to explain, as if it were unpardonable

mortal sin on my part not to have remembered.
Am I to burn in my chair for no worse fault
than pulling out the plug? Am I to bear
an eternal blame because the Pacific Ocean

disappeared down the pipe and sucked the sky
down with it? The edges of this sheet
of paper are beginning to brown, slightly,
but there is no definable smell of burning

in this house, this room. This window encloses
two leafless peach branches on which I count
fifty twigs and then give up. It will be the
fifty-first on which a sparrow settles,

cock sparrow, he picks under each wing
distinctly, so many times for the left,
so many for the right, one loses count.
He is not there now nor will be yet.

I should be used to it, the way numbers
won't go by numbers, the injustice of it
that finds me guilty. A sparrow has not fallen
to the ground. Do you smell burning?

II

It is not what you say,
it is not the way you say it,
it is not words in a certain order.

Look out the window.
                              It is on the page.
Examine the page.
                              It is out the window.
Knuckle the cool pane.
                              It is in the bone.
Why is the mud glassed,
                              with mangroves
bedded in the glass?
                              Why is the cloud
inverted in the glass?
                              Why are islands
in the Gulf stained blue
                              grained green with
interior lighting
                    by Hoyte?
                              Why not?

TO AN UNFORTUNATE YOUNG LADY WHO AFTER ATTENTING SIX PUBLIC READINGS BY THIRTY POETS ASKED, DOES ANYONE CARE?

How right you are, my dear,
Let us make an example of poetry.
It is possible, even for poets,
to live without it, so many do,
and to live with it, most of the time
impossible.
         Isn't it the rumble
of something loose behind,
or a fumble
in the back seat of the mind?
Or an innumerable company
of the heavenly host crying
rhubarb rhubarb rhubarb rhubarb
with obbligato innumerable other
syllables in several languages,
some dead?
         Does anyone care?
One man's rhubarb is another man's
artichoke and that's the reason why
the poetry of earth is never dead
dead dead.
         Rhubarb to you,
my dear, with cornflakes and cream,
every glorious carefree day and night of your life.

THIS BEACH CAN BE DANGEROUS

The fatalities of his nature cannot be disentangled from the
fatality of all that which has been and will be.

— Nietzsche

WARNING
They came back, a well known face
familiarly transfigured, lifelikeness only
cancer, coronary, burning, mutilation
could have bestowed, they came by millions
and a friend or two calling me by my name
and my father, by a name no other could know.

BATHE BETWEEN THE FLAGS
Each with the same expression, his own,
mirrored in the sand or the mind, came back
the way they went calling like winter waves
pick-a-back on the humped horizon they rode
the strong disturbed westerly airstream
which covered the North Island.

DO NOT BATHE ALONE
It was their company that made it possible
for me to walk there, cracking the odd shell
with the butt of a manuka stick,
happy to the point of hopelessness.

TO DOUGLAS LILBURN AT FIFTY

My fiftieth year had come and gone. So Yeats,
in the course of one astonishing poem,
letting the fact drop, his timing perfect.

Toothless warriors, nonagenarian burgesses,
mumble the sweet cake, the spittled crumbs.
Somebody will blow out all the candles.

If you had your way, would you compose a score
with fifty bass drums gunning the day down
in self-salute? What do we expect?

A poor look-out for honest pastrycooks,
all the same, for the economy generally.
Come on, be a quinquagenarian!

It is only for one day. No two are alike.
Each has its singular fascination.
You are fifty only once.

The lightest of touches on the shoulder, this
unreckonable reminder, will it alter
the weather even a shade?

The written score affirms
shades, alterations, novelties,
the days and the midnights between the days:

in part, you will be persuaded to allow,
the music affirms, makes room at least
for silence to loom in

larger than in the hills where it first harboured,
eavesdropped upon, spied upon.
The idea was never to break it!

Is it fiddlers' armpit sweat, the punished
bellies of drums, bespittled brass,
cock-pitted against silence?

Is it bloodbeat, waterdrop, all manner alchemical
electronic tinctures? *'Tis magic,*
Magic that hath ravish'd me!

Hang up blonde promontories, MacDiarmid's oils.
Take down my book, some poet's attitude.
Set a silence to catch a silence.

Eavesdropper, what are you overhearing now?
Blow out the candles. Praise the cake.
Indulge the birthday guest.

1965

WHAT WAS THAT?

Now I heard in my dream
        or dreamt I heard
                the Last Trump
                        it was not loud
seraphic brass
        made nobody jump
                sing glory glory
                        or the damned scream

it was not loud
        more of a hum
                than a vocal murmur
                        a unison
without voices
        no star performer
                blowing up the graveyards
                        tooting on a cloud

it was the single sound of
        all our deaths
                unison of our last
                        confusion
stopped breaths
        unison without blast
                or lambsblood bath
                        world without end

Socrates died so
        willingly Jesus
                not without a struggle
                        gave up the ghost
and a mother pleases
        to smother her baby
                in the Bronx or the Urewera
                        some other pillow

brain-tissue splashed
        fractionally after
                the bullet-hole appeared
                        in the gib board
freesias and catheters
        perfumed the ward
                in a hospice for the dying
                        the Boeing crashed

the Trump played on
        like a sea in my sleep
                or the thumb-stopped ear
                        where my blood can listen
to the river of itself
        nobody rose calling
                deep to our deep
                        last unison.

A REFUSAL TO READ POEMS OF JAMES K. BAXTER AT A PERFORMANCE TO HONOUR HIS MEMORY IN CRANMER SQUARE, CHRISTCHURCH

Jim, you won't mind, will you,
if I don't come to your party?
One death is enough, I won't kill you
over again, ritually,
being only one other poet
who knew you younger and never better,
I would hardly know under which hat or which crown
to salute you now —
bays, or myrtles, or thorns,
or which of them best adorns
that grave ambiguous brow.

The quandary's mine, yours too,
Jim, isn't there always too much
we don't understand, too much that we do?
Winged words need no crutch,
and I've none for you.

March 1973

TANTALUS

Tantalus, Tantalus, how are you getting on,
up to your guilty neck in the black river,
nothing to drink or to eat for an ever gone
and an ever to be?
                            Tantalus,
pick yourself a plum.
                            Tantalus,
dip your chin, drink.
                            Tantalus,
what's wrong with you?
                            God,
he's hopeless!
                Tantalus!

AN ABOMINABLE TEMPER

*H.A.H. Monro, 1814–1908, sometime Judge of the Native Land Court,
New Zealand, writes to his daughter, Ada Morrison.*

I

What little do I know?
Really very little indeed.
You suggest that I write it down.
Well, Ada, I shall try.
As much as I remember,
having forgotten the most.

We, whoever we are,
have seen the century out.
So conveniently, I might
have gone, that hundredth Hogmanay.
Raw 1901
is a socket my tongue touches

unhopefully. I take up my pen,
not without a little pain.
A hard frost again this morning,
a sharp frost, needle to the bone
as I crook my knuckle to the pen,
a black frost. I dip and scratch
like an old fowl. Winter

comes last for us all.
A fogged window, the gaslight
fizzing in the afternoon —
I feel the steel nib searching
skull bone, wrist bone.
Having forgotten the most,
dear Ada, I am writing it down,

the little of what I was told
by my father and my mother,
by this last light in my mind,
blue bead on a black wick,
which leaves most things dark.
I think my grandfather was killed

in a sea battle. Trafalgar?
Why not, if it suits you?
Any other battle would do.
This winter light's too dim
for embroidering by,
supposing I had the talent.

II

I am writing it down, as you say,
for my children and grandchildren,
or to oblige you, Ada.
I dip, and scratch.
What judgements did I scratch?
What claims? Whose lands?

Maori lands, when I was judge?
I am writing about my father.
He had an abominable temper —
That's written now.
When only a small boy,
he was taken to sea by his father,

the naval officer, who hoped
for a son in the same service.
In fact, he detested it.
I've often said, no wonder,
if the father and son were cursed
with the same bad temper.

Did my father hate his father
for a temper like his own?
No love was lost between him
and the sea, I'm sure of that.
I've often said, that first
voyage might have been his last —

I would not be sitting, Ada,
in this cold small city,
drizzling my winter away
out of the blinding mountains
into the blinded sea,
where the English trees don't care

what hemisphere this is
or month of the year,
and a hundred years are too
many, and too few.
I am writing about my father.
Quite a young man, he obtained

in his native Edinburgh,
some government situation.
I forget what, precisely.
I conclude it had a connexion

with the French wars, at all events
Waterloo was the end of it.
Othello's occupation was gone.

He could have had cash compensation
for the lost employment, or
he could name any colony for
his grant of land. The climate
in Tasmania was said to be healthy.
He sailed in the *Minerva*.

III

Six months at sea, with my mother,
my brother William, my sister
Marie — *tempestuous*.
I write down the one word
I ever heard of it.
I am sure, well chosen. It can hardly
have improved my father's temper.

But how promising it looked,
that Hobart landing!
Grass to the backs of the cattle
on the block my father chose.
It was her life's regret,
my mother would often say,

some blundering Sydney office
gave 400 trumpery acres,
Robinson's to my father,
and his fine block to Robinson.
Greener than the grass, my father
abandoned his rightful claim,

took money and lost a fortune.
He gained, in spite of it all,
a friend, Lieutenant Gunn,

ex-Imperial Army,
six foot six in his socks,
Commandant of Birch's Bay
convict station. Gunn

made me his special pet,
danced me on his knee.
A bushranger shot his arm off.
My father had his post,
with convict servants and all,
an eight-oared gig on the Derwent,
and a home rent free,

till the timber trade failed.
My father sailed
his own twenty-ton cutter
over to New Zealand.
Hell upon earth he found
at the Bay of Islands.
Hokianga, on the contrary,
agreeably surprised him,

the Maori a better class,
and so were the settlers,
several of them retired
army and naval officers,
highly respectable people
residing at Hokianga.

IV

My father found a purchaser there
for the twenty-ton cutter,
Count Dillon, a British sea-captain,
who obtained his title of Count
from a grateful French Government
for some service or other connected

with the mystery of La Pérouse's
expedition. Just what, precisely,
escapes me. He was a Count,
a reward, I am sure, as gratifying
to him, as it was inexpensive
to France. Back again to Hobart

my father sailed in a trading schooner,
chartered the brig *Brazil Packet*,
captain and crew, took us all aboard
for New Zealand. So far, dear Ada,
so near, perhaps I should say,
I have picked my thread for you,

my child, my other children,
your children, their children,
great-grandchildren of mine,
among others, Arnold, John, Allen,
great-great-grandsons Wystan, Timothy, Simon.
I dip, and scratch the hyphens,

not without a little pain
the steel nib searches
wrist bone, skull bone,
testicles, time stitches
hyphen by hyphen this hand-me-down
garment we wear in our turn,

shrunk in the wash, or threadbare.
I am twitched from behind
as I crook my knuckle to the pen.
I am writing about my father.
Peace to his loins, dust somewhere now
in San Francisco. The last voyage,
of which I write nothing.

V

A mouth made mountainous with mere sand
if ever dung yellow dunes were mountains
opened that morning to suck our ship in.

Out of many inlets, branches, root-breathers
of mangroves intaking, expelling pungent air,
a little strong for my taste now, not then,

mucus of a strange mother smeared us over
from head to foot. We were less visitors there
than visceral as hydatid worm to host.

Underfoot at Horeke the ground swayed civilly,
steadied, at the suggestion of our steps.
We lugged our worldly goods ashore,

    item tables and chairs
    item window sashes and doors (2)
    item bricks for the chimneys
    item one ton of flour
    item a team of four bullocks (£100)
    item a cart
    item a plough
    item harrows

On a block of land bought from the natives
the erection of a dwelling-house proceeded,
my mother, my two sisters and I meanwhile

accommodated in the house of a settler.
No sooner built than burned to the ground,
all our possessions with it. An accident,

at least I never heard anyone blamed for it.
My mother and sisters stayed on with the settler,
my father and I, my brother, our boy interpreter

(till more supplies could be obtained from Hobart)
roughed it in a hut the Maoris built for us,
one room, provided with

    item one frying-pan
    item four halves of coconut shell for cups
    item mussel shells stuck on reeds for spoons

Clearing the land went on, a hundred Maoris
were employed on this. If I remember rightly,
the daily wage was half a fig of tobacco —

eighteen figs to the pound, sixpence per pound.
Labour was not dear in those days.
Not that as a child that would have occurred to me.

Burned to the ground, a smouldering heap
heaves into memory, he and his household goods,
cold ashes now. This charred fag-end of me

pokes here and there. All fires are accidents,
if one happens to be ninety years of age,
most accidents have done, as we say they will.

VI

Re-supplied from Hobart, my father had built
a large weatherboard house, outhouses, boatshed.
He enclosed several acres and made a garden.

Like the Garden of Eden, I am tempted to say.
If it had been less like — indeed, dear Ada,
you know your Bible, I hope, as well as I do.

Yes, it was a pleasant life at Hokianga,
only for my father's abominable temper
we could have been very happy,

with a hundred head of cattle, as many goats,
innumerable pigs, fowls, geese, ducks, turkeys,
a beautiful six-oared gig rowed by six Maoris

(boys, we called those in our regular employ)
and the shooting and fishing. My father kept
his bad temper entirely for home consumption,

outside his family he never quarrelled with anyone.
The bad times came, the garden went
the way of all gardens from the first, I suppose.

Depression swept the Colonies,
Australia bankrupt, New Zealand fallen to zero.
Sails were few and listless on the Hokianga.

Disobedient to my father,
the timber trade failed again, the Maoris felled
no more kauri to make him spars for Chile.

Heke took an axe to the Flagstaff instead,
at the Bay of Islands. The War in the North began.
My father chartered a ship, the barque *Bolina,*

to carry us all, with his other belongings,
including the hundred cattle, south to Auckland.
I grew to manhood, married, you and the rest

came into the world. I write nothing of that.
Last light leaves most things dark, the nearer
the darker. Our secrets keep themselves.

VII

Did he love nobody?
Nobody him? Dear Ada,
I do not imagine my father
got me in a fit of temper,
whatever the connexion was.
Such things, if possible at all,
one prefers to think unlikely.

Can you, yourself, imagine
what the feeling was, my feeling
when my semen left me lonely
and you lonelier?
An absurd question. Precisely,
or I should not ask it.

Ask God why he does such things.

VIII

Was he of a romantic disposition?
Peter I mean, my father.
Born the same year as Keats
who shuddered at the sight of old women,
horrors! they knew too much,
and peppered his tongue
to taste the claret better,
I am sure he was otherwise preoccupied
in his native Edinburgh.

Was it smelly between the sheets?

What in the name of God and Robbie Burns
and the nine merry Muses was he doing
at Hokianga, not caring half a fig
of tobacco while the timber was profitable,
he with his gentlemanly tastes,

and the better class he never quarrelled with,
cherishing besides

> item one pair brass-barrelled black-nippled
>   spring-daggered percussion duelling pistols
> item one *Poems* of Robert Burns, Edinburgh,
>   1812
> item one Holy Bible?

IX

My mother's maiden name was Alcock,
granddaughter of an Englishman.
County family. It took his butler
all day to clean the silver plate.
He in his dotage left the estate
to some other relative.

                    This fool
of a grandmother of mine! My mother
was robbed, the second time, of a fortune.

My mother's younger sister Jane
died, unmarried, long, long ago.

X

In the beginning was the four letter Word
Tetragrammaton, an angry father.
The pistols will be sold for fifty pounds
by my grandson Tremayne to Arthur Morten,
collector of old firearms, whose collection
will pass on his death to the Canterbury Museum,
Christchurch, New Zealand.
Allen will get the Bible and the *Poems*.

I speak as a fool, fools shall repeat after me.

This prophecy Allen *shall make,*
for I live before his time.

AN INCORRIGIBLE MUSIC, 1979

CANST THOU DRAW OUT LEVIATHAN
WITH AN HOOK?

I

An old Green River knife had to be scraped
of blood rust, scales, the dulled edge scrubbed
with a stone to the decisive whisper of steel
on the lips of the wooden grip.

You now have a cloud in your hand
hung blue dark over the waves and edgewise
luminous, made fast by the two brass rivets
keeping body and blade together, leaving
the other thumb free for feeling
how the belly will be slit and the spine severed.

The big kahawai had to swim close
to the rocks which kicked at the waves
which kept on coming steeply steaming,
wave overhanging wave
in a strong to gale offshore wind.

The rocks kicked angrily, the rocks
hurt only themselves, the seas without a scratch
made out to be storming and shattering,
but it was all an act that they ever broke
into breakers or even secretively
raged like the rocks, the wreckage of the land,
the vertigo, the self-lacerating
hurt of the land.
               Swimming closer
the kahawai drew down the steely cloud
and the lure, the line you cast
from cathedral rock, the thoughtful death
whispering to the thoughtless,

Will you be caught?

II

Never let them die of the air,
pick up your knife and drive it
through the gills with a twist,
let the blood run fast,
quick bleeding makes best eating.

III

An insult in the form of an apology
is the human answer to the inhuman
which rears up green roars down white,
and to the fish which is fearless:

if anyone knows a better it is a man
willing to abstain from his next breath,
who will not be found fishing from these rocks
but likeliest fished from the rip,

white belly to wetsuit black, swung copular
under the winching chopper's bubble,
too late for vomiting salt but fluent at last
in the languages of the sea.

IV

A rockpool catches the blood,
so that in a red cloud of itself
the kahawai lies white belly uppermost.

Scales will glue themselves to the rusting blade
of a cloud hand-uppermost in the rockpool.

V

Fingers and gobstick fail,
the hook's fast in the gullet,
the barb's behind the root
of the tongue and the tight
fibre is tearing the mouth
and you're caught, mate, you're caught,
the harder you pull it
the worse it hurts, and it makes
no sense whatever in the air
or the seas or the rocks
how you kick or cry, or sleeplessly
dream as you drown.

A big one! a big one!

A BALANCED BAIT IN HANDY PELLET FORM

Fluent in all the languages dead or living,
the sun comes up with a word of worlds all spinning
in a world of words, the way the mountain answers
to its name and that's the east and the sea *das meer,
la mer, il mare Pacifico*, and I am on my way to school

barefoot in frost beside the metalled road
which is beside the railway beside the water-race,
all spinning into the sun and all exorbitantly
expecting the one and identical, the concentric,
as the road, the rail, the water, and the bare feet run

eccentric to each other. Torlesse, no less,
first mountain capable of ice, joined the pursuit,
at its own pace revolved in a wintry blue
foot over summit, snow on each sunlit syllable,
taught speechless world-word word-world's ABC.

Because light is manifest by what it lights,
ladder-fern, fingernail, the dracophyllums
have these differing opacities, translucencies;
mown grass diversely parched is a skinned 'soul'
which the sun sloughed; similarly the spectral purples

perplexing the drab of the dugover topsoil
explain themselves too well to be understood.
There's no warmth here. The heart pulsates
to a tune of its own, and if unisons happen
how does anybody know? Dead snails

have left shells, trails, baffled epigraphy
and excreta of such slow short lives,
cut shorter by the pellets I 'scatter freely',
quick acting, eccentric to exorbitant flourishes
of shells, pencillings, drab or sunlit things

dead as you please, or as the other poet says,
Our life is a false nature 'tis not in
the harmony of things. There we go again, worrying
the concentric, the one and identical, to the bone
that's none of ours, eccentric to each other.

Millions die miserably never before their time.
The news comes late. Compassion sings to itself.
I read the excreta of all species, I write
a world as good as its word, active ingredient
30 g/kg (3%) Metaldehyde, in the form of a pellet.

IN THE DUOMO

I   RECITATIVE

This is the rock where you cast your barbed wishes.
    That is the clifftop where you hang by the eyes.
    Here is where Leviathan lives.

It is all in the walls of one great shell incised.
    The instructions look simple, the trouble is the smoky
    ambiguous morning sunlight, the heights inside

the cathedral are blurred. So much for art, which only
    comprehends the introversions of arches,
    lunettes, capitals, where the sunlight slowly

floats up towards their rock-hung perches
    motes moths wings claws human hands fluttering
    prayers kites clapping gustily to barefoot beaches,

the tidiness of a carved by time discoloured
    eminence being magnetic to such poor untidy
    littles or nothings,

bits and pieces, yet 'of such' is the highly
    esteemed 'kingdom of heaven', what else?
    Imagine an enormous face, conceive it smiling

to an accompaniment of birds and bells
    down blurred clifftops, makebelieve masonry,
    by interior sunlight extinguished at eye level

which is rock bottom. Here the linens, the sacred
    silverware are arranged and the blood is poured
    by experienced hands which do not shake

serving up to Messer Domeneddio god and lord
    the recycled eternity of his butchered son,
    this mouthful of himself alive and warm.

This is homoousianus, this is the cup
    to catch and keep him in, this is where he floats
    in a red cloud of himself, this is morning sun

blotting the columns, the ogives, the hollowed throne,
    smoking the kite-high concavity of the cliff.
    This is the question, *Caught any fish?*
                            Say, *No.*

I am teaching Leviathan to swim.

II   A PROFESSIONAL SOLDIER

Ma ficca le occhi a valle che s'approccia
    la riviera del sangue in la qual bolle
    qual che per violenza in altrui noccia.

That's every one of us, man and woman and child.
    We all boil together when we boil
    up to our necks in the river so ardently imagined

(*Inferno* canto twelve lines 46–48),
    merely to exist being even for the gentlest
    the rape of another's breath or bread.

Gian-Battista Montesecco's problem was believing
    everything he read, the divinest poets
    told the sublimest lies, common sense was as rare

then as now, and that no such river existed
    for stewing damned humanity was much too big
    and flat a contradiction for this hired soldier,

throats cut, cities pillaged, assassinations,
    no job too small, go anywhere. His theology
    was eschatology, death judgement heaven hell,

he put last things first where they belong.
        There's life to be got through yet eternity's only
        a matter of time a hell of a long time.

Killer without qualms, he never forgot his basics,
        they scared the daylights out of Montesecco
        as nothing on earth could do, to do him justice.

III   A TURNING POINT IN HISTORY

It had to be an offering acceptable
to God, for which good reason, and for others
of a practical nature they decided the cathedral
was the place, and the time High Mass.

The flood of a king tide, the deepest sounding
where the big ones are, the holiest lure,
the tackle secure, the steel and the stone
scraped crosswise *in hoc signo*, can you beat it?

Where the pavement is cold underfoot
and over it full flow, high blood, High Mass
brings purple and princelier scarlet
scuffing the sea floor, graining the green,

and the other poor fish and the drab
discolorations of plankton, il popolo del dio
threadbare in Tuscan shoddy, miraculous draught
in the visible and invisible nets.

Hot hand for the gold, he got cold feet,
Montesecco did. He told this fat cat Pazzi,
I'll do you a fair day's kill for a fair day's pay,
but the banquet's where we settled for, am I right?

You keep your side of it, I'll keep mine,
I'll dagger you a dozen Medici at anybody's table
except Christ's. Two will be sufficient, Pazzi said.
Who's paying? And Montesecco, Who's going to burn?

You can stuff the whole deal and to hell with the money
where it comes from. There's an Englishman down there
eternally boiling for chilling his man at Mass,
when they lifted up the Host he stuck in the steel.

A crick in the neck isn't the worst you get
staring at the judgement in the roof of San Giovanni
and the damned people the size of a skinned eel
in Beelzebub's teeth and the fire from Christ's left foot.

And you're caught, mate, you're caught!

I'll take my chance of the pit, Ser Jacopo,
but I'm waiting till I'm pushed if it's all the same,
I'm not jumping. To which Pazzi, What if I tell you
this is for Rome, the holy father himself

blesses the act? Not on for double the money,
Montesecco said. And might as logically say
another half chiliad later than this latest
photographer studying for Bonechi's *Guide*

Ghiberti's regilded doors of paradise
and the godsize Jesus dooming in the dome,
not counting the time eternity takes one day
mopping up the bloody mess on the floor below.

IV   26 APRIL 1478

So they had to find somebody else
whose numinous nightmares
didn't unman his mind for the day's
churchmanlike chores,
whose mortal infirmities,
profane daydreams, dirt
in the ears and the nose, the involuntary
or surreptitious fart,

lascivious leakages,
the sea-cock under the cope,
were the daily wick, wax, oil and soot,
the smell of the shop,
for whom agnus and sursum corda
and gloria in excelsis,
candles on the lips, made light
of the darkest policies.

Pazzi found two priests
for the cathedral job,
Volterra's Antonio Maffei,
apostolic scribe,
Stefano curate of Montemurlo;
putting first things first,
whichever were last, they judged
the time right for murder.

Ite missa est.
The rite being said and done,
in a scarlet stir the hit-men edged
each to his man.
Lorenzo dropped his shoulder
quicker than Maffei struck
his fumbled blow and the blood ran down
from the nicked neck.

Blood fell, the rumpus rose
under the haughty summits
from the fractured glassy sea
to the mistiest limits,
and where was the other priest?
Stefano got no closer
than a dagger's draw from the mark
at the *ite missa*,

and the two young Cavalcanti
joined Il Magnifico,
and they knifed it out in the sacristy

to save Lorenzo,
leaving his brother dead
where he had to die
face down, by the Pazzi's jabbing steel
dancing wasp time.

Giuliano de' Medici
bled where he had to bleed,
bedrock flat on the church floor
in the cloud he made
of the strong bestial smell
of dissolving clay,
their offering to the oldest god
that holiest day.

V   AN OLD HAND

I tried from the cathedral
    yesterday and had no luck,
        Mrs Dragicevic said.

Slaty grey strata
    angled and squared abutted
        the clubfoot of the cliff

where she perched, this plump
    vigilant bird, in her blue
        quilted parka, pointing her

4.0 m. fibreglass pole
    over each big wave that walked
        white from the west

with a long bearded howl,
    broke roaring into a run
        for the rocks to come.

And the spot was a good one,
    the cathedral, so long as you kept
        your head for heights

and the big ones came,
    il magnifico and his brothers
        to the turn of the tide,

having to, having to come
    leaping to the holy lure,
        an acceptable offering

to the blooding hand, the scaling,
    the scarlet clouded pool,
        the necessary knife.

DICHTUNG UND WAHRHEIT

A man I know wrote a book about a man he knew
and this man, or so he the man I know said, fucked
and murdered a girl to save her from the others
who would have fucked and murdered this girl
much more painfully and without finer feelings,
for letting the Resistance down and herself be fucked
by officers of the army of occupation, an oblation
sweet-smelling to Mars and equally to porn god Priapus.

What a fucking shame, this man the one the man
I know knew decided, if you want a job done well
do it yourself, and he did and he left her in a bath
of blood from the hole in her neck which he carved
in soldierly fashion, a way we have in the commandos,
after the fuck he knew she didn't of course
was her last, and a far far better thing, wasn't it?
than the bloody fuckup it would have been if he'd left her
to be unzipped and jack-the-rippered by a bunch
of scabby patriots with no regimental pride.

And he had this idea, and he mopped up the mess
and he laid her out naked on a bed with a crucifix
round her neck for those bastards the others
the sods to find, furious it must have made them.
And the man I know who knew this man or some other
man who did never forget this fucking story,
it wouldn't leave him alone till he'd shown this goon
who actually did or said he did or was said to have done
the fucking deed what a better educated man
would have done and thought in his place.
And he wrote this book.

Experience like that, he exclaimed,
thrown away on a semiliterate whose English
was so imperfect you could hardly be certain
that what he did and what he said were connected,
let alone, by no fault of his own,
ignorant of the literature on the subject.
What can you do, with nothing but a cock
and a knife and a cuntful of cognac,
if you haven't got the talent?

A big one!

A COOL HEAD IN AN EMERGENCY

I

It will be back next minute
next week or tomorrow, if tonight
by the street lamp's negligence
it escapes, and the bells

yelling, the horns,
boots at the trot, motors racing,
doors wide with fright,
blotted faces looking

silly in an 'embarrassed
silence', the moment after,
will have been all about nothing.
No, not exactly all

or precisely nothing either,
but the word of a name escaped
custody, not even a man's or
absconding god's,

but the word of a name
scrawled by the roots of a tree
and the bole and the branch three-parts bare,
of what stood there

'in lawful custody',
escaped the cells and the rooms reserved
for the torturer's use, the mind's
painstaking hell.

II

The shock waves ringed, the shamefaced
street lamp reddened because
of what never should be but in truth
so commonly is

let slip to the dark,
where the tip of the tongue plays blind
man's buff and the wanted word
baffles the breath.

What's lawful here?
What's high or solid enough to keep
what's inside in? What's death
but a defect of memory?

III

It will be back, it will be
the beginning in the word, this *ginkgo*
safe in the cells, sludging the kerbstone
with colours of its fall,

frog's belly, canary's breast,
loquat or lemon or think of a thicker
yellow of a million mullioned glazes,
iridescences, buttered

sunlight. And think a little further,
up that street there's no necessity
to think anything at all, except of
an early winter gale,

the word of a name,
eyes in the usual places, the near side
of death's door daubed with autumnal redundancies
and verdurous chromatics.

BRING YOUR OWN VICTIM

I

For Isaac the ram,
 for Iphigeneia the goat,
under the knife in the nick
 was the substitute.

The rule was never to notice
 what had taken place
by the sea, in the thicket, the thing
 was your sacrifice.

Agamemnon didn't inquire
  nor did Abraham,
would the highest settle for a goat
  or oblige with a ram?

The heavens might be humane
  but you never knew,
you sharpened your knife, you did
  what they said to do.

II

History began to be true
  at a later time.
The gods got into the act
  and they played our game.

You killed your mother because
  they said you had to,
and before the agon was over you knew
  you must have been mad to.

Bring your own victim
  ruled from then on,
conscience cut its milk teeth
  on the live bone.

Brutus knew that the blood
  had to be Caesar's,
Caiaphas and Pilate found
  no proxy for Jesus.

You sharpened your knife, you steeled
  yourself, the wound
twisted the knife in the hand,
  the knife in the mind.

Man or beast you bought
    on the hoof hung dead,
neither the cloud nor the covert sun
    commented,

and you never knew
    what hung by the other hook
in the heart, your blessed sacrifice
    or your damned mistake.

III

You stood with an altar
    at your back, the grave
at your feet, no substitute offering
    to burn, wave, or heave.

You knew there was never nothing
    miracles wouldn't fix,
alone with your life, alone
    with your politics;

alive, alone, one-upping
    war, pestilence, famine,
happy in your Jonestowns, Hiroshimas,
    happy to be human,

happy to be history
    in a galaxy of your own
among the spitting and the shitting stars
    alive, alone.

Spillage of bird blood,
    fish, and flesh went,
the spoonful in the uterus, the aged
    and incontinent,

under your steeled thumb:
    so to imagine
slaughterman, overman, everyman,
      time's eminent surgeon.

THINGS TO DO WITH MOONLIGHT

I

Holy Week already and the moon
still gibbous, cutting it fine
for the full before Jesus rises,
and imaginably gold
and swollen in the humid heaven.

First, second, and last quarters
dated and done with now,
the moon pulls a face, a profane
extemporisation,
gold gibbous and loose on the night.

Hot cross buns were never like this,
the paschal configurations
and prefigurations could never have
nailed the moon down
to the bloody triangle on the hill.

By the spillage of light the sea told
the cliff precisely where to mark
the smallest hour when I woke
and went out to piss
thankfully, and thought of Descartes,

most thoughtful and doubtful pisser,
who between that humid light
and the dark of his mind discerned

nothing but his thoughts
e. & o.e. as credible, and himself

because he thought them, his body
had a soul, his soul had a body,
an altogether different matter,
and that made two of him
very singularly plural, *ergo*

sum couldn't be *sumus*. He thought
deeply and came up with the solution
of blood in spirit, holy adhesive,
God, singular sum
best bond for body and soul.

II

And the height of the night being humid,
thickened with autumn starlight
to the needed density and the sea
grumbling in the west,
something visceral took the shape of an idea,

a numen, a psyche, a soul,
a self, a cogitation squirmed
squirmed, somebody standing there
broke wind like a man
whose mind was on other things.

His back to me and black
against the gibbous gold
of the godless moon, still blinking
the liturgical full,
something stuck its ground like a man

in a posture of pissing out of doors,
thankfully by moonlight, thinking
of pissing, experiencing the pleasure

and the pleasure of thinking
of pissing, hearing also the sea's

habitual grumble. Descartes?
I queried, knowing perfectly well it was.
And he to me, Your Karekare doppelgänger
travesties me no worse
than the bodily tissue I sloughed in Stockholm —

no wonder I caught my death
teaching snow queen Christine,
surely as her midnights outglittered
my sharpest certainties
an icicle must pierce my lungs

(at five one midwinter morning,
the hour she appointed for philosophy
by frozen sea, freezing porches)
and my zeroed extension
wait there for the awful joyful thaw.

There's the customary stone I'm sure,
with the customary lie incised,
the truth being I exist here thinking,
this mild March night.
As for the thought, you're welcome.

III

No less true it was I, meaning me,
not he that was physically present
pissing, and metaphysically
minding the sepulchre
not to be opened till after the full moon.

Cogito. I borrowed his knife
to cut my throat and thoughtfully
saw the blood soaking the singular

gold humid night.
Ergo sum. Having relieved myself

of that small matter on my mind,
I leaned lighter on my pillow
for a gibbous moon, a philosopher's
finger on his cock,
and a comfortable grumble of the sea.

MORO ASSASSINATO

I   THE TRAVELLER

All the seas are one sea,
The blood one blood
and the hands one hand.

Ever is always today.
Time and again, the Tasman's
wrestler's shoulders

throw me on Karekare
beach, the obliterations
are one obliteration

of last year's Adriatic,
yesterday's Pacific,
the eyes are all one eye.

Paratohi rock, the bell-tower
of San Giorgio recompose
the mixture's moment;

the tales are all one tale
dead men tell, the minor
characters the living.

Nice and all as it was
and is, the dog-trotting sun
of early April nosing

the 'proud towers', to sit
at Nico's tables
on Zattere, and to watch

the Greek and the Russian ships
dead-slowing up the Giudecca
towards mainland Mestre's

raffineria, red-guttering
lanky steel candlestick:
nice and all the Chioggia

car-ferry making the long
wave wheelspoke from the bows,
slap-slop to the feet of the old

angler who trolls
past the Gesuati church, the pizzeria,
the house Ruskin lived in,

and to sit, deciphering
the morning's *Corriere*:
the lengthening anguish of

Eleonora, la Signora Moro,
now her fifth week begins
of unwidowed widowhood,

here and not here, to sit
by the sea which is all one,
where Paratohi is neither

steel stalk nor bell-tower
and either is Paratohi,
deciphering *Corriere*.

The tears of Eleonora
splash black, dry on the page,
the weather map, the fifth week

'after' the bloody abduction.
Ever remains today,
and the hands one hand.

II   AN URBAN GUERRILLA

> The real stress came from life in the group . . . we were
> caught up in a game that to the present day I still don't fully
> see through. — MICHAEL BAUMANN, 'MOST SOUGHT AFTER'
> GERMAN TERRORIST

It was a feather of paint
in a corner of the window,
a thread hanging from the hem
of the curtain, it was
the transistor standing on the corner
of the fridge, the switches
on the transistor, the way they were placed
in a dead design, it was where
the table stood, it was the label
Grappa Julia on the bottle
not quite half empty,

the faces that came and went,
the seven of us comrades
like the days of the week repeating
themselves, themselves,
it was cleaning your gun ten times
a day, taking time
washing your cock, no love
lost, aimlessly fondling
the things that think faster than fingers,
trigger friggers, gunsuckers.
People said, Andreas Baader

'had an almost sexual relationship
with pistols', his favourite fuck
was a Heckler & Koch. Not that sex
wasn't free for all and in all
possible styles, but not all of us
or any of us all of the time —
while agreeing, in principle,
that any combination of acbdefg
encoded orgasm, X being any
given number — got our sums right.

Dust thickened on the mirror,
the once gay playmate,
on the dildo in the drawer,
dust on the file of newspapers;
silence as dusty as death
on the radio, nobody can hear
the police dragging their feet;
sometimes we squabbled, once
could have shot one another
in the dusty time, we had to be
terrible news, or die.

III   LAMPOON

Nobody less than the biggest
        would do, and who was that?
Five times Prime Minister, the top
        Christian Democrat.
Two hours on his feet that day,
        talking the Catholics round
to live with the Communists' power
        in the parliament of the land:
President next of the butcher State,
        or the next to die
the death of an old crook, come at last
        to the reckoning day.

Normality was this car's
warm vinyl under the buttocks,
and the driver's nape,
the knuckles of his hand on the wheel,
the knowledge of exactly where
I was going, and why, and how,
point by point of my discourse,
A could be coaxed and B persuaded
and the State saved again.

Normality was the guns
worn close to the body of each
of the guards, good friends, composing
my escort sitting beside me,
and behind me the second car
completing the squad provided
by the Ministry of the Interior:
cheap at the price, when you think
of the Titians in the Borghese.

Normality was the moment's
mixture, moment by moment
improvising myself,
ideas, sensations, among them
the lacquered acridities
of ducted air in the car,
accelerations, decelerations,
nothing to be trusted further
than the mixture's moment.

Normality was no less
what it had to be, the ambush,
the crashed cars and the guards
gunned down dead in the street;
and the car that carried me next
here, to the dark classroom
of the Prison of the People.

Normality is, do you follow?
a condition very like mine.

The child I was would have known
better than the man I am,

when they tripped him, trapped him,
ripped his shirt, emptied his bag,

caught him, laughed him to tears,
rubbed cowshit into his hair,

the irreversible justice
of the wrong once done, the victim's

yes to the crime. Who knows
he had to be punished knows

how the women who wipe away
the tears and the shit

heal no hurt but their own.
Tell the bullet to climb

back up the barrel and close
the wound behind it. They carried me,

carrying the child who could teach me
my case was not so special.

Our household consisted
of, at a guess, half a dozen
comrades, both sexes, and a few
more, coming and going,

never forgetting one
supremely important person
for killing when the time came,
worth something alive

but how much, and for how long?
Understand, it was not a spacious
apartment, our elderly prisoner
had his own room;

the Prison of the People
was a tight squeeze, how long
would it take to squeeze the brain
till the fuses blew?

Not that we gave it a thought,
wasn't the State on the block
and the front page yelling rape,
and the cameras in at the fuck

and the dirtied pants scared off
the arses of the Bourses,
when we took him alive and we left
five dead in the street?

Not a thought. We slipped out for the papers,
read them ten times. We photographed
him, his shirt open, an unsmiling smile

on his lips, hung behind him the Red
Star banner and the words Brigate Rosse.
Christ! They printed it all. Next thing

we sentenced him to death. They printed this.
He wrote letters, we willingly accepted them
for delivery, Fanfani, Zaccagnini, Andreotti,

Cossiga, Dell'Andro, Eleonora his wife.
Did we seriously expect these would procure
the political deal, the exchange for our comrades

gaoled by the State, their liberty for his life?
'An episode in a war', terror for terror,
an honourable swap. So his letters argued.

He knew us better than they, adduced Palestinian
precedent, humane principle, the party interest,
all that shit. What did he, or we, expect?

Jesus wrote no letters to Judas or Caiaphas.
It was he or Barabbas, and that was another Rome.
Not known at this address. Try Simon Peter.

Silence in Jesus Square, his Demo-Christians
denied him by protocol, *il vero Moro è morto
il 16 Marzo, ultimo suo giorno di libertà.*

Consenting silence in the house of the Left,
Christ's communist other woman, three in a bed
with Rome, last word of his long clever speeches,

grosso orchestratore. And among themselves
read in his letters forgery, torture, drugs,
practices in the Prison of the People

which 30,000 police, etc., could never locate.
*Dead, by the party line, a just man we once knew,
of whose visible blood we shall be innocent.*

See ye to it.

Can the same w.c.
receive the faeces of judge, executioner
and condemned man for 54 days,

in hearing of each other for 54 days
(and he, at an age to be father and grandfather,
with Jesuit's mastery of his Marx and his Mao,

knew us better than we knew ourselves)
and nobody be changed? 54 days
were the count-down, the Prison of the People

shrank like the ass's skin every time
the w.c. flushed, and we cleaned our guns,
and the newspapers yellowed, the execution

wouldn't wait, the silence outside
and the nothing more inside were the only orgasm
now, out of the barrel of a gun.

VI   THE LETTERS

His letters. How can we know
who it is that speaks?
Covertly delivered by terrorist *postino*
to the press, *Messaggero, Vita, La Repubblica,*
from the Prison of the People,
so-called, an address unknown,
by what light were they written?
Under what drug? It is one
who writes with his hand, his signature,
la grafia sembra autentica.

True, I am a prisoner
and not in the best of spirits,
nevertheless believe me
this handwriting is mine,
so is the style.

Believe, do not speculate
about the effect of drugs,
my mind is clear, what I write I write
of my own will, uncoerced.

Get me out of this.

But I am, you would say,
not I but another who is not to be
taken seriously, not one word
in reply to my arguments.

My darling Noretta, After a little optimism,
fleeting and false, as it turns out, something
they said, I misunderstood, I see that the time
has come . . . no time to think
how incredible it is, this punishment
for my mildness and moderation . . . I have been wrong
all my life, meaning well, of course . . .
too late to change, nothing to do but admit
you were always right. What more can I say?
Only, could not some other way have been found to punish
us and our little ones? . . . I want one thing
to be clear, the entire responsibility
of the Demo-Christian Party by its absurd,
unbelievable conduct. Friends have done too little,
fearing for themselves perhaps . . . It has come
while hope hung by a thin thread, suddenly
and incomprehensibly, the order
for my execution . . . Sweetest Noretta,
I am in God's hands and yours. Pray for me.
Remember me tenderly, take our dear children
in your arms. God keep you all. I kiss you all.

(and writes) Monday, 24 April 1978,
newspaper *Vita* to Benigno Zaccagnini,
leader in extremis to party secretary.
I repeat, I do not accept
the unjust, ungrateful judgement of the party.
I absolve, I excuse nobody.

My cry is the cry of my family, wounded to death.
I request that at my funeral, nobody
representing the State, nor men of the Party,
take part, I ask to be followed by the few
who have truly wished me well and are therefore worthy
to go with me in their prayers, and in their love.

VII   THE EXECUTIONERS

Christ set it going and ascended,
leaving the engine running.

The R4 is a small popular car,
but a man could hunch himself

through the hatchback, the prisoner did,
as the guns instructed.

He looked his best that day,
thanks to the girl comrade

who washed and ironed his shirt
(by Ninarelli of Bologna, initialled A.M.),

the singlet and the long johns.
He took a shower, dressed himself,

knotted the blue necktie.
Only at the last moment I noticed

the socks were wrong-side out,
but the cars were ready by then.

A gesture with guns. Get in.
Silence was the last dignity possible

to the doubled-up foetus he made
in the baggage end of the R4.

We shot him there and then,
the first of eleven bullets

clipped off the thumbnail of the left
hand raised by a stupid reflex

of the giant foetus in a dark blue
suit with cuffed trousers.

It squirmed, shrank, squirted red
and Gesù! he saw them

coming, the rods in our hands,
at one metre's range

the Beretta 7.65s
had to hit the left hunch-breast

eleven times, the grey head
whiplashed, nodding to the shots

yes yes yes yes
        yes yes yes
yes yes yes yes.

VIII   9 MAY 1978

Circumvesuviano is the railway
to Ercolano, Pompeii,
Torre Greco and other incubations
of Neapolitan poverty.
If you want ghosts for your money,
dig for yourself.

They are all dead as nineteen hundred
years or the moment after.
They do not live in memory or imagination
or history, or any other

223

of death's entertainments. Poems
don't work any more.

Back from a day among the ruins
to Piazza Garibaldi,
the Alfas, Fiats, Lancias, *tutto klaxon*;
the stone bonneted Liberator
rides nowhere any more and what's in a statue
but rocking-horse shit?

It is five in the afternoon.
Il Mattino, page one, X-nine columns,
Edizione Straordinaria,
MORO ASSASSINATO.
You're a guest, in a stricken house,
eavesdropper, easy tourist.

One of Rome's mediaeval gutters
is Via Caetani, near Jesus Square.
They parked the R4 with its riddled man.
You will visit the spot, there will be
mourners and flowers, many weeks,
both withered and fresh.

IX   THE POOR

The poor publish their grief
on doors and doorways,

the black bar printed above
and below the name of the dead,

or needing no name,
per mio marito, mia moglie,

mio fratello, the scrap of newsprint
20 by 10 centimetres

pasted to the joinery in the masonry
centuries have nibbled,

the day's news, *Death was here.*
Dreamlessly nonna nods

into her ninetieth year,
where she sits, catching the sun

at the dark doorway;
over her, in black and white

run off at the *tipografia*
round the corner, which is always busy,

Per Aldo Moro

----

strikes off one more.

AN INCORRIGIBLE MUSIC

It ought to be impossible to be mistaken
about these herons, to begin with
you can count them, it's been done successfully
with swans daffodils blind mice, any number
of dead heroes and heavenly bodies.

Eleven herons are not baked in porcelain,
helpless to hatch the credulities of art
or to change places, e.g. number seven
counting from the left with number five,
or augment themselves by number twelve arriving
over the mangroves. Thirteen, fourteen, fifteen,
punctually the picture completes itself
and is never complete.

The air
and the water being identically still,
each heron is four herons,
one right-side-up in the air,
one up-side-down in the tide,
and these two doubled by looking at.

The mudbacked mirrors in your head
multiply the possibilities of human
error, but what's the alternative?

The small wind instruments in the herons' throats
play an incorrigible music on a scale
incommensurate with hautboys and baroque wigs.

There's only one book in the world, and that's the one
everyone accurately misquotes.

A big one! A big one!

YOU WILL KNOW WHEN
YOU GET THERE, 1982

A RELIABLE SERVICE

The world can end any time
it likes, say, 10.50 am
of a bright winter Saturday,

that's when the *Bay Belle*
casts off, the diesels are picking
up step, the boatmaster leans

to the wheel, the white water
shoves Paihia jetty back.
Nobody aboard but the two of us.

Fifteen minutes to Russell
was once upon a time
before, say, 10.50 am.

The ketch slogging seaward
off Kororàreka Point,
the ensign arrested in

mid-flap, are printed and
pinned on a wall at the end
of the world. No lunch

over there either, the place
at the beach is closed. The *Bay
Belle* is painted bright

blue from stem to stern.
She lifts attentively. That
will be all, I suppose.

A TOUCH OF THE HAND

Look down the slope of the pavement
a couple of kilometres, to where it empties
its eyeful of the phantoms of passers-by

into mid-morning light which tops it up again
with downtown shadows. There has to be a city
down there and there is, and an 'arm of the sea',

a cloud to sprinkle the pavement, a wind
to toss your hair, otherwise your free hand
wouldn't brush it from your eyes, a welcome

touch of sincerity. As they pass down hill
away from you, their backs, and uphill towards you
their faces, the ages, the sexes, the ways

they are dressed, even one 'smile of recognition',
beg an assurance the malice of your mind
withholds. Look down, confess it's you or they:

so empty your eye and fill it again, with
the light, the shadow, the cloud, the other city,
the innocence of this being that it's the malice

of your mind must be the ingredient making
you possible, and the touch which brushes
the hair from your eyes on the slope of the pavement.

THE WEATHER IN TOHUNGA CRESCENT

It becomes 'unnaturally' calm
the moment you wonder who's going
to be first to ask what's happened
to the wind when did we last see

or watch for it animate the
bunched long-bladed heads
of the *ti* tree and all the dials
fidget in the sky and then it did

and we breathed again? The moment
comes when the bay at the bottom
of the street has been glassy a moment
too long the wind is in a bag

with drowned kittens god knows
when that was and which of us
will be first to say funny what's happened?
And it won't be a silly question

when it's your turn in the usual
chair to stare up into the cloud-cover
in which a single gull steeply
stalling dead-centred the hole

in a zero the stillest abeyance
and vanished into the morning's
expressionless waterface
'not a line on paper' your finger

pricks as if it might but won't
be lifted for something say switch
off the life support system of the
whole damned visible material

world quite calmly would that be
fair to the neighbours or the birds
other ideas? Seven oystercatchers
at a standstill a study in black

and red beaks all the better to
stab with are modelling for Audubon
mounted on sand in the frame of your
own choice with nothing to shift

the cloud around the morning could
easily be dead mirror to mouth
not the foggiest hope fluttering
the wind-surfer lies flat on the beach

failing actual wind a pressure from
that quarter north-east as it happens
and another pressure like time
squeezes the isthmus the world you

didn't switch off so that coolly
as you recline bare-armed looking
up the spongy firmament has begun
drizzling the paper's getting wet

put the pen down go indoors
the wind bloweth as it listeth or listeth
not there's evidently something
up there and the thing is the spirit

whistle for it wait for it
one moment the one that's one too
many is the glassiest calm an
'intimate question' for the asking.

YOU GET WHAT YOU PAY FOR

One more of those perfections
of still water with houses
growing like trees with trees dipped
in first light
           that pearl of a
cloud excited by sunrise
may or may not be priceless
fine weather is not what it
was and you pay more every
day yesterday's blue was of
a depth and a brilliance you
don't find now
                rich eccentric
having wisely ingested
his cake has it too dying
among treasures the weather
troubles him very little
you too Ananias keep
back part of the price
                   it all
hangs by a breath from the south
you too pushing seventy
wishing the weather were here
to stay the morning's moment
free
      knowing that it is not.

A FELLOW BEING

I

How is it that the thought
occurs
            over again of not
being (myself that is being
not) Dr Rayner
                        and that when
it does that same moment the thought
of being him
                        he being
dead for one thing and in
the light of such darkness
a fellow being?
                        The syllogism
bubbles like
                        a fart in a bottle
all men (major term) are
mortal all
            doctors (minor term)
are men
            therefore all
doctors
            divinity dentistry
laws letters sciences cats
horses Dr Faustus Dr
Syntax Dr Slop and Thomas
the angelic Dr are
                        (were)
mortal alas
            there's a stone
with four names on it press
clippings photographs the year was
1931
      therefore
as things stand in the 'poetry
of fact' he's dead enough and I'm

alive (enough)
        the sillyolgism
says that makes two of us and
what are we going to do about
that
    sub specie
aeternitatis
        Anyway the
thought occurs and it's a fact
'attested by'
        the occurrence from
time
    to time.

II

A yellowing sunrise
heightens the cliff
deepens the sea
        the
wink of a lizard's
eye ago
    that's eighty
years
    and we're young
and getting rich isn't
the answer we want
to get big
      'a big fish'
already the American
Dental Parlors with
46,000 pleased patients
nothing to the money
he married
      more of that
later
    what else did
the sun that comforts my

233

westward windows
offer
      to his gaze and
grasp?
        I've a use for
this valley
        the same one
what else did he 'see by the
dawn's early light'?
a rare and a dreadful
vegetation
        vast bole by
swollen bole
          a sickness
peculiar to the soil
of the island stuffed up
into the sky jamming the
exits to the world
valley and belly
tumoured
        a case of
gigantism
        (pathological)
bole by bole sheer as
Karnak
        oh skip it
said the old priest of Ammon
what's holy about Karekare
sheer's sheer in Egypt
we know our geometry
moon-rockets are bigger and
dildos are smaller
refinery chimneys
aren't trees
        (repeat trees)
Dr Rayner looked north
with an eye to the uses of
surgery and the cost
of extraction

                    measuring
the height of the ridge
                        made it
1000 feet and too
steep for a tramway but
by God I'll
            Timber!
We've come and we'll stay till
there's not a stick standing.

III

Agathis australis a lofty
massive
                massive! tree
100 ft. (30 m.) high
sometimes far
higher with columnar
                        columnar!
trunk 3–10 ft. diam.
or even more
                more!
spreading head of great
branches geysers pumping
cloudy jets clouds forming
dissipating
                sap is rivers
pouring the wrong way
up
    up!
            always on the
boil fruit a hard ovoid or
globose cone which falls to
pieces
            when ripe scattering
compressed winged
                        winged!
seeds

235

a forest a throw
where the March sun thrust
and thudded among the great
branches
            till they came
and out there the sea's
full of fish and the myths all
dry on the beach

IV

and this god guy
                    see
cuts the dad god's balls off
be-cause the mum god
                        see
gets mad the way he kicks these
kids around
            see and
all this blood'n spunk sloshed like
she been blocked by these guys
they reckon was gods
                        see
and she's preg again this other
bunch of kids giants
                        they reckon
and he chucked his dad's balls
in the sea and that's how this other
chick got born that's what wet
dreams is about
                all balls and
bloody great lumps of fat
'dya reckon
                a rust-pimpled
car clatters down the valley
surfboards lashed tight
                        the boys
balance beautifully

                              half-erect
riding the boards arabesquing
green bellies translucencies
another wave rides fills bursts
pours upward
                    dry on the beach
a 'mature female' reads the
Woman's Weekly snuggling
bare breasts in warm sand
scallop and *tuatua* shells
lie around
                    unoccupied.

V

The soul of F. J. Rayner incarnated
in Toronto graduated doctor
of dental surgery Chicago

and there one-fleshed a
meat-packer's heiress happy couple
'holidaying in Delaware Park N.Y.'

top-hat and redingote side by side
in a motorised sulky of the
period c. 1897 thereafter 'toured

the world' not excluding Auckland
New Zealand where the above
mentioned stone bears also and

only the names of 'his friends'
2 Moodabes 1 Cole 'remembering his
sterling qualities and great

kindness' the soul of the doctor
sits at his study desk it
wears a starched Edwardian collar

cuffs necktie and pin it is
looking straight at me with a look
of an expression arrested yes

'a straight face' generally speaking
success doesn't smile the soul
of the doctor is no exception

its hair parted a little to the side
its moustache is a seal's the right
hand closed not clenched the left

rested on the desk shows one
big ring its trousers are confident of
'covering the loins and legs'

a well-tailored imagination
is the mufti of the soul
of the doctor behind his left

shoulder the barque *Njord* loading
timber an antique telephone
squats at his elbow

Rayner speaking *Doctor* Rayner
long-distance to Wellington
the threaded voices

looping around lakes volcanoes
you can tell the Minister
he can cut it up for butcher's blocks

or toothpicks for all I care
that's my price for the finest
kauri in the colony I can ship it

to Sydney or Manila or the moon
for double the money the money
talking the soul's language

which sits as if spiked
upright on crossed buttocks
reminded that there's a pain

commoner and more mortal than
the toothache and a chair
perfectly designed for the purpose

of holding the soul in an erect
posture the way they will say
'the eyes follow you' and why

do the eyes do so? You can't
flap them off like flies you've
got to do better than that.

VI

Other ways of putting the same
thing an abstraction a sum
of money
            big deal

            £1,000 Reward
for any dentist practicing in Auckland today who
can prove that he is the Originator of Painless
Dentistry. We are Auckland's best and largest
dental Concern. ELECTRICITY USED IN ALL
DEPARTMENTS.
            ODONTUNDER
makes pulling and filling painless. We have
purchased the secret of its manufacture . . . we
pull more teeth positively painless than all other
dentists. Our references are twelve thousand
patients a year. Call in the morning and have your
bad teeth out, and go home in the evening with
new ones, if necessary.

We make our best set of teeth for £3 3s fitted
with our Patent Double Suction, which positively
stops dropping down.
AMERICAN DENTAL PARLORS, Queen &
Wellesley Sts., *Auckland*
Dr. RAYNER

whom Eliot R. Davis nonpareil
colonial brewer hotelier racing
man high-class pig breeder could
'only say' he found

a most genial man and the cheeriest of company at
all times. A dentist by profession and an extremely
clever businessman with an immense number
of commercial interests. He had a huge forest of
kauri timber on the West Coast near the Manukau
Harbour, out of which he made a small fortune.

mile after mile precipitously
rifted ranges the cliff-bottom
beaches Whatipu Karekare
Paratohi Rock waist deep offshore
Piha Anawhata
                    having told his
nephew / secretary Prouting who
told Dick Scott (historian) 20
years was too long to wait in a
pond the size of the U.S.A
to become a big fish in a pond
like New Zealand I could be big
right away if anything bothered me
I could just eat it
                    an abstraction
one thing becoming another
'kind of poem' not leaving the
thing intact
                    all those trees and
Ethel his wife a lyric in her own

right 'a very wealthy woman' having
'a financial interest in Universal
'Pictures Hollywood' the movies
hit Queen Street

     an abstraction registered
as the Hippodrome Picture Company
and plenty more

      'a splendid cook'
in the opinion of Eliot R.
recollecting Moose Lodge later Cole's
where the Queen slept

       long after
and the doctor's well-equipped launch
The Moose for trolling the lapping lake
waters of Rotoiti

      'the finest
grilled trout imaginable'

        Ethel
whose money 'it was generally felt
he was turning to good account'
travelled much of the time in Europe and
the U.S.

    life being practical criticism
of the poetry of wealth

       is unspoiled
Nature any use after all and
what are we doing here?

       'unfortunately
in very bad health' she died
in Canada having left this country
not long before

     date omitted.

VII

Late among the locusts
to the ripest crop
'columnar' Karekare
valleys to the north
late among the locusts
the saw-teeth shining
for the swollen centuries
the locusts hadn't yet
eaten
            seven years
a few million board-feet
later and the big seas
which skittled the beach
tramway one wild
king tide and the bank paid the
doctor what he said
he sold that mill to
the Government
                        having
the right friends clearing
£18,000
and £100,000
royalties the sterling
quality of the man
and
        why don't you send
the money to America
Fred? they said
Kaiser Bill's at the gates
of Paris anything can
happen
            no it can't
God won't let it and
built himself a statelier
mansion in Almorah
Road Epsom Auckland
'magnificent view of the

harbour and landscape'
and there was *talk*

        doesn't he
know there's a war on?
What about those flashing lights
from the windows pro-German
don't tell me von Luckner's
not watching

           prisoner of Motuihe
island
      and why's he got that
Turkish bath with mirrors
all round and the *electric*
light under the mirrors and the
doors between the bedrooms
hidden in the wardrobes?

VIII

'lots of detractors the usual lot
of men who make good financially
or any other way' so Eliot R.

whose mum-in-law (1911) bought the
first Rolls-Royce seen in New Zealand
and who motored one day with the doctor

to Hamilton a hundred miles to the
music of boiling radiators
and exploding 'pneumatic' tyres

and who (Eliot R. that is) did
know there was a war on and sailed
to Sydney twice one month 'buying and

selling whisky in big quantities'
on which active service having been lucky
not to die pondered the all-wisdom of

the One who 'shapes our ends' ordaining
the *Wimmera* (poor Captain Kell)
must hit a mine and not the *Manuka*

preciously freighted with 'another batch
of whisky from the Americans' Charlie Macindoe
and not least if last Eliot R.

who lived 30 years more to put on record
appreciatively that the doctor 'a great
Bohemian always lived on the best'.

IX

The fatty fumes of Abels
margarine factory 'wafted'
on the north-easterly weather
heavy and warm this autumn
creep under low cloud-cover

up the affluently wooded
elevations of Almorah Road
the young executives and the
professional men understand
glossy pictures don't stink

the doctor's uplifted house
of home if that's the idea
is intact a stately shanty
by a World War I domestic
architect out of *Country Life*

in Hampstead it would've had more
knobs but if any fool's folly
ran to hallways two floors high
30ft long the wainscoting
wouldn't be Karekare *kauri*

stained rosewood colour or
the upper floors cladded
with weathering cedar shingles
and the shallow-pitched roof
so anxiously angled an

architecture of evasions
and asseverations *le style*
c'est l'homme Sir Carrick
Robertson 'prominent surgeon'
afterwards liked the outlook

over the trees the unedited
harbour views anybody's islands
a 'beautifully situated'
shabbiness too has its own
classical attributes

grubbiness its grandeurs under
the doctor's porte cochère
the latest cheesiest-lacquered
Japanese hatchback snuggles
long after half of the gardens

and the croquet lawn sliced
off in a storm of steel
pitched from the edge into the age
and the gorge of the motorway leaving
a house with nowhere to fall.

X

I might remember the year you
died but not for that reason
paths cross where nobody comes or
somebody's late it must have

been that in 1931
your soul could have dragged itself
as far as the dawn clifftop
over Anawhata or been torn

from death duties or been sucked
up and scaled off with the sea fog
or spilled into the creeks which drain
the steepnesses worming

its way the dragonflies and
the mosquitoes rise in their day
on wings of success humming
the way money hums and the saw-teeth

your life-cycle and mine
humming the hymn of it's finished
to the tune of it's just begun
fifty years 'later' the

questions open as the high-pitched
morning gapes to the sea
what was all the hurry? and who
on earth is that leaning into the

freshening westerly? *Agathis
australis* could've towered and
rotted in peace any number
of irrelevant centuries the year

I remember is the first I visited
the sun-drowning clifftop and

you died the two facts being
unconnected except I've come

where the paths cross the two of us
on collusion course the
'columnar' the elephant-limbed
conifers of this western

ocean toppled and rolled you
had only to lift your hand the
dank valleys delivered
shiploads ships houses theatres

railway cars the seeds are flying
down into the teeth of the wind
the bulldozers the week-end visitors
in March on my roof the bursting

cone wakes me like hail the soul
flies this way and that in the thinning
dawn dark where the paths cross and the
young trees know only how to grow.

AFTER DINNER

Arnold Wall, 1869–1966

At ninety he told the press,
I suppose you are going to ask me
how I manage to live so long,
and so well.
                    Five years later,
facing me across his table,
having lifted the glass of red
wine to an untremulous
lip, and set it down

with a steady hand, he remarked
that he once possessed the whole
of the *Comédie Humaine*
in a Paris edition. Couldn't
remember now what became of it.

Between him and his death's
left foot the gangrene was
no secret, already in the door
and pressing hard, in a white fold freshly
dressed for dinner.
                        Other whitenesses
were summits, mountain faces,
alps both Southern and Swiss,
Tibet, one icy toehold
after another, still climbing now
in the thinnest air, the last
of all those ups and downs.

Having read many books, taught some,
and written a few, after dinner
announced, as it were, a decision,
I have been here long enough.

A little after that, Lawrence?
D. H. Lawrence? Terrible young man.
Ran away with my friend Weekley's wife.

All true, as it happened. Twice
the mortifying foot, from under the table
published his pang, the grimace no sooner
read than cancelled, very civilly.

A PASSION FOR TRAVEL

Absently the proof-reader corrects
the typesetter. According to copy
the word is exotic. He cancels
the literal r and writes an x.

A word replaces a word. Discrepant
signs, absurd similitudes
touch one another, couple promiscuously.
He doesn't need Schopenhauer

to tell him only exceptional intellects
at exceptional moments ever get any
nearer than that, and when they do
it gives them one hell of a fright.

He's exercised, minding his exes and ars.
If Eros laughs, as the other philosopher
says, and if either word's a world
'offering plentiful material for humour',

that's not in copy. After dark,
that's when the fun starts, there's a room
thick with globes, testers, bell-pulls
rare fruits, painted and woven pictures,

pakeha thistles in the wrong forest,
at Palermo the palm lily *ti australis*
in the Botanical Gardens, Vincento
in white shorts trimming the red canoe

pulled the octopus inside out
like a sock, *Calamari!* The tall German
blonde wading beside, pudenda awash,
exquisitely shocked by a man's hands

doing so much so quickly,
Calamari! Those 'crystalline'

aeolian shallows lap the anemone
which puckers the bikini, her delicacy.

Short of an exceptional moment, if only
just! In his make-do world a word
replaces a white vapour, the sky
heightens by a stroke of the pen.

THE PARAKEETS AT KAREKARE

The feathers and the colours cry
on a high note which ricochets
off the monologue of the morning sun
the long winded sea, off Paratohi posturing
on a scene waiting to be painted.

Scarlet is a squawk, the green
yelps, yellow is the tightest cord
near snapping, the one high note, a sweet-sour
music not for listening. The end is
less than a step and a wink

away as the parakeet flies.
Darkness and a kind of silence under
the cliff cuts the performance,
a moment's mixture. Can scavenging
memory help itself?

What do I imagine coloured words
are for, and simple grammatical
realities like, 'I am walking to the beach'
and 'I have no idea what the sky can mean
by a twist of windy cloud'?

What's the distance between us all
as the rosella cries its tricolour
ricochet, the tacit cliff, Paratohi
Rock in bullbacked seas, my walking eye
and a twist of windy cloud?

DIALOGUE WITH FOUR ROCKS

I

High and heavy seas all the winter
dropped the floor of the beach the whole mile
exposing more rocks than anybody
imagined the biggest surprise a
reef the size of a visiting beast
you have to walk round
                              a formation
out of the gut of the gales the noise
the haze the vocabulary of
water and wind
                    the thing 'demands an
answer'
          I know you do you know me?

the sea shovels away all that loose
land and shovels it back underfoot's
a ball of sand stitched together with
spun lupin and looping spinifex
making it look natural
                              little
as you like to think nothing's either
covered or uncovered for ever.

II

A wall of human bone the size
of a small church isn't easy
to conceive
               neither is the rock
which overhangs me overhung
itself by cloud-cover cupping
the uproars of up-ended seas
and overhanging us all the
hot star which nothing overhangs
the wig it wears is trees knotted
by the prevailing westerlies
'chapleted' with clematis and
kowhai at this height of the spring's
infestations of white and gold
a cerebrum behind the bone
'thinking big'
                  proportionately
to the size of the thing
                     doesn't
have to be visible if it
stoops to speak so to speak the word
of a stony secret dislodged
the creator knows he's made it!
his mate matter
                out of nothing
a tied tongue loosed the stony ghost
before all of us talking all
at once in our own languages
the parakeet's brilliant remarks
the fluent silences of the
eel in the pool
              I think the rock
thinks and my thought is what it thinks.

III

A rock face is creased in
places in others cracked
through to itself I have

never climbed though children
sometimes do up to the
chin of the cave below

I always look up though
something else is always
uppermost a cloud scuds

past the sun reappears
yellow lichens ashy
patches thicken sicken

on the skin of the face
of the rock from spots the
size of the iris of a

mouse's eye to a smashed
egg the rock is wetted
by a weeping lesion

long after the rain stopped
it looks down I look up
a wink is sufficient.

IV

Memory is a stonier
place at the farm they called it
Rocky Gully blackberry
claws me back where I'm crawling

pistol-gripping the rifle
at arm's length after the hurt
hare my two bullets in its
body and couldn't reach it

where the third aimed blindly hit
home recesses of mother
rock overhang me and the
sun the rock offering no

choice of exit under the
one skin hare and hound I catch
myself listening for the shot
in the dark I shall not hear.

AN EXCELLENT MEMORY

Brasch wrote 'these islands' and I
'two islands' counting one short,
and 'the islands' in our language
were remoter, palmier Polynesian chartings,
a there for a here.
                    The cartographer
dots them in, the depth of his blue
denotes the depth of the entirely
surrounding water.
                    The natives,
given time, with the help of an atlas,
come to recognize in the features of

the coastline a face
of their own, a puzzled mirror
for a puzzling globe.
                          'Always in these
islands', that was Charles Brasch
getting it right the very first time.

Pat Laking knew it by heart the whole sonnet
all the way down to 'distance
looks our way' and it did,
over the martinis in Observatory Circle,
Washington D.C., demanding by way
of an answering look nothing more
than an excellent memory.
                          That was
8 November 1974, just about
midnight, give or take a few minutes.

THE OCEAN IS A JAM JAR

Hearing my name in the barnsize bar
of the Tokomaru pub where you cross the road
and walk into the Pacific
Rua made me a small
comically deferential bow
spreading his hands as far
apart as they could go
'You are a *haapuka*!'

and I affecting modesty
comically flattered
flatteringly comic with
hands a bit closer together
'No not a *haapuka* a *kahawai*'

and Rua closing his hands
to the little fish size
perfect at this game
'Perhaps a *maomao?*'

a long way off in the city
in another sort of bar
one stuffed rainbow trout adorned
the wall and a mirror swimmingly
reflected the weed and the cloud
a jam jar full of tadpoles.

IMPROMPTU IN A LOW KEY

None of those was Eden
   I was as far
from that as from this, one's
   own personal
infancy of orchard
   grass grasshoppers
and a Black Prince apple
   or ten summers
later the long breath held
   bursting under-
water in Corsair Bay
   and breaking
surface from the deep green
   dive,
        the breathless
exhalation tweaking
   the neck, half-blind
fish snapping at sunlight.
   None of those was
anywhere near,
           neither was
   the summer come

of sex, give me a hand
  I'll take it.
Fifty onces and sinces,
  paradises
are statistics, I'm as
  far as *ever*,
the older one gets the
  better one gets
the hang of it all the
  essential
onceness.
        Visitors dig
other people's Edens
  there's a sign in
Sicily GROTTA DI
  POLIFEMO,
when you get there you see
  why Homer was
blind as a bat and the
  town football pitch
is netted all round with
  rusty wire.
Interesting,
        the way
  the English say
round the corner and the
  Romans *cento*
metri.
      I'm a stranger
  here myself,
sorry,
      give me a hand.
  You heard what the
man said, keep right on you
  can't miss it.

ORGANO AD LIBITUM

For beauty with her bande
These croked cares hath wrought,
And shipped me into the lande,
From which I first was brought.
— Thomas, Lord Vaux, 1510–1556

I

Time's up you're got up to kill
the lilies and the ferns on wires
the brightwork the sorrowful silk
ribbons the cards the cars

the black twelve-legged beast
rises the dance begins
the six shoulders heave
you up the organist sits

with his back to you and your hobbling
pomp *largo* it says
e grave his fingers walk but
none of the feet is in step

he polishes the stool he rocks on
the bones of his arse he reaches
for a handful of stops he's nodding
yes to your proceeding

perched on a mountain with
'rows upon rows of pipes
set in cliffs and precipices'
growing and growing 'in a blaze

of brilliant light' that sort
of stuff is packaging
printed matter only if only
there were more to it than that

(shriek!) you could see 'his body
swaying from side to side amid the
storm of huge arpeggioed
harmonies crashing overhead'

in a cloud a bandaging whiteout
'his head buried forward towards
a keyboard' busier than God
and you that wool-shed sleeper

the one who saw in his dream
was it Handel high among the icefalls the
big wig nodding mountainously
swaying playing the instrument

had to be big enough to drown
Sam Butler's rivers up there in
Erewhon chapter IV and climbed
uselessly towards the source

of the music this isn't a dream
west of the main divide
Nowherewhon sounds no trumpets
this afternoon everyone present is

wide awake nobody's dreaming
least of all you (you) steady there
hand on *taihoa*! the organist's
fingers trot he breathes through

dusty curtains a husky
vox humana out of dusty
pipes fat candles for Sister
Cecilia's jig-time fingering

diddledy-dancing you down
hold tight there brother in the box
saying after me 'It was
no dreme: I lay brode waking' and

II

saying after me it was *raunchy*
and heavy with lilies in the chapel of
Walerian Borowczyk's blue (blue)
nunnery
        she leaned she fondled the
keyboard the pipes blew kisses
to the mouth her virgin sisters
dressed the altar-table dusted
the pews
        every one a beauty
(beauty) 'dangerous; does set danc-
ing blood' Fr Hopkins S.J.
specialist
        swaying she swept up
nympholept handfuls flung
on the bloodstream a sister playing
organo ad libitum jiggetty-jig on the
woodcutter's cock and the butcher's
block
        Paris having the rottenest
summer for years the crowds
packed in out of the rain to the
Cinéma Paramount leaving
Montparnasse to the web-footed tourists
and the taxis
        dead in her bed
by toxic additive smuggled and
slipped from the knickers to the coffee cup
the gaunt Mother lay
        and they danced
their hot pants down on the stony
gallery for joy of their nubility
crying 'La Mère est morte!' they
swung on the bellrope naked making the
bell-mouth boom at the sun
            one
sneeze of the gusting equinox

whipped the doors from the bolts and up
went the scarlet skirts of the cardinal
dead leaves and fingers
                              flying
to the roaring organ the guffaw
of the daylight and the rain pouring
from the outside in
                              the movie's
over
        will you get up and go?

III

The organist blows his nose folds
his music switches the power off

getting into the 'waiting cars' they
postpone the politics of eternity

till time permits which is after the
cards the flowers the municipal

oil-fired furnace the hole
in the ground one after after

another thereafter before you
know where you are you were.

IV

No bookshelf in the room
                              the Gideons'
bible in the drawer the last occupant
never opened is a black book
lying in wait
                    lucky you brought
your bedside paperbacks prismatic

blue green yellow purple
one celebrated psychiatric
teacher and there's this marvellous
meteorite or enormous
boulder of Magritte a motto for
Sisyphus beneath which you are that
prone figure folded in scarlet perfectly
composed exposed in a
window for anyone who cares to know
what it's like in these rooms for sleeping
off life
      'O Faustus lay that
damned book aside read read
the scriptures' watch out for the
fish-hooks in the small print

V

                          mark
the exits fasten your bible-belt
for take-off
           'the unlikely event
of an emergency'
                 he sits with his
back to you 'busier than God' his
instrument flashes the crash is
programmed the music is magnified the
size of the side of an antarctic
volcano
         you disintegrate there
buzz buzz
            with or without your
loved ones and a face the mirror has
forgotten.

VI

        After is a car door
closing
      chlomp
a blinking light a wide gate
the main road
        chlomp
can I take you anywhere?

VII

Hands on the wheel and eyes on the road
reprieved into the time of day they notice
a yellow bus turning a tired female trundling

groceries 'belief in a hereafter'
wasn't so difficult was it? hardest of all
to believe what actually happens come to think

the difficulty was never to have believed
willingly in heat o' the sun or winter's rages
nor that here after all the hereafter hadn't much

going for it notwithstanding the beauty of
the language nor been listening
when the little dog said you can't eat it and you

can't fuck it sour grapes dogs having no
souls if you believe the books and what's
so special about you in your situation

apropos eating and fucking and
who writes the books? only men who do both or
if no-one did wouldn't exist.

VIII

palingenesis
            five syllables' worth
of pure vacation
                round trip
                     returning
you don't know you've been
                         born twice not again
'Fie upon such errors!
                  To hear stuff of that
nature rends mine ears'
                  Panurge said but Arthur
(Schopenhauer) three
                hundred years after
rather liked the thought
                   looked forward to a
hereafter stocked with
                  genuine spare parts
good as new nothing to
                  burden the memory
naked on the beach
                now storms from the west
stand the sea on end
                  it's an instrument
big enough to drown
                accompanies you
all the way down the
                  'cold front' feathering
inland hanging its
                gauzes uncloses
closes teases you
                don't see anything
clearly
        taihoa!
              your replacement's on
his way
         you're naked
                as the fish bottled

'in its element'
                    lifted to the sun
and it's the same wave
                           spirits you away
out to sea while the
                       biodegradable
part picks up its heels
                         recycles all its
degradations
                fresh
                      wreaths every time and
no resurrections.

IX

                      The organist
locks up the console
                      Handel
booms at the sun
                  Tiziano's
rapt airborne virgin in the Frari
was an assumption removed *per*
restauro in '74 that too was a day of
sun wind and rain
                  Domenico's
mother said and he quoted 'life
is bitter we must sweeten the coffee'
shovelling the sugar
                chlomp
'towards the source of the music'
                      chlomp
and they made the bell-mouth swing
swinging on the bell-rope
                    naked.

YOU WILL KNOW WHEN YOU GET THERE

Nobody comes up from the sea as late as this
in the day and the season, and nobody else goes down

the last steep kilometre, wet-metalled where
a shower passed shredding the light which keeps

pouring out of its tank in the sky, through summits,
trees, vapours thickening and thinning. Too

credibly by half celestial, the dammed
reservoir up there keeps emptying while the light lasts

over the sea, where it 'gathers the gold against
it'. The light is bits of crushed rock randomly

glinting underfoot, wetted by the short
shower, and down you go and so in its way does

the sun which gets there first. Boys, two of them,
turn campfirelit faces, a hesitancy to speak

is a hesitancy of the earth rolling back and away
behind this man going down to the sea with a bag

to pick mussels, having an arrangement with the tide,
the ocean to be shallowed three point seven metres,

one hour's light to be left and there's the excrescent
moon sponging off the last of it. A door

slams, a heavy wave, a door, the sea-floor shudders.
Down you go alone, so late, into the surge-black fissure.

THE LOOP IN LONE KAURI ROAD, 1986

A RAISED VOICE

Let it be Sunday and the alp-high
summer gale gusting to fifty miles.

Windmills groan in disbelief, the giant
in the pulpit enjoys his own credible

scale, stands twelve feet 'clothed in fine linen'
visibly white from the waist up, all

inferior parts masked, as my father
ascends three steps, is cupped like an egg.

The pulpit floor's eye-level, I look
up, Gordon Brown looks up, my father

looks down at his notes and begins in the
name of the father and of the son

and of the holy ghost amen, a voice
that says Jess to my mother, heightened

three steps, to which add the sanctuary
rise, the subdued pile of the Axminster

runner. Panels of pale-coloured wood
liturgically pointed assemble

to enclose and to elevate the voice:
is it soft *kahikatea*, so readily

riddled by the worm of the borer
beetle but ideal for butter-boxes

or heart *kauri*? the rape of the northern
bush left plenty for pulpits and pews.

Gordon Brown, grocery and general store,
before kneeling always pushes one

oily vessel up clear of his head, the
tin lampshade clashes, the pulley squeaks.

I'm looking up into my thought
of my father, my certainty, he'll

be safe, but what about me? What else?
A voice descends, feet scrape, we all

stand up. The scent my mother wears is
vera violetta. That can't be it.

MOULES À LA MARINIÈRE

It took the sun six hours to peel
the sea from the gut, black underwater
dries out grey underfoot, 'cleft for me'

to look down. The dull thought of drowning
ebbed with the flood, this orifice entices
wide open, gargling, warm at the lips.

Not all the way down. The deepest
secretions don't drain, still you can 'feel'
what's below the bottom of the tide,

knowing more than's good for you: seabed
rock wetted perpetually with spectral
colours, quotations lifted from

life into stony text, epigraphies
remembering shot-silk offals, trapped
green weed, petrifying mauves,

muddy cysts, mucus, your own interior
furnishings, glands, genitalia
of the slit reef spilling seawards:

walls all scabby pink, sprayed-on starfish,
gluey limpets, linings of the gut which
swallowing a wave throws up an ocean,

it smells of your nature, sickishly.
Hold on tight, by one hand, stripping
off the mussels, quick! with the other

into the bag, don't count cut bleeding
fingers. The tide scrapes the bottom,
blinded and a bit fouled with sand

the slack of the swell drools, fills, empties
refills, your jeans are sodden
to the crotch, that's wet enough, the bag's

heavy enough: do you really want more
mussels, old swimmers, do you need
more drowning lessons? Here it comes, one

ten-foot wave after another, it's
all yours now and it's up to you down
in the gut and the blind gut

in the wet of your eye gorging
moules à la marinière,
an enormous weight! Nothing to the

tonnages of water lightly climbing
your back. Picked off alive and
kicking in the rip, did you 'feel'

unaccountably unsurprised by
how natural it all is, in the end,
no problem, the arms and legs have only

to exercise the right allowed by law,
last words, the succinctest body-language.
You're innocent. The sea does the rest.

DO NOT TOUCH THE EXHIBITS

A gulp of sea air, the train
bites off a beach, re-enters the rock.
A window, a blind cathode, greyly reflects,
Plato sits opposite, his nose in a map.
Where you're going's never what you see

and what you saw, is that where you went?
Is there a reef with an angler on it
whose rod makes a twitching U?
Has he landed his fat silver-gilt
dorado, smack! on a pan in the mind?

Why can't I cut corners and have them?
Daylight chips in again, with cypresses,
olives, loquat (*nespola* the Japan
medlar, not the ones you eat rotten,
the other sort, butter-yellow, sweet

embedding slippery outsize pips),
artichokes, the native littoral
cultivations, rivermouth litter,
punctured cans, plastic bottles,
and behind (supposedly) the weatherish

pink and chrome villas gingerly
seated, shutters to seaward,

the Ligurian blue, too much of it.
Or weathering the long cape
another fisherman whose limping

boat I'm overhauling? a file
of red and white Martini sunbrollies
wheels in, peels off, drops back.
A brace of NATO frigates present
unmuzzled guns, 'optional extras'.

Beachcombings, introjections,
best stuffing for tunnels. Venus
on her lee-shore *poco mosso*
paroled from the Uffizi, screwed
to the wall under the baggage rack,

space reserved in the mind, goes
where I go, my side of the glass
beneath which our family motto's pinned,
è pericoloso sporgersi
indelibly incised on steel.

Rapallo, London 1983

ON THE ROAD TO EREWHON

The Author wishes it to be understood that Erewhon is pronounced
as a word of three syllables, all short — thus, E-re-whon.
— Samuel Butler, preface to *Erewhon*, 1872

Once past the icefalls and the teeth of
noon, already descending the pass,
out of a cloud blackened by lightning,
if mirrors can spell and maps don't lie,
that's the Erewhon road, the ambush

can't be far. Gigantic statues shock
you down to size. Before the Hyksos
their senate debated what's to be
done with you. They have mouths the mountain
blast vociferates in, a people

had need of these or these of themselves
were in need *causa sui*. Inhuman
syllables, harmony that howls and
hails, halting you. Patches of old snow
squeak underfoot. Goat-tracks, lost writings.

Six or seven times larger than life,
of great antiquity, worn and lichen
grown. They were ten in number . . . I saw
that their heads had been hollowed. Fear,
pain, hate, cruelty once chopped into stone

stare out again, each head *a sort of*
organ-pipe, so that their mouths should catch
the wind. Earthly, unaccompanied
voices empty wind into wind, mist
into mist, rock into rock, these ten

commandments. Eight of them still seated,
two had fallen. The God who thinks aloud's
the worst, your own shadow's a friendlier
fright. Physical, *superhumanly*
malevolent faces look back, too

hard for your nature to bear, only
the legs and how fast they can carry
you the hell out of here *as though one*
of them would rush after me and grip
me . . . If it were just one of those dreams

where running gets you nowhere! This is
the mirrored map, the Erewhon road,
where you came from is where you're going,

the hammers in the brain keep time with
feet pounding downhill, the rivers are

swollen in the mind's eye. Back there, in
the cloud the trumpeting heads perform
their own *Te Deum*. Panicky antiphons
die down in the blood. You can shiver
suddenly, for no reason at all.

BLIND MAN'S HOLIDAY

I

Is the word 'adult'? Utamaro's engulfing
vulvas, deep thought! Füssli's girls muscling in, a
moist-handled glans, *shockingly indelicate*,

poor wretch! Flaxman said, *looking ineffably
modest*, one didn't blame the widow Füssli's
thrift, who stoked the kitchen range with them, making

sea-coal burn bluer. Was less at stake for Bruno
in Venice, incinerated, ineffably
for something ineffable? Ashes, in the end.

Stuff your pillow-book with metaphysics for
the best bedside read, it takes the place of what
takes place, pictures or *pensées*, the same thing.

The picture in the mind revives, our poet
noticed, and so do I. These agreeable
sensations moved over and made room for *sad*

perplexity, and back again, having once
orbited the earth. I re-enter, entering
you. The mind's too full of itself, to make sense

of Pascal or the creed of Saint Athanasius
damp and hot from the press, 'would you believe it?'
What does God smell of but the dust of hassocks,

wine, laundered linen, a creation of Patou
fingertipped behind the ears? Angel surrogates
shinny up and down the fire-escape, flapping

at bedroom and bathroom windows, all fingers
and feathers. She's too full and he's too busy to
notice much, only *gleams of half-extinguished*

thought, in the light of what takes place, no other
light really than these, which take the place of it.
A particular darkness forgets our visits.

II

What happened? What's happening? Somebody drew
a funny face on a big shell, BANG! you're dead
all of you, Ol' Bill ducks his helmet, it flies

past grinning, or bounces off a parapet.
In a serious oil-painting nobody gets
obscenely eviscerated, the war artist's

a dab hand at cosmetic bandaging, he
patches up with white, with a fine tip adds red
for the head-wounds, mostly in the scalp and brow,

the eyes of the wounded are forget-me-not
blue, gun-flashes vermilion, virginal pink
for the faces, like begonia blooms in shit

which is khaki *dunnest smoke*, old-masterly
murk *that my keen knife see not the wound it makes*
nor Heaven peep through. Heaven does. One painted

274

star blinks benignly. A child in the sun sees
it all in The Queen's Gift Book where Adam hides
because he is naked. My bank manager's

choice is a framed cauliflower cloud, the atoll
vertically blown up out of a silk-screen
ocean. Glass catches the light. Entering, I

turn it to the wall, unwilling to pre-empt
the untriggered fact, the picture in the mind,
the job in hand. Its relevance is obscure.

III

What's pain time? Your long wire, Alvin Lucier, sings
to the oscillator, end over end, glistens
in your darkened gallery. This is our midnight
ride in a wet gale banging the heads of the trees

together. Quartz watches don't keep it, humane
quackery knows what's quickest for capital
offenders, mortal inhalation, 'lethal
injection', make up your mind, how would you like

to die? In a flash, a puff, *an unconscionable
time a-dying* the king said or was said to have
said? Duration is public, the intensity
private, God's wink, a lifetime, a million years.

Where are we now? Between gulps of gas, that's twice
I've asked, this time he answers Saint Luke's, meaning
the supermarket not the church, I grunt back
gratefully, meaning neither, the hospital's

any minute now by pain time, a quick fix could
conveniently snap the wire, drop the dumb ends
in a puddle of terminal quiet, no
more random glistenings, no sound-images

whipped off the street. I want it stopped. Where are we?
The ambulance corners with a shrug, straightens,
windshield wipers egg-scramble headlights, greens, reds,
ambers, unquantifiable messes of wet

incandescences. Squatting, he holds the gas
bottle as steadily as he can. I lie
still too. The driver's shoulder's a dark function.
It's an 'essential service' we all perform,

Monday is beginning, Sunday's casualties
unloading still, full as a party balloon
with pain the mind bobs unserviceably while
somebody is brought in dead. I want my shot

and a couple of 50mg
indocid is all I'm getting if that's true
about the key to the cupboard where they keep
the morphine and the sister who comes on duty

at five, that's four hours more of this, the
bloody sheet keeps slipping off. You get the picture?
Amnesia, muse of deletions, cancellations
revives, revises pain, a ride in the dark.

LO THESE ARE PARTS OF HIS WAYS

and to make up my mind about God before
he makes up his about me put myself
in Wallace Stevens's place and
God wherever he pleases
and a precious pair of us that makes

two minds in two minds each about
the other or say four deadlines
in search of a Last Supper

r.s.v.p. time running out
no entry on the diary's blank last

fly leaf's dateless day
numinous yesses and noes making
minds up alters nothing materially
can you see God changing his or
being in more than one about

anybody's finally settling
for 'naturally' the right one like
in the event of malfunction aborting
the count-down? our recreation's
chess he's white and I'm black

the board expands infinitely
at an infinite speed like Pascal's point
with mirrors which mirror mirrors
behind each of us his lips think
in his native Russian one forefinger

pauses on a pawn's or a bishop's
bonnet when it lifts we both know
that move's for keeps operations
belong to control where celestial
software lisps eternal

zero-zeroes to the pacemaker
aorta *soft drum* the screen's bare
of digits all circuits locked *prepare to
meet thy God* have you an appointment?
belief hung in mid-mind between

the ethereal and the dustiest
answers let it hang! whose creature
whose creator to believe him into
existence or out of it? the heart
grows obsolete bottled protons

of an irrefutable *might*
majesty dominion and power poke
infernal noses into heavenly
business mutually assured
destruction keeps both of us guessing

demonstrable changes in the forms
of matter like fire-storms hanging
fire *Et O ces voix*
d'enfants chantant DIES IRAE
DIES ILLA exist in a mirror

a lifted forefinger for God's sake
whose? playing for keeps
my playmate's one unbelievably small
particle and who knows whose dust's
on fire in whose mind's eye?

GARE SNCF GARAVAN

The day doesn't come to the boil, it guards
a banked-up flame under a cool first light.
Madame tethers her Siamese to the doorway
of the Gare SNCF, the shadier side
of the tracks where we mustn't stray.

The tracks are bare, the pines don't stir, the haze
is international, Cap Martin is a thing
in the mind's eye of 'that eternal sea',
Bordighera just one more. Behind the doorway
of the sanctuary, something rings, Madame is

answering. I am questioning a blossom of
some nameless yellow creeper about the excitements
of life on a warm wall. Pussy is overweight,
so is Madame, but active, panties and *collants*
hang from an upper room, over the yard side

of the Gare, the seaward, shaded by the dark
eyelashes of the pines in a light that is not
explicit. Landward the Alpes Maritimes lean
scarily steep-to, by the Gare clock
I can relax, nobody's yet begun saying

'to the mountains, fall on us', only indistinct
voices drop from the lemon-gardens, the villas.
A frequent service. Madame emerges, bearing her
official baton, producing a train from Nice,
Italy's minutes away, an old-fashioned thought,

an old-fashioned iron expostulation of
wheels, fluttering doors, interrupts nothing.
So much at risk, a miracle that so much gets
taken care of, Madame picks up her cat from
the *quai* and cuddles it, conversing with friends.

Menton, London, 1983

CANTO OF SIGNS WITHOUT WONDERS

I look where I'm going, it's the way
        yesterday's and the day before's clouds
        depict themselves over and over

an affluently planted skyline:
        the clouds lay the whitenesses on thick
        over the bluenesses. The impasto

is unsigned, there's a kind of an impression
        of lettering rapidly rubbed out
        before I can read, pasted over again

and rewritten, the name of a famous
        product, the thing that's everything,
        the sky being prime space, anyway

279

the most public part of this universe.
    Speculative thunder is noises,
    contused vapours, colours into which

my eyes walk: high-flown language, logo and
    sign of a brand of which 'the authors
    are in eternity', at least some

country we never trade with. My eyes
    walk a tight wire made fast to a cloud,
    securest anchorage, the weather

man's promise of 'settled conditions'.
    Underfoot, the pavement keeps falling
    away step by step where I'm about

to pass the pianist's open door
    some *chant sans paroles* escapes: his patched
    iron roof leaked, he spread a tarpaulin

over the Steinway: two of his cats
    stare from the shade of the hydrangea.
    The pavement is still falling, my eyes

walk not precisely stepping high across
    craters and cones, 'best parts' of our city:
    volcanic pustules green a thousand

years, and for a couple of lifetimes
    these people, yesterday's and the day
    before's people, as far as the bluest

dilations of clouds and seas and names
    to call islands by. Less and less time
    remains, they purify their private

pools, uncapping the vials which protect
    from viral enemies: the prudent
    set aside sums for depreciation,

each year sell off a wasting asset,
    c'est la vie. The painter is freshing
    up yesterday's clouds by interior

light, he cleans his brushes, drinks a mug
    of instant coffee. The rusted VW
    meditates my other car is a Rolls.

As they walk, those two, side by side,
    his hand fondles the blueness of her
    jeans, her thready rondure and the stitched

name of Levi Strauss, below the patch
    seeking. She takes the hand. The sign is
    what the maker means. Much more than that

calls for an impossible presence
    of mind, I look where I'm going and
    that way they depict themselves, yes

that's all for today, my eyes wired
    to a system there, feet falling in turn
    on the pavement which is falling away,

unsigned whitenesses, unsigned bluenesses.

A SIGHT FOR SORE EYES

They wrap mountains round my eyes,
they say 'look' and it's all what they say
where the colour, that's another word is
deepest blue, and that's the colour of
the wind, blowing this way, warm and dry
coming from the mountains, visibly.

I have eyes in the back of my neck
too, the sun is mumbling the day's news
over my head. In so many words.
My morning bath was warm, out of a tap.
This garden is just one year younger
than I, 'girdled round' five years ago

with six-foot galvanised iron on
rimu posts, the sawn timber elsewhere
supports the Number 8 fencing wire
with one barbed strand, a little rusted.
The new vicarage is a 'bungalow',
the veranda faces north by west,

casements are fashionable magic
again, since the double-hung sash went
out, opening on the forms of pain, of
mumbled words, mountainously pronounced.
Too small to see over, I can thread
my line of vision through a nail-hole

in the iron. I give it a tug.
The mountains have shifted at their moorings,
shudder and heave clear. The biggest wind's
in that quarter, it loosens the snows,
the Green Road is under water, old
Mr and Mrs Troon in a boat

are 'taken out' repeated in a dream
of the Troons, the Troons! What have I done?

What are the Troons doing 'taken out'
in a boat in the dark up Green Road,
old and ugly and wet? The wind was
never so dry and warm or the smell

of sheep so sour or the dust so thick
in the macrocarpas. The mountains
are the colour of wind, the highway
north is a pillar of dust by day
half-blinding riders and dogs, westward
the river still rises. My mother

bathes my eyes with boracic, she ties
up torn dianthus, delphinium, phlox
wasted on the alluvium the storm-
waters have been scraping seaward since
the sun mumbled the first implanted
word. My mother grows it all from seed.

THE LOOP IN LONE KAURI ROAD

By the same road to the same
sea, in the same two minds,
to run the last mile blind or
save it for later. These
are not alternatives.

So difficult to concentrate! a powerful
breath to blow the sea back
and a powerful hand to haul it
in, without overbalancing.
Scolded for inattention,

depending on the wind, I know
a *rimu* from a *rewarewa*
by the leaf not 'coarsely serrate',

observant of the road roping
seaward in the rain forest.

A studied performance, the way
I direct my eyes, position
my head, 'look interested'.
Fine crystal, the man said,
you can tell by the weight,

the colour, the texture. The dog
steadies, places a healthy turd
on the exact spot. We like it
in the sun, it keeps our backs
warm, the watertables

dribble down the raw red cutting
the road binds, injured natures are
perfect in themselves. We liked it
at the movies when they nuked the city,
and suspended our disbelief

in doomsday, helping out the movie.
NEW YORK STATE jogs past me,
rib-cage under the t-shirt stacked
with software, heart-muscle programmed
for the once round trip,

crosses my mind, by the bridge
at the bottom, the road over which
and the stream underneath are thoughts
quickly dismissed, as we double
back, pacing ourselves.

Concentrate! the hawk lifts off
heavily with an offal of silence.
Forget that, and how the helicopter
clapper-clawed the sea, fire-bucketing
the forest, the nested flame.

There is a law that governs all artistic creation, of which Kondrashov had long been aware, which he tried to resist but to which time after time he feebly submitted. This law said that no previous work of his carried any weight, that it could not be counted to the artist's credit. The focal point of all his past experience was always the canvas on which he was working at the time; for him the work on hand was the ultimate expression of his intellect and skill, the first real test of his gifts ... only *now* was he really finding out how to paint! ...
— Alexander Solzhenitsyn, *The First Circle*, tr. Michael Guybon

SURVIVORS

Night falls on an unusual scene of public
rejoicing. A whole head taller than the crowd,

astride my father's nape, I can see the *jets
d'eau* the fire brigade pumps across the lake,

ebulliently spouted, illuminated.
Rose-coloured spectaculars blown to waterdrops

float off briskly, lifted into the dark
as the land-breeze variably puffs. Up above

searchlights find nothing but weather and themselves
(a dustier glare is where I see those headlamps

juddering for ever and all the way home
and hear the motor fire steadily) because

it's the end of the war, these are survivors
by the long wash of Australasian seas

a diminuendo of bells, guns, and prayers and
all these people simply enjoying themselves.

A wind freshens across the park, the crowd begins
thinning towards tomorrow. Climb up and see.

NARITA

Turning its eyes from side to side, inquiring
brightly, the head of the worm issues
from the door for arrivals.

The door for departures is where papers are
handed in. There are many of these,
all numbered. Never look back.

Between the two the meantime is all there is.
It passes of itself. Your cabin
crew girls are for off-duty

fantasies. Abaft the loo the tail section
ruptures, the sky inhales heavily,
a change of plan is announced,

all four hundred, some gifted or beautiful
or with greedy heirs, have to die now,
only to make sure of you

this instant sooner or later than you think.
The prettiest accessories, like
silk scarf, matching lipstick, badge

of rank are brightness fallen from the air, you
will never see it. The uniformed
personnel most pitiably

heaped, colours of daedal feathers, the smells of
burning, a ring'd finger, a baby's
foot bagged for the mortuary.

No, you will never see it. Wish yourself then
the best of Lucifer's luck. This indoors
world's roof is geodetic,

as good as any heaven, and better lit
than the broad daylight it simulates,
out of hearing of the rising

and the falling scream and sight of the nearest
numbered gate. Picture to yourself some
small green hills with ginkgo trees.

THE VESPIARY: A FABLE

Its thoughts are modular, they attach themselves
to the young tree, the soffit of the back porch,
a grey box with multiple apertures where

its visible business is with legs and wings
purposefully hesitant, the unseen venom
is contingent, the sting for later inquiry.

I write. Those writings which we now identify
doubtfully as such yield nothing. I transcribe
tapes of the period recovered from pack ice,

leaning hard on the crude systems in use today.
I construe gaps, blips, ambiguous phonemes
and learn that the day after the first confirmed

sightings country children were sent home early
from school, a pet goat found stung dead on its tether.
Townspeople who'd never heard of honey dew

ran out into the streets, crying and silent.
Unopposed meanwhile, our oceanic nation's
defences in traditional disrepair,

the feral Vespoidea victory in their grasp
thrust inland, seized ornamental trees, PVC
downpipes breeches of abandoned guns ditched

cars, open mouths, armpits, natural nests
of which the naturalness has taken centuries
issuing the safe side of history's mirror.

I write. The past itself encoded itself
known only to itself and is dead, and we
live in our different style. No one knows how

many millions perished while our two species
achieved symbiosis by selection, between
this beach and that mountain 'under Capricorn',

in an agon of orifices, host and guest,
legs, wings, damp secretions. Now the dark swarms, my
lips mumble words over the busy bodies.

I write. The bones of the last boatpeople from
the north and the west lay somewhere under the dunes
where dogs dug and we played. When I was a kid

that's what we said. The safest thing's to touch nothing
on the beach, the back of the cave, the riverbed,
never leave the nest in the bush, where you were born

and suckled. A mother's cry stings me in my
mind's ear stuck to the tape, another tongue trapped
in the dead of time, *Attention! les guêpes!*

THE PUG-MILL

At his age, he must know what it is
to have hands of clay and a child looking on.
A life by dug-out light under the hillside,
he has copied so often the one

thought baked in the bones of his wrist, there's
no obvious excuse for stopping now, so long
as there's a next there's no last. I am this child.
I watch Mr Prisk raise his left hand

eye-level (his own) as high as where
a bit of unweeded green light leaks beneath
a punky window-sash and pull on the rope's
knotted end. Up above in the sun

his horse hears the bell and stumbles out
of a doze into the collar and begins
orbiting the pug-mill, plods a muddy zodiac
which in its turn turns. Clotted clay buries

the workbench again. With palping palms
he stuffs his mould, that's one more circle squared, one
more brick the desert will keep. A contribution.
Its damp six faces sparkle dully

because of the sand which helps them slide
out whole into the system we inhabit here.
Is there anything outside? The hillside steepens
till baffled it stops, this way by blue

air that way by blue water, a third
which escapes between I'm running barefoot home
Corsair Bay, Flea Beach, pines of the town Domain
past the burned-out house with one dead brick

chimney standing. They are asking *Where-
ever have you been?* I tell them *Helping Mr Prisk.*

CONTINUUM

The moon rolls over the roof and falls behind
my house, and the moon does neither of these things,
I am talking about myself.

It's not possible to get off to sleep or
the subject or the planet, nor to think thoughts.
Better barefoot it out the front

door and lean from the porch across the privets
and the palms into the washed-out creation,
a dark place with two particular

bright clouds dusted (query) by the moon, one's mine
the other's an adversary, which may depend
on the wind, or something.

A long moment stretches, the next one is not
on time. Not unaccountably the chill of
the planking underfoot rises

in the throat, for its part the night sky empties
the whole of its contents down. Turn on a bare
heel, close the door behind

on the author, cringing demiurge, who picks up
his litter and his tools and paces me back
to bed, stealthily in step.

A TIME OF DAY

A small charge for admission. Believers only.
Who present their tickets where a five-
barred farm gate gapes on its chain

and will file on to the thinly grassed paddock.
Out of afternoon pearl-dipped light the
dung-green biplane descended

and will return later, and later, late as
already it is. We are all born
of cloud again, in a caul

of linen lashed to the air-frame of the age,
smelling of the scorched raw castor oil
nine whirling cylinders pelt

up-country-smelling senses with, narcotic
joyrides, these helmeted barnstormers
heavier scented than hay,

harnesses, horsepiss, fleeces, phosphates and milk
under the fingernails. I'm pulling at
my father's hand *Would the little*

boy for selling the tickets? One helmet smiles
bending over yes, please yes let me,
my father hesitates, I

pull and I don't let go. Neither does the soul
of the world, whatever that is, lose
hold of the load, the bare blue

mountains and things hauled into the time of day
up that steep sky deepening from sea-
level all the way west again,

this paddock, the weight of everything, these people
waiting to be saved, without whom there's
no show, stay in place for ever.

A hand under each arm I'm held, I'm lifted
up and over and into an open
cockpit *Contact!* Gnome-LeRhône

fires ninefold, the chocks kicked clear, my balaclava
knits old sweat and foul oil, where tomorrow
was encloses me now.

THE GAME OF TAG, (1989-1997)
from EARLY DAYS YET, 1997

The Erewhonians say that we are drawn through life backwards; or again that we go onwards into the future as into a dark corridor. Time walks beside us and flings back shutters as we advance; but the light thus given often dazzles us, and deepens the darkness which is in front. We can see but little at a time. . . . ever peering curiously through the glare of the present into the gloom of the future, we presage the leading lines of that which is before us, by faintly reflected lights from dull mirrors that are behind, and stumble on as we may till the trap-door opens beneath us and we are gone. . . . The Erewhonians say it was by chance only that the earth and stars and all the heavenly worlds began to roll from east to west and not from west to east, and in like manner . . . that man is drawn through life with his face to the past instead of to the future. For the future is there as much as the past, only that we may not see it. Is it not in the loins of the past, and must not the past alter before the future can do so?

Sometimes, again, they say that there was a race of men tried upon the earth once, who knew the future better than the past, but that they died in a twelvemonth from the misery which their knowledge caused them . . .

— Samuel Butler, *Erewhon*

THE UNCLOSED DOOR

Freshened by any wind, sanitised
with pine and cypress, the slaughterhouse

is cool as a church inside. High rafters
too. A gallery. The hooks hang ready.

Nothing else intercepts the day's late
blaze across the Seven Sleepers' chins

and Cooper's Knobs, on this point between
adjacent bays, only a blotched light

293

can get past, as the wind in the trees,
fidgeting to the doorway. The door

on its iron track having been wheeled back
wide enough, the small boys, me and Bob

Crawford, can see in. One of the men
turns our way, in the act of closing his

left hand on the lamb's throat, at the bass
viol the right, the bowing hand slashes

deep! *in blood stepped in so far* will up
to the eyes or the ears be enough?

They're all busy now, the hosing down
will have started. Add water and sweep

shit pellets puddled blood, the outfall
gulps, discharges over the rock-face

misting all the way to the green bay
water, with a noise of waters, where

the round stain dilates. An enrichment.
I think the children had been silent, all

this time. I will have pulled my bike, off
his, on the tree. Nothing alters this.

A SOUTH ISLAND NIGHT'S ENTERTAINMENT

Somebody mistook
the day, or how

will we have found
ourselves denied

entry, by chained
gate, padlocked

bolted door of an
empty dark shed

of a hall, miles
from the next town-

ship, as many from
the last lit lamp?

The night itself
unpunctuated,

no Southern Cross,
no Pointers, no

cartwheeling, hand-
standing giant

Orion, aka
Urine (born cauled

in a sacrificial
Boeotian cow's

pelt, pissed in by
no fewer than three

grateful gods) no
moon. Heavy cloud.

This my ninth year
under them all gets

darker by the minute.
What's visible here?

Not the crab tropic's
maidenliest stars

twinkle-twinkling
on my grandmother's

East Anglian
wedding night, swapped

now, for a sphere
beyond the circuit

of the shuddering Bear.
Eastward our austral

Pacific sands,
our high snows west-

ward. Our meridian
threads a chained gate

which brings us up
all standing, my father,

my mother, her
mother, and me.

Shut out. Wrong day.
Wrong side of the screen

where a New Age
was to have unreeled

itself, stormed this
barn in drizzling light.

Unreeled the fat
man's quaking back-

firing automobile.
Silent. His arse-

over-kite exit.
Silent. The Metro

Goldwyn lion's jaws
parted. A World

War One great gun
discharged. Silent.

A cloud that was
the city. A painted

scream. Silent, only
for the lady playing

'Rustle of Spring'
in an empty dark

shed of a hall.
Nobody comes.

Only our feet go
crunch-crunch in and out

of step as they fall,
all the way home.

A BUSY PORT

I

My turn to embark. A steep gangplank
expects me. An obedient child,
I follow my father down.

It happens that the sun will have topped
a black hill beside the time-ball tower,
and found the spot of a fresh

tear on Bob Hempstalk's cheekbone, whose wet
red eyes blink back seaward where he leans
for'ard at the wheel-house glass;

one hand wipes an eye, the other shakes
a half-hitch loose, unlashing the wheel.
A man's tears, obscene to me

caught looking. Too late now. The time-ball
drops. Quayside voices (not for my ears)
discuss the dead, bells repeat

ding-ding across the wharf. Brightwork traps
the sun in brass when I next look up,
following my father down,

who made the trip himself many years
past. The old rust-bucket gets up steam.
Frequent sailings from where we live.

II

Winched aboard still warm over the for'ard
hatch the morning's bread hangs by a breath
of its own. It smells of bed.

An enriched air. The urinal under
the wharf drip-feeds, the main steam below
sweats. Darky Adams, deckhand

engineer stoker bangs his firebox
open, slings in a shovelful, slams
the insulted flame back home,

thick acrid riddance topples the way
smoke rolls by its own weight, in an air
that barely lifts, off the stack.

One jump clear of the deck the plank dips
with a short uneasy motion, deep-
sea talk to the paddler's foot

out of my depth, deeper yet, off the Heads,
our Pillars. Pitching like a beer-can.
I'm hanging on tight, can't hear

clashes from the stokehole for the wind
yelling, crossed on the wheel he's yelling
back, 'Ay, bit of a stiff breeze'.

Eyes that last I saw in tears can read
abstruse characters of waves, on course
between them, our plunging bows.

ANOTHER WEEKEND AT THE BEACH

Turn left at the sign. Lone Kauri Road
winds down to the coast. That's a drop
of about five hundred feet. Look out
for the waterfall, the wooden bridge,
the mown grass, the pohutukawa glade.

The western horizon will have slid
behind the mask of an eye-levelled
next eyeballing wave. Park here. Proceed
on foot. The spot has barbecues with
MALE and FEMALE dunnies in a figtree

thicket, wrong hemisphere, implausibly
fruiting. Tracks cross the wind-sifting dune
skyline of unkempt lupin, marram,
spinifex's incontinent seed-
vessels bowling downwind, the way I've

come and come, how many thousand times
to no other conclusion, the back
of a broken wave, and found no word
or forgot or omitted to write
it down, *Ah, quelle écriture de la*

différance! l'orthographe derridienne
for every thing's everything. Then why
not phytoplankton, the algoid bloom
any less than those offshore purples, this
beached medusa, polythene waste, bubbled

sea-froth, tincture of a present spume
spattered up the sands? Mind where you pick
your mussels and *kina*, these tides may
secrete indigenous toxins. Deadly
to the text. Shall I copy it again?

THE GAME OF TAG

AFRIKA POET HERO DODGER FELIX DEVOE
CURSE EXIT CICERO BEASTIE SAINT THANKS
FOR THE TAG AFRIKA POET '93
         — Graffito, Lone Kauri Road

Seven thigh-thick
hamstring-high posts,

embedded two
metres and cemented

in, where the side
of the road burst

into bird space,
tree-toppling all

that plunging way
down. A clean-cut

horizon shapes
daylight. A gap.

Where the sea glares
back at the land's

shiftiness. Hefty
planks mounted strap-

wise, post to post,
invite my spray-

gun-toting rival
to sign A-F-R-I-K-A

P-O-E-T-92
who will have caught

up with himself
at the next bend

where the road slipped
again, and again

tagged the white paint-
edness of a new

barrier A-F-R-I-K-A
P-O-E-T-93. The paint

is for the poetry.
And signed off. Skid

marks in the gravel.
And powered the old

Falcon around, like
a bat out of Hell. Gave

Death the fingers.
Shook the dreadlocks

from his eyes, for
his best shot. Darkly

incontinently
lets fly, spattering

name after name.
A crumbling road.

Where have they all
gone, with CICERO

BEASTIE and me
and which of us

leads the way down
post and plank not-

withstanding, car-
apaced in Korean

steel, to be wrapped
round a bole two

hundred years thick,
two hundred feet

below? One wild
wheelie and we're off.

Rain-forest soon
repairs its ruins.

Dead men's dental
records and cellphones

tell no lies. Rust
finishes the job

(almost). One chip
of red Perspex

under a stone
in the stream was

his (whose?) tail-light.
A-F-R-I-K-A P-O-E-T

writes, and I quote
THANKS FOR THE TAG.

LOOKING WEST, LATE AFTERNOON, LOW WATER

*The typical tidal range, or difference in sea level between high and low tides,
in the open ocean is about 2 ft (0.6m), but it is much greater near the coasts.*
— Desk encyclopedia

Our beach was never so bare. Freak tide,
system fault, inhuman error, will it

never stop falling? After dark, said
the tables of high water and sunset

pasted on the wall, which don't deceive.
Come on down for a walk while there's light.

A wall of pale green glass miles above
head high alongside, complete with fish

crossing, is what will have been the wave
once it has broken. Leviathan is

the beached cachalot we left Bob Falla
filleting for science, the ebb to wash

away these fifty years, each one smaller
than the last. Come down, this is today

delivered factory fresh, in colour
heated by the late sun. Time to try

looking on the bright side, or join those
Great God! (says the poem) who'd *rather be*

suckled in a creed outworn: but whose
cast-off cult's to be the lucky one?

Great waters, unfinished business, done
blind to the deadline. From that rock to

this tree was *tapu* and it sticks. Thin
pickings, Tangaroa, this is *pakeha*

story time, only Okeanos and
sister Tethys having it off: the way

they love makes hairy cliff-hanging seas
roll drums on the sand, the three-metre swell

flat on the seabed bangs the pubes,
very ancient and fishlike they smell

close to. Divine all the same. Dangerous,
not to be approached, least of all by

mortal man whose years are four-score plus
tomorrow night. While I count the three

strong swimmers carried past out of sight
round the North Rocks the whole shoreline shakes

underfoot again, dead friends call out
not to be heard. Look west, what looks

back is blood-orange nightfall, the stooped
sky drowning another sun overboard

where the horizon was: till it snapped
those deep-sea moorings and will be heard

oncoming, the sound of a scream. *tsunami!*
tsunami! splintering deadwood of the boat

I lost half a life ago, swept
away with a judgement on the work

she's amateur built but your friends won't know.
Last seen, one inflatable rescue

craft stood on its tuck, bows to skyward
in fast failing light, a turning tide.

THE SCRAP-BOOK

I

The light in the window blew out in a strong
draught only to return wearing a black mask,
behind William Woon's chair, which he draws up close

to the desk. A roundhouse swing from the nor'east
rocks the plank walls from blocks to purlins. He trims
the Miller Vestal's ragged flame, lays the scrap-

book open by the burning oil, finds a clean
pen, writes *Detained* (flourishing the big D)
at the Mata, Mr Monro's, during a gale

of wind, October 4, 1841.
Blood sample of Peter Monro, where do I
come in? The book doesn't say. Might as well ask

this heart-murmur I've got, how Edinburgh rock,
chipped like a golf ball cleared Arthur's Seat the day
after Waterloo, first bounce Van Diemen's Land,

holed up next and last a thousand sea miles more,
Ngapuhi country, MacGulliver's last landfall.
Not by this light. The rain pisses down, the tide

crawls up the creek, reads the mangroves' million false
scents. No way out of the Mata but by water
neither gig nor canoe can live in tonight.

II

Puts pen to the recto, lovers have left no room
on the verso, who damply dream of gravestones
and each other's names *May mine alone attract*

thy pensive eye! On a night like this, God help
poor sailors and lovers too, and the Reverend
William, who wishes it all further. As if

the Mata weren't further than ever God's writ
ran till the day before yesterday, and He
outnumbered thousands to one by the *iwi*

of the *tangata whenua*, and outgunned since
the musket spoke with tongues, not without a bang.
And writes against the wind, fishing for a poem

gilled in the drift-net of his mind, and pulls up
'Music', hymnodist Wesley's ghostly sixain
warning! Addiction can endanger the soul

and steal our hearts away from Thee. And subjoins
The Saviour, lover of storm-bound souls, starred
twice with a criss-cross ink-blot, *In Hoc Signo.*

III

Lifts the pen and listens for the wrath to come.
Hears nothing but the clock striking some small hour,
the crack of a *kauri* branch dropped by the gale.

The lovers are as dead as they ever dreamed.
Mildew has freckled the page, dulled the once-gilt
edge, browned the black longhand. All the lights are out,

it's blowing like the hammers, the power lines are down.
The scrap-book sheds loose pictures of lost homelands,
times long past, northern steeples and thatch, Maori

stockades. *Detained at the Mata*, what else does
the book say? The radio confides the latest
rape and Rugby. Another branch thumps the roof.

EARLY DAYS YET

I

Lift out front seat-
cushion. Unscrew
filler-cap. Insert

large funnel. Spike,
and up-end four gallon
can of Big Tree

Motor Spirit. Let
flammable contents
flow *pingle-pangle-*

pingle through fine
gauze filter. Your new
1919

Model T is now
fuelled for the week's
pastoral mileage,

Hororata, Kowai
Bush, Darfield. Three
Holy Communions per

gallon today (Sunday)
and by the time we
bury old Mrs. Hole

(Tuesday, Halswell
Churchyard) not much
left in the tank. Still,

miles better than the doctor's
barge-size guzzler,
and the right image

for the poor *The Lord be*
with you the pews creak back
And with thy spirit.

II

This world's the one
you are in. Replace
front seat-cushion.

Advance Throttle (on
left of steering-column)
and Spark (on right)

a few notches. Walk
to front, pull Choke
wire, engage starting-

handle, swing vigorously
up, release the moment
motor fires, and fires.

A great while ago
the world began, with
hey, ho Bang!

309

And where will it all
have ended? That
was a great way off.

III

This corrugated
iron outbuilding
doubles for cowbail,

garage. In a manger
Cow Beauty tongues
her rock-salt, rolls

the big lump over, and
over the milk-pail
my mother's hands

tug, squeeze, tug *pingle
pangle*. The New Age
enters, in reverse

gear, my father at the
wheel brakes, gets back
in gear, turns towards

Torlesse Range which is
twice blue, once for the
noon sky, deeper again

for the *massif*. No time
at all, that straight
lonely road locks us

both in with a high
head wind, unhingeing
nor'west slammer. I don't

see him any more
distinctly, for
dust of the earth,

his own. It closes
behind. The spirit
fires. Driving, driven,

swaying, keeps time with
his body, old habit.
Any old song the

motor beats out finds
words in his head
O forest, green

and fair, O pine-
tree, waving high,
How sweet your cool

retreat, How fresh
and fair A great
way off's too near

by far, the dust's
at our eyes already,
with a high warm wind,

with a whiff of japanned
seat-cushion, a shudder
with a skitter of rubber

on a rutted macadam,
with hey, ho, Bang!
And with thy spirit.

A FACING PAGE

Behind the eyelids the giant in the sky
is probably sightless, but that can't be known.

Cruciform from full-stretched arms his black robe drops
the whole way to the city. His fingers point

down at our rooftops. We don't know about him.
He knows all about us. By the fire the child's

nightgown is warmed for bed. The book's entitled
Under the Sunset by Bram Stoker M.A.

my mother's copy in green cloth board 8vo
has nearly lost the spine, a few threads hold,

her childhood and mine. Tucked and kissed for the dark,
I shut my eyes too tight on a picture-book

for waking to loosen. Locked on to where people
believe in themselves, engraved fingers point down.

INVESTIGATIONS AT THE PUBLIC BATHS

At nine fifteen a.m.
on the first day of his eighty-
first year. Why don't I

first-person myself?
I was hoping nobody would ask
me that question

yet. The strong smell of
chlorine for one thing, one thing
at a time, please.

For instance, there's always
this file of exercyclists
riding the gallery

over the pool. Bums
on saddles, pommelled crotches.
The feet rotate, the

hands grip, or hang
free, or hold open a book,
demonstrating how

the mind is improved
without progression, if not without
rumbling noises and

lascivious absences.
How free-standing engines enjoy
their moving parts,

privately mounted
overhead. There's also the deep
and the shallow end

between which the body
swims and the mind, totally
immersed, counts

and keeps count. I think
sixteen, touch tiles, turn again,
with underwater eyes

follow the black line.
Touch, thinking seventeen, turn
thinking eighteen

and enough. Whatever's
thinkable next or only the peg
where I last hang

my clothes. A destination.
The gallery rumble-trembles, the riders
always up there were

an abstraction blooded, a
frieze the wrong side of the urn.
One grins, catching

me looking, lifts
a tattooed hand. I wave back. So.
You know how it is.

PACIFIC 1945–1995

A pantoum

> ... if th'assassination
> Could trammel up the consequence, and catch
> With his surcease, success; that but this blow
> Might be the be-all and the end-all ... here,
> But here, upon this bank and shoal of time,
> We'd jump the life to come ...
>   — *Macbeth*

Quantifiable griefs. The daily kill.
   One bullet, with his name on, his surcease.
'The casualties were few, the damage nil' —
   The scale was blown up, early in the piece.

One bullet, with his name on, his surcease.
   Laconic fire, short work the long war mocks.
The scale was blown up, early in the piece —
   How many is few? After the aftershocks,

laconic fire — short work! The long war mocks,
   dragging out our dead. What calibration says
how many is few, after the aftershocks
   of just such magnitude? We heard the news,

314

dragging out our dead. What calibration says,
　　right! You can stop crying now, was it really
of just such magnitude? We heard the news
　　again, the statistical obscene, the cheery

right! You can stop crying now, was it really
　　the sky that fell, that boiling blue lagoon?
Again, the statistical obscene, the cheery
　　salutation and bright signature tune.

The sky that fell! That boiling blue lagoon!
　　Jacques Chirac's rutting tribe — with gallic
salutation and bright signature tune —
　　thermonuclear hard-on. Ithyphallic

Jacques! Chirac's rutting tribe, with gallic
　　eye for the penetrable, palm-fringed hole —
thermonuclear hard-on, ithyphallic
　　BANG! full kiloton five below the atoll.

Eye for the penetrable, palm-fringed hole,
　　whose trigger-finger, where he sat or knelt down —
BANG! full kiloton five, below the atoll
　　had it off, bedrock deep orgasmic meltdown —

whose trigger-finger, where he sat or knelt down,
　　fifty years back, fired one as huge as then
had it off bedrock deep, orgasmic meltdown —
　　whose but Ferebee's? — Hiroshima come again! —

fifty years back, fired one as huge as then
　　fireballed whole cities while 'People ... copulate, pray ...'
Whose but Ferebee's — Hiroshima come again! —
　　bombardier, U.S. Army? *Enola Gay*

fireballed whole cities while 'People ... copulate, pray ...'
　　Not God fingering Gomorrah but the man,
bombardier, U.S. Army. *Enola Gay*
　　shuddering at 30,000 feet began —

not God fingering Gomorrah, but the man,
    the colonel her pilot who named her for his Mom —
shuddering at 30,000 feet began —
    'Little Boy' delivered — her run for home:

the colonel her pilot, who named her for his Mom,
    flew her to roost (at last) in the Smithsonian.
'Little Boy' delivered, her run for home
    lighter by the Beast's birth, her son's companion:

flew her to roost (at last) in the Smithsonian:
    are tourists' hearts and hopes, viewing her there,
lighter by the Beast's birth, her son's companion?
    Jacques' Marianne's delivery, is that near?

Are tourists' hearts and hopes, viewing her there,
    pronounced infection-free and safely tested —
Jacques' Marianne's delivery, is that near? —
    What effluent, what fall-out's to be trusted?

pronounced infection-free and safely tested
    for carcinogenic isotope unseen fall-out —
what effluent, what fall-out's to be trusted?
    The Beast once born, who's answering the call-out?

For carcinogenic isotope, unseen fall-out,
    for the screaming city under the crossed hairs,
the Beast once born. Who's answering the call-out?
    no time even to know it's one of THEIRS —

for the screaming city under the crossed hairs,
    'The casualties were few, the damage nil' — ?
No time even to know! It's one of theirs —
    quantifiable griefs. The daily kill.

October–November 1995

AN EVENING LIGHT

The sun on its way down torched the clouds and left
them to burn themselves out on the ground:

the north-west wind and the sun both drop at once
behind the mountains. The foreground fills

with a fallen light which lies about the true
colours of absconded things, among

which I place this child whose tenth birthday happens
to have been my father's, that will be

a hundred years next Thursday. We were to meet
at a time of precisely such radiant

discolorations, the city of his mind.
The smallest leaf's alight where he looks

at the riverside willows, the painted iron
glows cold where he holds the garden gate.

The butcher's horse drops golden turds which steam
in sundown chill, an old man minds where

he walks, whose viridescent black assigns him
to an age before the city was,

I take his (my father's) hand: we follow him,
bowler hat, silver-topped stick, the hand

knuckled into the small of his back, which aches
to think of riding wet to the girths

and stirrups cutting up a country the size
of England with a sackful of pegs.

Under the one fallen firelit sky the Ngai-tahu
kainga and excavated *paa*

mark time by moa-bone middens, oceanic
migrations. What gospel will my father

preach to Tuahiwi, counting communicants
and the collection? A lamp-post cab-horse

blows into its nosebag, the old man fumbles
at his fob, his gold Waterbury's right

by the Post Office clock. By this light the city
is instant history, my father's mind.

THE BELLS OF SAINT BABEL'S, 2001

TEN STEPS TO THE SEA

I

Repeat this experience
wilfully.
Instruct this
experience to repeat
itself.

II

With or without
vicarious detail for all
verities of this place.
Me too.

III

Plenty of that
already. Kikuyu grass
underfoot, thunderheads, purple-
patched sunshine offshore, onshore
the high dunes, the hollows of
wetted sand, rabbit shit.
Foot of a cliff, arm of a stream
where fallen yellow bloom
degrades.
September sickness.
El Niño weather.

IV

One wild, white
arum leans landward a little, round
which in its pool, drip-fed off
a slimed rock-face, is arranged the sky
for inspection.

V

A remark
for the rising sun. I see
by what blinds me.

VI

Telling us about
his cancer, he said: 'They can control
the pain till there's well really
no pain, but then there's no reality.'
He said: 'I try to balance
the two, as little pain
as possible, as much reality
as possible.'

VII

One moment before
that cloud bursts and the flash
flood swipes, I'm across
safely, seeing stringers, planks
gadarening down into the tide
which rises to receive them. There
goes our bridge. How the upstream
railing splintered, the deck duck-
diving, you'd never know now.
Good as new.

VIII

The pain is the dog
not heeding the whistle, on account
of scenting a rabbit or an old
turd, his own possibly, or snuffing
ashes of a Sunday campfire because of
the slab and the grate provided there.
Will he follow?

IX

Up and over the sandhills? Not much
help in the sea's habitual heave,
sprawl, grumble, hiss.

X

In reality,
no. A step in the right direction.
The pain is this wind, which blows the whole
time, uncontrollably.
In your face.

THE KINDEST THING

Rear-vision glass
   knows what comes up

out of whatever
   concealed exit

I've left behind
   me. These cross-country

highways hide little
   for long, and least

when driving east
   one of those bright

spring mornings. Green
   acclivities drop

back. Sheep with them.
   What comes up next

comes fast, the ute
   probes left, probes right

(how can hurrying
   mirrors keep up?),

overtakes me
   with a long blast

storms past into full
   view carrying

at gathering speed
   what was concealed,

only heard, the dog
  half-hanged, roped

by the neck, raving,
  clawing at the tailboard

forefeet can't climb
  back over, hind-

legs cruelly danced
  off the tar-seal.

Bare road between us
  lengthens. Away

out of sight, how long
  will it have held,

that rope, till it parts?
  And the ute's gone,

the dog's flung down
  and I brake, short

of the strangely small
  body, the one

coin-size blood spot
  at the jaws. Convulsed,

gets to its feet.
  Convulsed, falls over.

And I'm joined here
  at the roadside by

the Maori boy who
  saw it all, from

that house, the first
   before Kawakawa.

Where there's a vet.
   Pick the dog up.

Put the dog down.
   These hurts can't heal.

At the vet's, yes,
   green with a white

logo on the cab.
   And he, not council

car? Got the number?
   And I, that speed!

You're joking *Drunk* —
   stoned, more likely,

on the hemp, cash
   crop around here.

And he, Ranger's job,
   picking up strays.

We put them down.
   Kindest thing, most times.

THE CAKE UNCUT

I

Not him — he's where
no fears can find

nor torments touch
him — it's his Mum

has the details,
who told the head-

master, who talked
to the press.

       Dad
only just gone

for the takeaways
at KFC,

when he says — quiet,
sort of sudden,

you'd hardly know
it was him speaking —

'Can't wait any more
for Dad, I've got

to go now — no,
just tired again,

like yesterday' — that
was when I knew

how it had to be,
like he said, *now*.

II

We're very religious
people. We sing,

we pray to God
to make the lump

go away, if that's
His will — it still

swells up, and up
so big you'd never

believe, it could
be a football

there in the leg.
The lady kept

at us, why don't
you see the doctor?

Try everything.
What harm can that

possibly do?
Made him sick — no

way would he keep
anything down —

medicine killing him, we
threw it all out.

Never went back.
No one's come near

till the police —
God knows we've done

nothing like what
they said — his life's

necessities — our own
heart's blood was his

if it would save him —
I always hear

him say *now*, the moment
before it was.

III

Funny dream.
                Dad's
in bed with me
and that come-dom

thing on, and says
how do you like

my Mexican hat?
That's where we're going

when the Lotto money
comes, people get

cured there, like that
kid on the talkback —

something about
apricot stones —

IV

Shame not to cut the
cake with his twelve

candles on. God'll
have you up and running

again, for your
birthday, I'm saying

and we'll all see
the Millennium in —

he'd've loved that so,
every minute, even

knowing, all along,
what never was meant.

THE BELLS OF SAINT BABEL'S

I

After those months
at sea, we stank

worse than the Ark.
Faeces of all

species, God's first
creation, cooped

human and brute,
between wind and

water, bound for
this pegged-out plain

in the land called
Shinar, or some-

thing. Give or take
some chiliads, I'll

have been born there.
Saint Babel's tower

with spire (sundry
versions of that)

stuck not far short
of a top (Wait

for it!) gilded
to catch first light

or last flame flung
by the torched snows

farthest west.
                    Four
shiploads of us.

Under its breath
a warm land breeze,

wind of our coming,
breathed Shit!

Lightered ashore,
our cabin trunks,

rust-freckled steel-
braced outside, inside

compartments kept
things lavendered,

smothered memories
of sweats and smears.

For laters. Boxroom
dry dreams, our child-

hood's indoors, wet
holiday games . . .

II

We wanted it
above all (except

heaven) to make
the world out there

aware, if there's
any such world,

as if to cry
Look! Look at me!

Very old story.
Some other time.

Before all this.
Before history ran

out of excuses . . .

III

I, the present
writer, that is,

can see the Rev.
F. G. Brittan,

octogenarian
of stertorous

pulpit delivery,
who also told

the time by the ding
and the tink-tink

simply by a squeeze
of his silver watch:

seated beside
the vicarage fire

'after Service':
who, babe-in-arms

(his mother's) came
ashore that day

where four ships lay
under the steep

hills, beyond which
an unbuilt city was

unpaved wetlands,
too near, too far

from unclimbed alps.
Settlers made shift

improvising
themselves. In shock.

Still do. Still are.
Only the games

they play . . .

IV

To relocate the
roof of the world,

obviously Everest
has to be moved —

South Latitude
thirty-three West

Longitude one-
seventy-seven, where

Kermadec Trench
ten thousand metres

deep floored with 'fine
volcanic ash,

aeolian dust'
drowns mountains.

New Zealand side
of the Date Line

meaning, those shores,
Raoul Island, any

Kermadec reef
cries to the sun,

Me! Me! This day
dawns first on me,

you won't find that
in your King James

nor Maori story
of a half-god's

trap for the sun,
that sun . . .
                    which one?
Which thousand years?

v

Next time you look,
he will have stepped

out of the shade
the West Front casts

into a sun-stuffed
ambulatory called

Cathedral Square.
His buttoned black

gaiters encase
his shanks. The Dean

of Saint Babel's
rig of the day.

One more step, he's
joined by a friend,

silk hat, frock coat,
silver-knobbed cane.

Their morning walk.
What makes the tower

burst but thunderclappers
newly hung, high

peal deafeningly
detonating,

the Dean's delight,
Are not those bells

Divine?
            Silk hat,
hand cupped on ear,

shouts back, What's that?
and Gaiters, Divine!

And he, What? What?
Can't make it out —

Sorry, Mister Dean,
can't hear a word

for those DAMNED BELLS.

THE POCKET COMPASS

(i.m. G.E.T.)

We stood at the timbered railing just one steep
rain-forested mile above the sea
the upper rail being level enough
to lay your pocket compass to copy there

the compass-rose, for me to get my bearings
by, for you to see our world the right
way round. The blaze of a late sun half
blinds us. Later my chisel will have incised

the upper case cardinal points, years after that
the rotted rail will have been replaced,
pencil or chisel can't replicate
the rose in the mind's eye, indelibly true

north by needle. I paint it over again
in sight of the sea with one more sun to drown.

FOR PETER PORTER AT SEVENTY

A pantoum

Clock-watchers all for whom the digits tick
our momentsworth of years. Nine sevens brought
a six and a three and a Grand Climacteric.
Take one more seven, this one's next to a nought,

our momentsworth of years. Nine sevens brought
small pickings, and what's so special about ten?
Take one more seven, this one's next to a nought,
shall we count on time to fetch the same again?

335

Small pickings! And what's so special about ten
is the ninetieth psalm, that scary three-score *and*
shall we count on time to fetch the same again
like a birthday of the world, from where we stand?

Is the ninetieth psalm, that scary three-score *and*
ten years any good reason to rejoice
like a birthday of the world from where we stand?
new stars, in perfect time and excellent voice.

Ten years! Any good reason to rejoice,
day barely broken after that small Bang,
new stars in perfect time and excellent voice
sang together, together was how they sang.

Day barely broken after that small Bang
the young stars of your native Brisbane sky
sang together, together was how they sang
as we met, you fifty-plus, turned seventy I.

The young stars of your native Brisbane sky
out of our terrene earshot sang back shrilly
as we met, you fifty-plus, turned seventy I —
Consider the idle ant, the busy lily

out of our terrene earshot sang back shrilly,
ciphering not of an organ-pipe high wind —
consider, the idle ant, the busy lily
do nothing but rhyme — the high outback sound,

ciphering note of an organ-pipe high wind
continuo under the voice — your own, so many
do nothing but rhyme — the high outback sound
upfront, more of our hemispheres than any,

continuo under the voice — your own, so many
have made so few and fewer that come to mind
upfront more of our hemispheres than any —
And I, eight decades crowding me behind,

have made so few and fewer that come to mind —
a six and a three and a Grand Climacteric —
and I, eight decades crowding me behind,
clock-watchers all, for whom the digits tick.

FOUR POEMS AFTER PUSHKIN

I   WHEN AND WHERE

Where the big crowds come, the street,
the stadium, the park where the young
go crazy to the beat
and the heated bubble of the song,

thoughts running loose, I tell
myself, the years will have blipped past,
one by one the lot of us here present will
be gone into the dark. Someone's last

hour's always next, right here and now.
Deep under the bark of that great oak
my father's lifetime's told in rings, which grow
to outlive me too. Gently as I stroke

this child's head, I'm thinking, 'Goodbye!
It's all yours now, the season's crop —
your time to bud, and bloom, while my
late leaves wither and drop —'

And which day of which year
to come will turn out to have been
the anniversary, distant or near,
of my death? Good question. The scene,

will it be wartime, on a trip,
or at home or in some nearby

337

street, crashed coach or a ship-
wreck that I'm to die?

Cadavers couldn't care less where they rot,
yet the living tissue leans (as best it may)
toward the long-loved familiar spot
for its rest. Mine does, think of it that way.

Freshly dug. Young things, chase your ball.
Nature's not watching, only minding
by its own light perpetual
beauty of its own fact or finding.

                                        1829

II   THE UPAS TREE

Scorched unforgiving soil
burned off burned out
in summer conflagrations

half-way to the horizon
look for the Upas Tree
no other created thing
to be seen than this

grim guard

            the parched
steppes convulsed
at its birth
and a deathly day that was
loading root and branch with
instant poison
visibly in the heat of noon
sweated out by nightfall
globuled and beaded
thick thick

and clear
the concentrate
lethal
          the small birds
drop dead from the sky
outside the dripline of its leaves
the tiger
gives it a wide berth

only the black whirlwind
swarms up it and out again
with death to deliver
and any passing cloud
sprinkling its foliage
carries across the hot sand
its poisonous rain

'Find that tree
Bring back the deadly stuff'
his imperial master said
and off he went
and by morning brought
one resinous lump
and one withering branch
and fell to the rush-strewn floor
of the great tent
to die at the feet
of his Lord now possessed of
invincible power

and that power made
him such murderous missiles
as devastated
neighbouring realms
and subjected
them and their peoples
by life's death-dealing arts.

1828

This pig of a gale
      now screams, now drops
      to a baby's wail
      while it wraps
      cloud-cover around the sky
      where twisters of snow
      fall and flake as they fly.

Gusts fit to blow
      straws out of our thatch,
      or like someone's there
      at the window-catch
      stormbound, after dark —

dark enough in there,
      our tumbledown shack.

Grandmother dear,
      why wouldn't you speak
      just then as you sat
      by the window spinning?
      Was it nothing but that
      crazy wind's dinning?
      Had you just dropped off
      to the humming of the wheel?

Let's drink! That's the stuff
      to make us both feel
      better, old mate of my sad
      young life.
          Where's the jug?
      Things can't be that bad.
      Sing me the old songs,
      the one about the blue
      bird resting its wings
      far across the sea,
      the one about the girl

who got up so very early
before daybreak
to fetch water from the creek —

while this pig of a gale
now screams, now drops
to a baby's wail
and it wraps
cloud-cover around the sky
with its gusts that blow
those twisters of snow
that fall and flake as they fly.

Let's drink! little old
friend of my unhappy
youth, our glasses filled
with the gladdening stuff
smiling at grief.

1825

IV   THE TALISMAN

A warmer latitude.
An unvisited
beach.
Rocks wetted where
the last wave broke.
Some
such night as this lit
by a swollen moon's
foggy glow.
Somewhere
the Pasha (of these parts)
relaxing sucks at the
narghile the sweet
fume inhaling.
Was it

341

there this ravishingly
wise woman whose hands caressed
me pressed something small
into mine?
                    Keep it.
It's a talisman.
Keep it safe. It's got
powers that love gave.
                              Listen
while I tell you all
you need to know about
this precious thing.
                              Sick
it won't cure you. No
earthly use either in
the hour of death or day
of disaster.
                    Nor will it
win you the Lottery
crown you superstar
jet you happily home
(soured expatriate!) No.

But when cheating eyes
meet and you're aroused
oh my darling! (she said)
and lips after dark
unlovingly kiss
                    That's
when it kicks in — this
talisman of mine
                         you'll
never be two-timed
left for dead bleeding
newly from the heart!

1827

342

A NICE PLACE ON THE RIVIERA

The last act is bloody, however fine the rest of the play.
They throw earth over your head and it is finished for ever.
— Pascal, *Pensées,* XII. 210 (tr. A. J. Krailsheimer)

I

Refuge in San
Remo won't work

out. Local health
officialdom rules

La signora è
malata. Not

welcome this side
of the frontier.

France is not far:
why don't I try

cousin Connie
Beauchamp? Nice place

they say they've got
in Menton. She

and inseparable
Jinnie Fullerton.

This horrible cough!
Kind souls. Perhaps

their prayers will work
with a few more Hail

Marys thrown in.
Connie or Jinnie

(never mind which)
murmured 'The Lord

has delivered you
into our hands'.

II

'No personal God
or any such

nonsense' — Katherine
Mansfield Beauchamp

to Murry, spouse,
from Villa Isola

Bella, Menton,
18 October

being much the age
Blaise Pascal was

(three centuries
back) to whom God

personally did
appear that day

'from about ten
thirty p.m.

till past midnight'.
Sick too. And wrote

'Fire', 'Jesus', 'God'
(ten times over) *and*

much more. They found
the parchment stitched

into his clothes
when they stripped him for

burial. Not known
like her, at this

address.

III

    And there's
his *Pensées*, where

I left the book,
this rickety desk,

the Villa's one
spare room, kept up

in her name. Here
the annual New

Zealander sweats
brief tenure out,

memorialising
her genius. I

brought profound Blaise
along, whose death–

mask eyeballs me
glazedly, from

the paperback's
cover, with eyes

they plucked I (learn)
out of his painted

portrait and poked
them in here

and they look it.

IV

Spring equinox:
lemon trees drenched

one minute, next
blast of the same

black sirocco
blow-dries bright green

under the shuttered
villa windows. Miss

Fullerton rose
from the escritoire,

having inscribed
her gift, the book,

from Jinnie, to
Katie, Saint

Joseph's day, nine-
teen twenty, *The*

*Imitation of
Christ*, (Thomas à

Kempis) in soft
red morocco,

title in gilt . . .
One Turkey rug's

length separates
the two. The *bonne*

brings coffee, liqueur.
That rabid wind

bangs shutters, dis-
colours the sea,

dishevels the world
outdoors. Beside

the demitasses
the Abdullahs in

their silver box,
the *Imitation*

waits to be read . . .
The climate here's

her only hope,
some doctor said.

Always a chance.

V

Your call, says Blaise.
Heads, there's God;

Tails, none. The coin
infinitely far

away spins itself
asleep, a still

spherical blur —
slowing, splits down

meridians, falls
over, face down,

face up. Your call.
God knows the odds

incalculably. Tell
me what your plans

are, for retirement.

VI

Pieces of his mind
by the thousand,

jottings on jumbo-
size sheets. Pierced

for threading string.
Tied in *liasses*.

Too sick, or just
ran out of time

sorting the huge
heap. Such heads as

PROOFS OF JESUS,
NATURE CORRUPT,

SO ARE WE ALL,
CAUSES, EFFECTS . . .

VII

Imitation — big
ask — of the life

he lived, the death
he died — if that

doesn't make two
of us, there's one

Christ lookalike
more than we knew.

VIII

Top-heavy *Alpes
Maritimes* grind

the sky small. Fast
forward, to autumn.

One of those two
women, who could

be seen watchfully
to cross the rail

tracks where they start
threading the rock

through to Liguria
halts, chestily coughs

in her handkerchief:
but has finished

writing her last
storybook; by now

consumption's two
years' gallop away

from Gurdjieff's
Institute, that

fatal torrential
haemorrhage, at

Fontainebleau,
stumbling upstairs.

IX

Fast forward again
top-heavy *Alpes*

Maritimes grind
the sky small. One

more dull day scraped
off a slaty sea.

FANTASIA AND FUGUE FOR PAN-PIPE

I

Engaged too long
too chastely. Was

that it? Anyway,
she broke it off,

my father wrote
'Pan', earliest verse

of his, to make
it into print

over his name,
the god revealed

as Tremayne M.,
Syrinx as Maud.

Twenty-odd pages
further on, more

forgotten poems
between his lines

and hers (called 'Song'),
both plaintively

lovelorn, obscurely
set down between

Oceanian winds
and waters. *New*

Zealand Verse. Walter
Scott Publishing.

London. New York.
1906 — Safe

distances, for
blushing unseen,

big breaths unheard,
'O cruel nymph' not

unwritten and
much more, his drift

of 'low-blown music' —
the words, the lips,

the pipes — 'who love
thee still' — so eaves-

dropping Nature
guessed, or his poem

supposes — Maud's
chips in, crying over

spilt 'joyous youth
gone in a night'.

Her feral horned
god's hinderparts

wore clerical grey
serge, irreversibly

decent disguise.
Afterwards (not

long) that *traveller*
came by . . . he took

her with a sigh . . . his?
hers? or theirs?

II

Had a hand groped,
grabbed, come away

with a moist fist-
ful to play black

hole tunes, the ones
Pan pistol-whips

the galaxies with?
Terrified mind

whines to itself
don't panic, don't —

answers the hoof-
beat. Words for things,

things back again off
the tips of tongues.

Lost names. Try not to
think about that.

III

One world war later.
Not any more

the slender reed,
fifty-something Syrinx

drops in on one
newly-wed son

of Pan. I see
her, to my (not

small) surprise, seat
herself heavily

down on the foot
of the bed, hands

compress the ball
of a hanky, damp

from dabbing tear-
ducts. Someone said

she tells fortunes in
teashops, the dregs

of emptied cups,
to make ends meet. —

More tea? — quick look
at her watch — Oh,

thank you, no,

I'm running late, I
really must go.

IV

One lizard's wink,
two thousand years

(rounded out), since
Jesus called out

with a loud voice
it was all over,

that louder voice
downloads, this Greek

seaway hears GREAT
PAN IS DEAD — what

could be figured?
Who's being fingered?

And why's it got
so suddenly dark?

Nothing but those
four words themselves,

nobody spoke.
Printed now, like

Tremayne's, Maud's, mine.
Rolled up the beach

in a bottle, rolled
back into the surf.

Hoofprints in soft
and softening sand.

NOTES

VALLEY OF DECISION, 1933

Heavily revised in *Collected Poems, 1933–1973* (1974) and four poems omitted. For the 1933 text see Appendix.

AC (Foreword, 1933): Nobody who deprecates my conceit in permitting the publication of these first and no doubt ill-considered poems is likely to be convinced by any sort of apology I might make. I would say, however, that whatever conceit has led to their publication had no part at all in their writing.

THREE POEMS, 1935

The first two poems appeared originally in *Tomorrow* under the pseudonym Julian. Small revisions in *Collected Poems* (1974).

From ANOTHER ARGO, 1935

Besides Curnow's 'Doom at Sunrise' there was a poem by Denis Glover and one by A.R.D. Fairburn, with a frontispiece by Leo Bensemann. See Gordon Ogilvie, *Denis Glover: His Life*, Godwit, Auckland, 1999, p. 83.

From A CAXTON MISCELLANY, 1937

'Inheritance'. This poem was never reprinted in Curnow's lifetime but signals the turn to history in his next collection.

ENEMIES, 1937

Most of the poems were written in the second half of 1936 and had not been published previously. Extensively revised in *Collected Poems* (1974). See Appendix for 1937 text.

AC (Author's Note, 1937): This collection contains nothing which has not been carefully worked upon. There was a great temptation to include a number of pieces which seemed competently written, but which were merely (or chiefly) written in satisfaction of the desire to emulate some admired poet. Such work seems to me to be too common in New Zealand. The only hope is in poetry written on a genuine impulse to present in expressive form the material which naturally suggests itself — suggests itself, that is, uninfluenced by any notion of what is or is not fit subject matter for poetry. I have tried to avoid a preconceived idea of what poets in New Zealand should write about. And I have tried to show the possibility of a technical development pari passu with that of recent English poetry. Whatever may be said or written about a national literature for New Zealand, England remains at the very least the 'technical research laboratory', where the finest and most advanced work is done with that subtle material, the English language.

'Mountain Elegy'. AC (Author's Note, 1937): 'Mountain Elegy' was suggested by the Suite in B Minor for Flutes and Strings, of J. S. Bach. The first two parts were intended to follow the *grave* leading to *allegro*, and the *sarabande*, of the suite. But the poem developed of itself and on advice I deleted musical terms which I had used to separate the parts of the poem.

AC (Notes, *Collected Poems*, 1974): It must not appear that I knew the music musically. Among the few recordings I possessed in those pre-stereo days was one of this suite, played by the Concertgebouw orchestra of Amsterdam. I cannot remember any that I listened to nearly so often, or that delighted me more. It was in my mind's ear distinctly when I wrote the poem. Somebody may remember the charming verse mimicry of a *gigue* in J. C. Beaglehole's *Considerations on Certain Music of J. S. Bach*. I knew his poem, but what happened in my case was different, if only because I did not have his pianist's privilege and skill; if I was naive, it was not in supposing I could write verse that might accompany such music, only that the poem depended on the music, as I am sure it did.

This poem was originally called 'Mountain Rhapsody'. See Appendix.

NOT IN NARROW SEAS, 1939

This sequence, in poetry and prose, originally appeared in *Tomorrow* from 1937 to 1939; see that text in the Appendix. There were small revisions in *Selected Poems* (1982).

AC (Author's Note, *Collected Poems*, 1974): I have altered almost nothing in *Not in Narrow Seas*. It has its own accent. It sets its own limits of a time and a place with a peculiar severity. I suppose it could be called my contribution to the anti-myth about New Zealand which a few of us poets — and almost nobody else — were so busy making in those years. It had to be done. The country did not know what to make of itself, colony or nation, privileged happyland or miserable banishment: the polarisation was nothing new, and it is still with us, but we were the first to find poetry in it. I know that I wanted, for myself, to focus the vision sharply on a few details of a few scenes of New Zealand history, some of them distinct to me from childhood. I had not the sense of a poetic style, ready for use, that my elders Mason and Fairburn had; I had to improvise one for myself; but we had in common that instinct for a few particulars, sharpened by our antipathy to almost everything that satisfied — or seemed to satisfy — an older generation. I shared the antipathy, of course, with Denis Glover: each, in those days, wished he could write like the other, the last thing either of us could ever have done ....

AC (Author's Note, *Selected Poems*, 1982): *Not in Narrow Seas* had to go in entire, with a few minor revisions which will no doubt be noticed where such things have to be noticed. I have called it elsewhere, rather summarily, a 'contribution to the anti-myth about New Zealand'; but it was a poetic and personal need that got me into history (or 'unhistory'). The question of my country was, for me at that time, an intensely personal one. There is indeed a claptrap of the subject, we have heard enough of 'national identity', but this doesn't mean that it will go away. There is also, I hope, a poetry of the subject.

The 'Epilogue' was extensively revised in the 1982 volume. Originally the first lines of verses 1–4 and most of verse 5 were drawn directly from a 'Song' by William Blake. These lines were italicised in the 1974 collection. However Curnow must have subsequently discovered that Blake was himself drawing on a sixteenth-century poem by Thomas, Lord Vaux, 'The Aged Lover Renounceth Love'; he therefore altered the first lines of verses 1–3 to match Vaux's lines; the first line of verse 4 and most of verse 5 remained Blake's though in verse 5 he made a few small changes of his own (adding 'and false' and changing 'doth' to 'both').

From RECENT POEMS, 1941

This volume included poems by Curnow, A.R.D. Fairburn, R.A.K. Mason and Denis Glover. The anthology resulted directly from Curnow's saying to Glover: 'It's time we had another book, but it seems nobody has enough poems ready, what about joining ours with Mason & Fairburn if they can and will?' (AC to Terry Sturm, 7 October 1974). Four of Curnow's nine poems appear here and the remaining five in *Island and Time*.

ISLAND AND TIME, 1941

Curnow several times described what he was attempting in this collection, so influenced by the outbreak of war and the writing of French philosopher Henri Bergson (see 'A Job for Poetry: Notes on an Impulse', *Book*, 1, March 1941, reproduced in Allen Curnow, *Look Back Harder: Critical Writings*, Auckland University Press, Auckland, 1987, p. 24; and also Terry Sturm, *Simply by Sailing in a New Direction. Allen Curnow: A Biography*, Auckland University Press, Auckland, 2017, ch. 9).

AC (from a notice of the forthcoming book in *Recent Poems*, 1941): These poems are an attempt to place New Zealand imaginatively in the widest possible context of Time and the current of history; but the poems have each their separate occasions springing from the natural scene, the history, and the life of New Zealanders.

AC (from a cover blurb he wrote): These are frankly the poems of a New Zealander native & untravelled, convinced now that the need is for legend rather than for 'realism.' Mr Curnow has moved far from the mood of his earlier 'Not in Narrow Seas,' though the line of development may be clearly traced. His time-images provide him with a dynamic of his own, & though they represent no metaphysical system they give a humanity & a tragic sense wanting in the earlier work. There has been an increase in his technical range; and he has sought a variety of forms and images to sustain the imagination in its thrust across the Pacific and through Time.

AC (Author's Note, *Collected Poems*, 1974): Very soon after [*Not in Narrow Seas*], I was writing the poems of *Island and Time* and *Sailing or Drowning*. I had to get past the severities, not to say rigidities, of our New Zealand anti-myth: away from questions which present themselves as public and answerable, towards the questions which are always private and unanswerable. The geographical anxieties didn't disappear; but I began to find a personal and poetic use for them, rather than let them use me up.

'Sentence'. Written early February 1941 and, according to an undated letter to Betty Curnow, discussed with the German refugee poet Karl Wolfskehl. See Friedrich Voit, 'Karl Wolfskehl', *Out of the Shadow of War*, Oxford University Press, Auckland, 1998, p. 109.

'The Unhistoric Story'. AC (Notes and Acknowledgements, 1941): 'The Land of Beach ...' This reference, with others in the same poem, I have from J. C. Beaglehole's *Exploration of the Pacific*. From seventeenth-century Dutch sources the author gives examples of the belief in a fabulously rich country or continent somewhere in the south. Frederick de Houtman, coming on the west coast of Australia, thought 'that this must be the coastline of the "Beach" or "Locach" of Marco Polo, with its fabulous riches'. Visscher, Tasman's chief adviser, planned the discovery of 'all the utterly unknown provinces of Beach'. Gold was thought to be abundant there, and some hoped to profit by the inhabitants' supposed ignorance of its value.

AC (Author's Note, *Selected Poems*, 1990): 'Vogel and Seddon howling empire ...' Sir Julius Vogel and Richard John Seddon, late nineteenth-century premiers of New Zealand. They sought 'wholesale annexations' of Pacific island territories by Britain: there were dreams of an oceanic empire under New Zealand rule.

'St Thomas's Ruins'. AC (Notes, *Collected Poems*, 1974, partially reprinted in Notes, *Early Days Yet*, 1997): By the St Helier's Bay road, Auckland, there stood in an open paddock the ruined and roofless walls of a small imitation-Gothic church, known as St Thomas's Ruins. The church is said to have been built by Bishop Selwyn, nostalgic for a place of worship recalling the stone churches of England. But it was ill-constructed; the mortar did not hold, so people said, because it was mixed with sea-sand. Selwyn's timber churches, like the St John's College chapel near by, have lasted 150 years and longer; ironically, this stone structure failed, and had been abandoned for many years when I first knew it in 1931. Since the poem was written, the ruin has been replaced, with no great loss, by a characterless stone building after a local builder's conception of church design.

'Crash at Leithfield'. Written during or after a holiday in December 1940 at Leithfield Beach and refers to an accident in which two pilots were killed nearby on a training mission on 11 December. Its details taken from the Court of Inquiry were written up along with a reprint of the poem by Cliff Jenks, *Journal of the Aviation Historical Society of New Zealand*, Dec. 2003, 46–47.

'A Victim'. AC (Notes, *Early Days Yet*, 1997, slightly revised from 1941): The occasion of this poem, if not the impulse, and some narrative detail, I owe to J. C. Beaglehole, *The Discovery of New Zealand* (Wellington 1940) and to the portion of Tasman's journal quoted by him.

The note heading the poem in the 1941 edition ran:

Jan Tyssen, one of the four Dutch killed by Maori when Tasman called at Murderers' Bay in 1642, sees his death as a ritual sacrifice reconciling the unborn with Time.

However in the 1974 *Collected Poems* and in all subsequent appearances Curnow altered this to remove the last part of the sentence and changed the title from 'The Victim' to 'A Victim'. The effect of the revisions was to make the religious resonances of the poem less specifically Christian.

'Wild Iron'. Curnow wrote this poem, also a Leithfield poem, at the same time as Denis Glover was writing his famous poem 'The Magpies'. See Ogilvie, *Denis Glover*, p. 123 and Sturm, *Simply by Sailing in a New Direction*, ch. 9.

SAILING OR DROWNING [1943]

'In Memoriam 2/Lieutenant T.C.F. Ronalds'. Ronalds, who died on the Allied front in Tunisia, was a cousin of Curnow's.

'The Navigators'. This was one of 'Four Pacific Sonnets', appearing in the Caxton journal *Book*, 5, 1942, and the only one which was reprinted. It was much revised. For the four sonnets see Appendix.

'To M.H. Holcroft'. Holcroft was a journalist, editor, essayist and critic; at the time of the poem's completion he was working for the *Southland Times*.

'At Joachim Khan's'. This sonnet was originally published in the first issue of *New Zealand New Writing* in late 1942 under the title 'Musical Criticism' but reappeared here retitled and much revised. Joachim Khan was a political science lecturer at Victoria University College in Wellington; he was Hungarian-born and a wartime refugee from Munich.

'Spring, 1942'. This is the last part of a long verse letter sent in November 1942 to Curnow's friend, printer and poet Denis Glover, now overseas on war service. For the full text see Appendix.

'Pantoum of War in the Pacific'. The choice of the form, of supposed Malayan origin, connected it to the eastern Pacific where the war was being fought. This poem too appeared in the first issue of *New Zealand New Writing*, under the title 'The seascape'. Though it did not in fact appear in *Sailing or Drowning*, Curnow placed it with poems from that volume in *A Small Room with Large Windows* (1962), Curnow's first selection from his poems, and in the 1974 and 1982 anthologies.

'Landfall in Unknown Seas'. AC (Notes, *Collected Poems*, 1974): 'Landfall in Unknown Seas' was written during 1942, and before the year ended, Douglas Lilburn had composed the music for strings which so splendidly complements and illuminates the verse. Both were undertaken for the National Historical Branch of the Department of Internal Affairs. What this really means is that the late J. C. Beaglehole, O.M., asked me to write a poem about Tasman's voyage, to be part of a commemorative volume designed by him for its tercentenary. This book, *Abel Janszoon Tasman and the Discovery of New Zealand*, was produced by the Department for official and private distribution; it was entirely John Beaglehole's conception, both as historian and typographical designer. It consisted of his own specially written essay with a new translation of Tasman's log, and the poem. When I had finished, I showed the poem to Lilburn, then living in the old brick apartment block on the site now occupied by the Christchurch Town Hall. I would have called, as I so often did, on my way to work at *The Press*. I hoped it would strike him as a subject for music. By great good fortune it did, though part of the fortune was (I am glad to think) that we knew each other's minds so well; no one would have been quicker to perceive it, than Lilburn, if the poem and his music could not agree. With an immediate response from Beaglehole and from Joe (afterwards Sir Joseph) Heenan, then head of Internal Affairs, the music was completed and the first performance arranged; it took place in Wellington on 13 December 1942, three hundred years to the day since Tasman had first sighted New Zealand. I have not counted the many performances since: at least one for each of the thirty years including three in 1973.

'Attitudes for a New Zealand Poet'. In *A Small Room with Large Windows* (1962) the second of these three sonnets was presented along with the pantoum under the title 'Pacific Theatre, 1943'. In the 1974 volume he reverted to the original title and contents of the sequence; however in 1982 and 1997 he dispensed with the idea of a sequence and included the second and third sonnets individually. In the later volume he used the title 'Pacific Theatre, 1943' to refer only to the second sonnet beginning 'World, up to now we've heard your hungers wail', omitting the pantoum.

'That Part of You the World Offended So'. Note the allusion to T.S. Eliot's *The Wasteland* in the second stanza.

'World, up to Now We've Heard Your Hungers Wail'. The starting point for this poem seems to have been a famous scene in Webster's *The Duchess of Malfi*, alluded to in the second verse; Curnow had seen the play performed in November 1942.

JACK WITHOUT MAGIC, 1946

As Curnow recalls, 'One day in 1945 he [Denis Glover] telephoned me to say he had an off-cut of handmade paper . . . enough for a limited printing of a small book; he wanted to handset something in Blado italic type. Did I have any poems? I did have a few, but no idea, till he spoke, of collecting them for print. The result was *Jack Without Magic*, an edition of 200 copies.' Introduction to *Denis Glover, Selected Poems*, Penguin, Auckland, 1981.

Six of the poems here reappeared in *At Dead Low Water* (1949). 'Dunedin' reappeared, heavily revised, in *Poems 1949–57* (1957).

'To D.G. Overseas'. D.G. is Denis Glover, who had enlisted in the navy in 1941.

'Darkness, Patience'. The final appearance of this poem was in *Selected Poems* (1982) where, unusually, Curnow revised the third line, altering 'O premature my legend' to 'So my precocious legend'.

AT DEAD LOW WATER AND SONNETS, 1949

Apart from the title poem, which had appeared in *Jack Without Magic*, and 'All Darkens but Her Image', this is a collection of sonnets, many of which had been seen in previous books. There are only twelve 'new' poems which intermingle with the previously published work.

'In Memoriam, R.L.M.G.' This sonnet recalls the burial of Curnow's grandmother, Rose Gambling, in 1931.

'To Fanny Rose May'. Addressed to Rose Gambling's sister, Curnow's great-aunt.

'Lili Kraus Playing at Christchurch'. Lili Kraus was a world-famous Hungarian-born pianist who had been interned in Java by the Japanese during the war. In 1946 she toured New Zealand where she was rapturously received.

'A Sonata of Schubert'. Lili Kraus played this sonata, Schubert's posthumous sonata in A major, written shortly before his death, on her second visit to Christchurch.

POEMS 1949–57, 1957

'Idylls in Colour Film'. These two poems were first written on board ship in April 1949. The collective title was first 'Intimations in Kodachrome' but Curnow changed it for this collection. 'Cristobal', stanza 5, was slightly revised for *Collected Poems* (1974), as was the first line of stanza 6 in *Selected Poems* (1982).

'Jack-in-the-Boat'. This poem based on a manufacturer's advertisement for a child's toy made it a favourite for children's anthologies, and for musical settings.

'Spectacular Blossom'. Written in late 1954 a few weeks after Curnow met Jenifer Tole and the beginning of a period of intense creativity. It was also the first of many poems Curnow checked out with C.K. Stead, as Stead recounts, *South-West of Eden: A Memoir, 1932–1956*, Auckland University Press, Auckland, 2010, p. 306.

A SMALL ROOM WITH LARGE WINDOWS, 1962

'A Small Room with Large Windows' first appeared in *Poems 1949–57* (1957).
The location is the sitting room at 13 Herbert St, Takapuna.

'An Oppressive Climate, a Populous Neighbourhood'. The only new poem in this collection. Begun while staying in an apartment at 526 East 85th St, New York, in July 1961 and originally two distinct poems. In the first completed version they were given subtitles, '1. The Dog' and '2. The People', under the general title 'Temperatures in the Lower Nineties'.

Poems from the 1960s

On the Tour. A broadsheet published under Curnow's own name by the Pilgrim Press. Provoked by the decision of the New Zealand Rugby Football Union to send an All Black team to South Africa which deliberately excluded Maori members.

'Capitoline Spring'. Begun in Washington in April 1961, offered to *Poetry* (Chicago), but put aside unpublished; later it provided ideas and images for *Trees, Effigies, Moving Objects* (1972).

'Visibility Almost Nil'. Unpublished, 1961. Presumably draws on his visits to San Francisco in 1961.

'Veterans Day in the Metropolitan Museum of Art'. Written in New York October–November 1966 but never published. The last page of the typescript has been heavily altered by hand and is not altogether clear. See Allen Curnow Papers, Alexander Turnbull Library (ATL) 4652-03.

TREES, EFFIGIES, MOVING OBJECTS, 1972

AC (Note, 1972): If I say these poems were *written* in the spring and summer of 1971–2, I mean that is when they were finished and found the order in which they now appear. A poet never stops trying to save poetry from poetry, to make something of it, not a spurious everything. Memory is always something, but if memory were ever good enough — even of a moment ago! — would we want poetry? Isn't this the necessary irritant? Because of it, memory is a thing of the present, a thing of the future too, if that is not already taken care of. Why should the irritant, in a particular spring and summer, fasten on these few things, not any of the many other conceivable *those*? The missing poem, the one that didn't get written, might have answered that. Has it perhaps got written after all? It ought to be the single poem of which these are the lines and spaces.

AC (added in Author's Note, *Selected Poems*, 1990, and Notes, *Early Days Yet*, 1997): It was in fact ten years earlier, the spring and summer of 1961, which I spent in Washington D.C., that the first notes for parts of this sequence were made: in particular II 'Friendship Heights', X 'A Framed Photograph', XIV 'Bourdon'. In XIII 'A Four Letter Word' the Maori names (line 3) are of trees in the New Zealand rainforest. *Tane* is the tree-god in Maori theogony: he raised the sky-father (Rangi) from the earth-mother (Papa) so that his fellow divinities had living space between. He is *Tane mahuta* (Tane arisen, or rising) in the form of the bole of a great *kauri* in the Waipoua forest, much visited by tourists though decayed over centuries.

I, XVII, 'Lone Kauri Road'. The location of the Curnows' bach, at Karekare, on the west coast north of Auckland.

XII, 'Magnificat'. Refers to a large statue of the Virgin Mary at Waikanae, north of Wellington, on the Kapiti coast. Sister M. Vianney, of the Presentation Convent in Paraparaumu, replied to Curnow's request for architectural information about the statue and her letter (adding to details in a brochure) provided several phrases eventually used directly in the poem:

> The material is not reinforced concrete — the statue is hollow in the centre having been built on a 2" x 4" scaffolding covered with many layers of scrim and finished off with a 3" plaster. (Incidentally there are 'steps' inside the statue, and a trap-door through Our Lady's head! This is used for maintenance, painting, electricity etc.) . . . (Sister M. Vianney to AC, 17 December 1971. AC Papers, ATL 2402-68.)

XIV, 'Bourdon'. There are close links between this poem and 'Capitoline Spring' (p.145).

AN ABOMINABLE TEMPER AND OTHER POEMS, 1973

AC (Notes, *Early Days Yet*, 1997): My great-great-grandfather Peter Monro (1793–1865) settled in the far north of New Zealand in 1835, five years earlier than the Treaty of Waitangi, by which Maori chiefs ceded a putative sovereignty to Queen Victoria, beginning the colonial period of New Zealand's history. His son's letter, written in old age to one of my father's aunts, is my primary source (see headnote to the poem). His *Poetical Works* of Burns is on my bookshelf, in remarkably good repair, considering its many sea voyages, and at least one fire since he bought and inscribed it, c. 1812, in Edinburgh. See also my note to 'The Scrap-book', below.

The book was complete in time for it to be included in *Collected Poems* (1974).

'To an Unfortunate Young Lady . . .' Refers to a Christchurch Arts Festival in March 1973 and the young lady mentioned was in fact Sue McCauley, later a well-known New Zealand novelist celebrated for her first novel *Other Halves* (1982), winner of both the Wattie Book of the Year award and the New Zealand Book Award for Fiction.

'To Douglas Lilburn at Fifty'. 'MacDiarmid's oils': Douglas MacDiarmid (1922–) is a New Zealand-born artist who has lived in Paris since the 1940s.

'A Refusal to Read Poems of James K. Baxter . . .' This poem was also occasioned by the 1973 Christchurch Arts Festival, and actually written on the stage while nine other poets read their poems. He immediately passed it to a journalist from the Christchurch paper *The Press* which printed it prominently the next day, 12 March, the actual day of the memorial celebration for Baxter.

'What Was That?' Written probably early in 1973 in response to the final illness of his mother.

AN INCORRIGIBLE MUSIC, 1979

'Canst Thou Draw out Leviathan with an Hook?' The title comes from Job, 41.1.

'A Balanced Bait in Handy Pellet Form'. AC (Notes, *Early Days Yet*, 1997): The Torlesse range (line 11) rises to 6000 feet, east of the main divide of the Southern Alps, to dominate this part of the Canterbury plains. Cf. my poems 'A Time of Day' and 'Early Days Yet', also 'On the Road to Erewhon' and my Note to that poem. The 'other poet' (line 31) is Byron, *Childe Harold's Pilgrimage*, canto IV, cxxvi. 1997.

'In the Duomo'. The subject of this poem is the Pazzi conspiracy, the assassination attempt, in April 1478 in Florence, by the Pazzi family on the two powerful Medici brothers, Lorenzo and Giuliano. The murder was to take place at a banquet but Giuliano was unwell and decided to skip the banquet so the venue was changed to the Cathedral, or Duomo, during High Mass. The original hired assassin, Gian Battista da Montesecco, now refused to go ahead for fear of eternal judgement and two priests, Maffei and Stefano, with members of the Pazzi family, did the deed, killing only Giuliano. The first and last sections of the poem are set at Karekare (see note to 'Things to Do with Moonlight'), where according to a neighbour, Mrs Dragicevic, a high cliff above the ocean was called the Cathedral.

'II A Professional Soldier'. 'Ma ficca le occhi . . .' These three lines from the *Inferno* of Dante's *Divine Comedy* are translated as follows in Charles Singleton's prose translation in the Bollingen Series LXXX, Princeton University Press, Princeton, 1970: 'But fix your eyes below, for the river of blood draws near, in which boils everyone who by violence injures others.'

'Dichtung und Wahrheit'. This poem was understood to refer to *A Soldier's Tale* (Collins, Auckland, 1976), a novel by Curnow's colleague, M.K. Joseph. It was strongly criticised in New Zealand in various reviews and considerable debate ensued. Peter Simpson reproduces an excellent response by Curnow to this controversy: '"Dichtung und Wahrheit": A Letter to *Landfall*', *Look Back Harder: Critical Writings, 1935–1984*, Auckland University Press, Auckland, 1987, p. 326. The note following the text usefully lists relevant letters, reviews etc.

'Things to do with Moonlight'. AC (Notes, *Early Days Yet*, 1997): 'Karekare doppelgänger' (line 58) names the place where the poem was written, on the steeply forested coast of the Tasman Sea, west of Auckland; I have spent most of my summers and weekends there since 1961. All four syllables are sounded, rather like English 'carry-carry'; a native (or instructed) Maori speaker might give the vowels different values, more like Italian, and stress the word differently. This Note is for the sake of the metre, since the name occurs elsewhere in these poems (v. 'Moro Assassinato', I, and 'A Fellow Being', II, VI, VII, IX).

'Moro Assassinato'. AC (1997): Parts of this poem inevitably owe a good deal to the Italian press, but in particular to the Naples daily *Il Mattino*, of 9 May 1978; to the news magazine *Panorama*, Milan, 13 June 1978; to *Corriere della Sera*, of 13 September 1978 (for seven letters of Moro, posthumously published). The German magazine *Stern* interviewed Michael Baumann (see motto of 'II. An Urban Guerrilla') in an 'underground hideout'; my source is an English translation of this interview, in *Encounter*, September 1978.

AC (1979, 1997): The character of the sequence *An Incorrigible Music* was decided, and most of the poems written, some months earlier than the kidnapping of Aldo Moro in the Via Fani, Rome, with the death of his five guards, on 16 March 1978. It was impossible to live in Italy from early April through June, reading the newspapers, catching the mood from chance remarks or no remarks at all, and not be affected. To this day, nobody knows where the 'Prison of the People' was. At the spot in Via Caetani, Rome, where the murdered man's body was left, in the Renault 4, about a dozen metres of wall were covered with private tokens of respect — handwritten papers, placards, flowers — from the ground to above head height. People came and went, or stood silently. That was mid-June, a full month later.

'A Reliable Service'. This poem recalls a fifteen-minute ferry trip from Paihia to Russell in the Bay of Islands.

'A Fellow Being'. AC (Acknowledgements, 1982): For 'A Fellow Being' I helped myself to detail from Dick Scott's account of F. J. Rayner (*Fire on the Clay*, Auckland, 1979) which also refreshed a memory of remarks by Aucklanders of an older generation. Of course, the historian is not answerable for the poet's conceptions. My uses of Eliot R. Davis's memoir (*A Link with the Past*, 1948) are, I think, self-explanatory.

Frederick John Rayner (1875–1931), a Canadian-born entrepreneur who married the wealthy heiress of a Chicago meat-packing business, immigrated to Auckland in 1900. He was a successful dental surgeon and also a property magnate with a handsome residence in the Auckland suburb of Epsom. In 1907 he purchased cheaply a large block of kauri forest on Auckland's west coast where for six years he cut and milled large quantities of kauri, selling out profitably in 1913.

'After Dinner'. This poem is a tribute to Curnow's uncle, Arnold Wall (1869–1966), who was a long-serving professor of English at Canterbury University College and also an amateur mountaineer.

'A Passion for Travel'. Draws on memories of visits to Sicily in 1974 and 1978.

AC (Notes, *Early Days Yet*, 1997): *pakeha*: Maori loan word for 'not Maori' viz. 'European', or 'introduced', 'not indigenous'.

'An Excellent Memory'. Pat Laking, the wife of the New Zealand ambassador to the United States, remembered perfectly a well-known sonnet of Charles Brasch, 'Parting', at a Washington reception which actually occurred in 1966, not 1974, as recorded in the poem.

'The Ocean Is a Jam Jar'. This poem was based on a playful pub conversation with a local Maori writer at Tokomaru Bay during a visit to the east coast in November 1979, which Curnow described at the time:

> Did you realise that I am *a Hapuka*, this title being conferred at the Tokomaru Bay pub by a Maori well read in NZ poesy? No, I said, 'only a Kahawai' — to which our Maori friend, 'Perhaps a Mao Mao?' I settle for that. (AC to Dan Davin, 14 November 1979, Dan Davin Papers, ATL 5079-075.)

The pub was also adorned with a stuffed rainbow trout, and a mirror reflecting a jam jar full of tadpoles. 'I hope it doesn't seem to assert more than it admits,' Curnow wrote to Stead. 'It was the irony of the two perspectives I suppose. I might well be one of the tadpoles — more likely the stuffed trout.' (AC to C.K. Stead, 12 June 1980, C.K. Stead Papers, ATL 8220-08.)

'Organo ad Libitum'. AC (Notes, *Early Days Yet*, 1997): 1. The quoted lines are grafts from *Erewhon*, Chapter 4 (see note to 'The Road to Erewhon', below). The parish organ changes to the mountainous instrument played by the transfigured Handel of Butler's dream, but this is 'no dreme, I lay brode waking': the cadaver is 'wide awake' to the knowledge of death, as it recites the erotic mystery of Wyatt's sixteenth-century sonnet. *Taihoa*! Maori loan word for 'wait a bit' or 'no hurry'.

II. The film is Walerian Borowczyk's *Intérieur d'un Couvent*, the quoted poem Gerard Manley Hopkins': 'To What Serves Mortal Beauty'.

IV. The 'boulder of Magritte', a detail of 'Le Cap des Tempêtes', adorns the cover of my paperback copy of Camus's *The Myth of Sisyphus*.

V. The antarctic volcano is Mt Erebus, on which an Air New Zealand DC10 crashed on a sightseeing flight, killing nearly 300 passengers and crew, 28 November 1979.

VIII. For 'Panurge said' see Rabelais, *Gargantua and Pantagruel*, Book III, chapter xviii (tr. Urquhart 1693): 'Panurge is a second Bacchus, he hath been twice born ... In him is renewed and begun again the palintokis of the Megarians, and the palingenesis of Democritus ...'

For Schopenhauer, see *Parerga and Paralipomena* (tr. Hollingdale): '... a clear distinction between *metempsychosis* ... and *palingenesis*, which is the *decomposition* and reconstruction of the individual in which *will* alone persists and, assuming the shape of a new being, receives a new intellect'.

IX. Domenico Parrani smoked the biggest Savinelli pipe in Italy and had some official role in the denomination of the country's wines. One day we (my wife and I) drove with him along the north Sicilian coast from Capo Skino to Capo d'Orlando, where it amazed him that we took our *espressi* without the usual sugar.

THE LOOP IN LONE KAURI ROAD, 1986

'A Raised Voice'. Set in St David's church at Belfast, north of Christchurch, this is the first of many poems drawing on Curnow's childhood.

'Do Not Touch the Exhibits'. '*è pericoloso sporgersi*': it is dangerous to lean outside.

'On the Road to Erewhon'. AC (Notes, 1986, Notes, *Early Days Yet*, 1997): A few lines and parts of lines are lifted, unaltered, from Butler's *Erewhon*, Chapter 5, 'The River and the Range'. A reader may be reminded of similar grafts in an earlier poem of mine, 'Organo ad Libitum'; these were from *Erewhon*, Chapter 4. The young Butler's four New Zealand years (1859–1863) were spent sheepfarming, on his own high-country station between the headwaters of the Rakaia and Rangitata rivers, flowing east from the Southern Alps to the Pacific Ocean; he called his land Mesopotamia, after the 'between rivers' of antiquity, and the name has stuck, at least for the trifle of another century and a quarter. Anyone born and bred, as I was, in sight of the same sea and mountains, enjoys privileged access to the region of Butler's opening chapters, drawn (as he tells us) from 'the Upper Rangitata district of the Canterbury Province (as it then was) of New Zealand'. It is a common terrain and climate: its mountains, rivers, and winds are the outdoors bearings of other poems I have collected here, 'A Sight for Sore Eyes' and 'A Raised Voice'; also for 'An Evening Light' and 'A Time of Day' (see below).

The terrifying statues guard the summit of the pass which Butler's narrator crosses, from the landscapes of reality, westward into the 'nowhere' of *Erewhon*. On which plane does he (or Butler) hear, back in England and telling his story, the bars of a Handel prelude, printed in the text, which remind him of the 'horrible' aeolian blasts of the Erewhonian statues?

'Blind Man's Holiday'. AC (1986, 1997): I The packets of Utamaro postcards any traveller can buy at a Japanese airport contain no examples of the eighteenth-century master's erotic art; nor do historians (I suppose) connect this genre peculiarly with the name of his Western contemporary Henry Fuseli, the adoptive name, that is, of the Swiss-born Johann Heinrich Füssli. It is a somewhat circumscribed modern taste which discovers them both in, say, some production of the Erotic Art Book Society — in company with Rembrandt, Rowlandson, Grosz, Balthus, Dali and Picasso. Does anybody know whether Sacheverell Sitwell guessed correctly that 'hundreds of these exceptionable drawings may have escaped Mrs Fuseli's kitchen range'? Or how deeply scandalised friends like Flaxman and Haydon actually were, learning of their existence at the time of the artist's death in 1825? My source is Eudo C. Mason, *The Mind of Henry Fuseli* (London, 1951), citing Benjamin Haydon's *Diary* and Allan Cunningham's *Life* of Fuseli.

II A First World War early childhood left a few of Bairnsfather's popular cartoons of trench warfare sharply printed on my memory. *The Queen's Gift Book* would be one of those sumptuously got-up volumes published under royal patronage in aid of patriotic funds; there were cosmetic paintings of scenes at the Front, like the retreat from Mons, in the lurid colour reproduction of the time.

III Alvin Lucier's 'long wire' was on loan to the Auckland City Art Gallery for a time in 1984, a wonderful contrivance, not only for the electronically translated sounds intended by the American composer, but visually as well. Voices or footsteps in the gallery, noises in the street outside, made a continuously changing murmur about almost everything. Not mere 'electro-acoustic natural photography', as someone described Luc Ferrari's *Daybreak on the Beach*: much nearer, even painfully, to one's sole self.

This poem, exploring the difficulty of describing intense pain, began with memories of a severe attack of back pain in December 1982. Curnow was taken by ambulance to Green Lane Hospital and then to Middlemore Hospital where he stayed several days. Its title is a now obsolete colloquial phrase referring to the twilight period of near darkness just before nightfall. In a letter to Stead he writes:

> I've known the title from childhood — my mother (or grandmother?) used it after nightfall, or just before it, if the light wasn't lit & perhaps only a bit of firelight. . . . The Blind Man has a holiday from being blind, everyone else being the same, we're all playing at blindness. (AC to C.K. Stead, 7 November 1984. AC Papers, ATL 4650-06 and C.K. Stead Papers, privately held.)

'*The picture in the mind revives,* our poet/ noticed . . .' The poet is Wordsworth and multiple allusions to his 'Tintern Abbey' follow.

'. . . *dunnest smoke*' and '. . . *that my keen knife see not the wound it makes/ nor Heaven peep through.*': see *Macbeth*, Act I, scene v, ll. 48–50.

'Gare SNCF Garavan'. For the phrase "'to the mountains, fall on us'" see Luke 23:30.

AC (From Author's Note, 1988): It will be seen that the book begins with the newest poems, followed in reverse chronological order by the five published collections, from *The Loop in Lone Kauri Road* (1986) back to *Trees, Effigies, Moving Objects* (1972). The logic of the collection favours this arrangement; besides, it agrees with my own perspective over these years, and perhaps the way past and present things shift about in some of the poems.

This reverse order was first suggested to Curnow by Robert Penn Warren's *New and Selected Poems* (Random House, New York, 1985). The quotation from Solzhenitsyn which is the book's epigraph reinforces this perspective.

'Survivors'. Another memory from childhood, this poem is set in Hagley Park, Christchurch on Armistice Day 1918.

'*by the long wash of Australasian seas*', from Tennyson's 'The Brook'.

'A Time of Day'. This poem recalls Curnow's brief flight in 1919 in an Avro 504K biplane. He wrote to his cousin G.C.A. (Ted) Wall, experienced in all aviation matters,

> It was while T was Vicar of Malvern parish, & we lived at Sheffield .... Some chaps — pilots with World War I service, I believe — took their aeroplane on a barnstorming tour in the country — using farm paddocks for airstrips, charging the locals to see the performance, and for short flights. I was one of a few children at Waddington School who sold tickets. The little girl who sold most tickets was too scared to take a free flight which was her reward. I pestered T and Muz [his parents] to let me go up in her place. I did .... (AC to Ted Wall, 21 September 1987, AC Papers, ATL 4650-11.)

THE GAME OF TAG AND OTHER POEMS (1989–1997)
in EARLY DAYS YET, 1997

'A Busy Port'. AC (Notes, *Early Days Yet*, 1997): The time-ball tower housed 'a sphere which at a certain moment each day is allowed to fall down a vertical rod placed in a prominent position, so as to give an accurate indication of time' (*New Shorter Oxford Dictionary*). At the port of Lyttelton, New Zealand, my busy port, it is a gothic-looking affair, the crenellated main turret supporting the ball and rod. There were quarters for (I imagine) the signalman who, as well as attending to the ball, hoisted flags on the adjacent flagpole, to announce and identify ships arriving off the Heads. The ball itself was for ships in port to correct their chronometers by. Technology will have changed all this but the tower remains.

Alas it no longer does: it was severely damaged in the earthquakes of September 2010 and February 2011 and, in a subsequent aftershock in June 2011, the tower collapsed. However there are plans to restore part of the historic building. The poem recalls an eleventh birthday treat promised by Curnow's father to accompany him, in his role as Port Chaplain, on a small steamship the S.S. *John Anderson* which serviced the settlements around the Lyttelton harbour. It is clear from earlier drafts that Bob Hempstalk weeps for the death of his wife.

'*with a short uneasy motion*'. From Coleridge's *The Rime of the Ancient Mariner*, Part 5, lines 386 and 388.

'*Eyes that last I saw in tears*'. The title of a short poem by T.S. Eliot.

'**Another Weekend at the Beach**'. **AC (1997):** *kina*, line 28: the edible sea-urchin *Evechinus chloroticus*. Maori loan word.

The trigger for this poem appears to have been an invasion of toxic algal bloom around the New Zealand coast in the summer of 1992–93. In the poem this becomes a metaphor for the fashionable literary theory of deconstruction, which Curnow describes as 'the deconstruction pestilence or pandemic' (AC to C.K. Stead, 8 April 1993. C.K. Stead Papers, ATL 8220-15.)

'**Looking West, Late Afternoon, Low Water**'. **AC (1997):** Tangaroa, line 24: Maori god of the sea, supreme god in some other parts of Oceania, or creator of the world.

Bob Falla. An eminent New Zealand ornithologist and Director of the Dominion Museum whom Curnow and Roger Duff dropped off, half a century before, at Waikuku Beach in North Canterbury to examine a dead whale.

'*rather be/ suckled in a creed outworn*': from Wordsworth's sonnet 'The world is too much with us'.

'*she's amateur built but your friends won't know*': these are the words of Brian Donovan, Curnow's neighbour, from whom in the 1950s he purchased a small boat which on one occasion got into difficulties.

'**The Scrap-book**'. **AC (1997):** Eighty-three pages are left, of the hundred or so the scrap-book had when William Woon wrote his entries in it, being storm-bound at my great-great-grandfather Peter Monro's house on the Hokianga in October 1841. It has lost one of its heavy black embossed covers, and its spine. Many pages are blank, others haphazardly occupied by sentimental verses, sketches, engravings of ships, houses, horses, clipped or copied from books or albums of the time. Woon's entries take one full page; another is filled by a pencil sketch of 'Horeke, from Manungu, Hokianga', where the stockades of Maori *paa* (strongholds) appear on hilltops across the water, and a *waka* (war canoe) paddles up the harbour past a small house in European style with its fence-posts behind the beach. Woon, a Wesleyan missionary, returned on 11 September 1844, to open the book again where he had written three years ago: he asterisked the earlier date, and added a pious couplet, still in the darker oscillation of his evangelical faith: '*See the rapid flight of time — How swiftly it runs away!/ May we now His favour seek — While it yet is called day!*'

I, line 17: Nga Puhi country. Dominant Maori tribe of northernmost New Zealand.

II, lines 9–10: *iwi* of the *tangata whenua*: literally 'tribes of the people of the land'. Common borrowings in New Zealand English.

'**Early Days Yet**'. **AC (1997):** The petrol tank of these cars was mounted under the high front seat, so that fuel reached the engine by simple gravity feed. A cost advantage, no doubt, over other cars of the period, though not without inconvenience to driver and passenger, who had to get out whenever filling was necessary. The gravity system could fail when climbing an exceptionally steep slope: the resourceful driver would then turn the car round, and proceed in reverse.

'*A great while ago/ the world began, with/ hey, ho*'. From the last verse of Feste's song at the end of *Twelfth Night*.

'unhingeing/ nor'west slammer'. The strong warm wind familiar to anyone who has lived on the Canterbury plains.

'*O forest, green . . .*' The words of a popular song Curnow remembered his father singing.

'A Facing Page'. AC (1997): In Stoker's story it was a city stricken by plague. Another illustration showed a very old man and a very young girl seated on the edge of a fountain in a public square. One of them, I forget which, holds out a consoling hand to the other.

'Investigations at the Public Baths'. Curnow was eighty in 1991 and this poem recalls a swim in the Auckland Tepid Baths (part of a regular regime) on the day after that birthday.

'Pacific 1945–1995'. AC (1997): The three words in quotation marks, quatrains 10–11 of this poem, are a theft from Robert Penn Warren's great Hiroshima poem, 'New Dawn'. My pantoum appeared also in *Below the Surface, Words and Images in Protest at French Testing on Moruroa* (Random House NZ, 1995).

At a time when Curnow happened to be tinkering with his earlier pantoum, 'Pantoum of War in the Pacific' (page 94), he was asked for a poem for the Random House anthology protesting against the French resumption of nuclear testing in the Pacific. The epigraph and first verse clearly hark back to his original but the rest of the poem takes its own way with assistance from Robert Penn Warren's poem. He thought it was 'the longest pantoum in the language'.

'An Evening Light'. AC (1997): The Ngai-tahu tribe (lines 25–26) occupied, and still claim, a great part of the South Island of New Zealand. A *kainga* is a Maori settlement, a *paa* was a fortified (stockaded) place or stronghold. In common European speech, *paa* is often used for any form of Maori settlement; infrequently and locally, *kainga* is heard in the corrupt form 'kaik'.

THE BELLS OF SAINT BABEL'S, 2001

'The Cake Uncut'. This poem, written in 1999, first appeared in a special millennial literary supplement in the *Sunday Star-Times* on 2 January 2000, although it had only the briefest mention of the millennium. Curnow added the third section before sending it to the *London Review of Books* in February.

'The Bells of Saint Babel's'. AC (Notes, 2001): For biblical allusions in (1) see Genesis, chs. 10, 11. My '. . . pegged-out plain/ in the land called/ Shinar . . .' may be identified, by a reader who happens to know the place and the history, with the newly named Canterbury Plains in the

South Island of New Zealand, and the 'four ships' with the first arrivals of the Canterbury Association settlers in 1850: who also set about building a Tower (with a 200ft spire) 'to make us a name, lest we be scattered'. Like the colonists of Shinar, the builders of Babel, they were generations shaped by a long voyage in unknown waters: one of them was F. G. Brittan, named in (3). The vicarage where he sits at the fireside still stands but is no longer a vicarage, and the timbered church that stood nearby now serves as an assembly hall to a city school some miles away. (4) The 'half-god' is Maui, most famous hero in Polynesian mythology, where a well-known story tells how he lengthened the day for the good of mankind, by casting a noose round the neck of the sun-god, slowing down his passage across the heavens. Maui stole fire, like Prometheus, and like Proteus could change his shape into that of any other living creature; he fished up the North Island of New Zealand (aka as *Te Ika a Maui*, Maui's fish). His hubristic challenge to the Goddess of Death (*Hine nui te Po*, Great Woman of the Night) was the end of him: his plan was to catch her asleep, and having taken the shape of a caterpillar, to penetrate between her legs; but the cry of a bird woke her and she crushed him there. In some versions the goddess strangles Maui, or tears him in the terrible jaws of her *vagina dentata*.

'The Pocket Compass'. A response from BBC Radio 4 to write a sonnet 'having some connection with a point of a compass'. AC writes: 'I tried first with the Petrarchan abba ... found myself choking, & invented a new one — not end-rhymes but syllable counts — 11/9/9/11, which nobody will notice, I expect. . . . There was once a compass rose drawn elegantly on our railing at Karekare by George Tole (Jeny's father), with his pocket compass beside him to get the points right. I chipped it into the timber, & was sorry to lose it when the rotting rail had to be replaced — that's what the sonnet is about.' (AC to C.K. Stead, 14 Sept. 2000. AC Papers, ATL 7574-79 and C.K. Stead Papers, privately held.)

'For Peter Porter at Seventy'. Commissioned by Anthony Thwaite for a collection to mark the seventieth birthday of poet Peter Porter. Another pantoum, which delighted Porter.

'Four poems after Pushkin', II. 'The Upas Tree'. AC (2001): Barring some likelier guess (or proof?) I am left with my own, which is that the story of the 'celebrated poison-tree of Macasser' could have reached Pushkin by way of Erasmus Darwin, the English botanist poet (grandfather of the more famous Charles) who had it from the report of a ship's surgeon, the Dutchman N.P. Foersch, published by the *London Magazine* of December 1783. Darwin's long poem, 'The Loves of the Plants' (1789, 4th edn. 1794) tells how '. . . on the blasted heath/ Fell Upas sits, the hydra-tree of death'. He bought the whole extraordinary tale of the tree's biocidal powers and wrote: 'This however is certain, though it may appear incredible, that from 15 to 18 miles round this tree, not only no human creature can exist, but that, in that space of ground, no living animal of any kind has ever been discovered . . . there are no fish in the waters, nor has any rat, mouse, or other vermin, been seen there; and when birds fly near this tree, they fall a sacrifice to the effects of the poison'. Pushkin transplants his Upas from Java to a steppes region of vast extent: its birth and growth are imaged as startlingly as its deadly effects; but it is man, in the person of a pitiless despot, a Tsar, who finds his own use for it, its potential (so to speak) in biochemical weaponry. The poem is dated 1828. While adding a story of his own, with its own satirical spin, to the tales about the Upas, he need not have troubled much about degrees of credibility. A modern dictionary entry, by the way, correctly mentions its 'poisonous milky sap', also indicated by its scientific name, *Antiaris toxicaria*, and its known use for poisoned arrows.

These four poems were the result of a commission from Elaine Feinstein to contribute translations of poems by Pushkin to a book to mark the centenary of that poet's birth (*After Pushkin: Versions of the poems of Alexander Sergeyevich Pushkin by contemporary poets*, Folio Society, London, 1999). Knowing no Russian, Curnow relied on the literal translations by Walter Arndt sent by Feinstein to the contributors.

'A Nice Place on the Riviera'. Curnow's last poem, probably begun in 1983 when on the Katherine Mansfield Fellowship at Menton, now recalling that time as well as Mansfield's period there in 1920–21. He had taken with him a copy of Blaise Pascal's *Pensées*, a strong presence in the poem. Connie Beauchamp and Jinnie Fullerton owned the Villa Isola Bella, where Katherine Mansfield (and later the Katherine Mansfield Fellows) stayed; their unsuccessful attempts to convert Mansfield to the Catholic faith also inform the poem.

'Fantasia and Fugue for Pan-pipe'. AC (2001): i–iii:'. . . (Mercury) still had to tell what Pan said to the nymph, and how she, scorning his prayers, ran off through the pathless forest till she came to the still waters of sandy Ladon . . . prayed her sisters of the stream to transform her; and when Pan thought he had at last caught hold of Syrinx, he found that instead of the nymph's body he held a handful of marsh reeds. As he stood, sighing, the wind blew through the reeds, producing a thin plaintive sound. The god was enchanted by this new device and the sweetness of the music . . . then he took reeds of unequal length and fastened them together with wax . . .' (Ovid, *Metamorphoses* Book I, tr. Mary Innes).

i:. . .*'traveller/ came by . . . he took/ her with a sigh . . .'* (William Blake, 'Never seek to tell thy love').

iv:'. . . since/ Jesus called out/ *with a loud voice/* it was all over, . . .' (cf. Gospels, Mark 16.34, John 19.30, King James version)

iv:'. . . this Greek/ seaway hears GREAT/ PAN IS DEAD. . .' '(heard) from the island of Paxi the voice of someone loudly calling Thamus . . . an Egyptian pilot not known by name even to many on board . . . and the caller, raising his voice, said, "When you come opposite Palodes, announce that Great Pan is dead". . . . Thamus made up his mind, that if there should be a breeze, he would sail past and keep quiet, but with no wind and a smooth sea about the place he would announce what he had heard. . . . So, when he came opposite Palodes, and there was neither wind nor wave, Thamus from the stern, looking towards the land, said the words as he had heard them, "Great Pan is dead". . . . Even before he had finished there was a great cry of lamentation, not of one person but of many, mingled with exclamations of amazement. As many persons were on the vessel, the story was soon spread abroad in Rome, and Thamus was sent for by Tiberius Caesar (who) became so convinced of the truth of the story that he caused an investigation to be made about Pan; and the scholars, who were numerous at his court, conjectured that he was the son born of the god Mercury (Hermes) and Penelope . . .' (Plutarch, AD c.50–125, *Moralia*, Loeb English translation). It was two centuries later that Eusebius, bishop of Caesarea, famous early Church historian, placed a Christian interpretation on the story: the death of 'Great Pan' signified the end of ancient paganism; the time of Tiberius coincided with the end of Christ's work on earth, with the downfall of the devils, as the old gods were seen to be by Christians. 'Great Pan' could be compared with the supreme Nature god known to the Stoics as Zeus-Cosmos, in some sense foreshadowing Christian doctrine. He was not (as Plutarch had supposed) one of the godlike *daimones*, still less the goat-like ('hairy') Pan worshipped by Arcadian shepherds. More than a thousand years after Eusebius, Rabelais again retells Plutarch's story, insisting that 'Great Pan' is none other than Jesus Christ: I quote from Peter Motteux's 17th century translation of *Pantagruel*, Book IV ch. 28, 'And methinks, my interpretation is not improper; for he may lawfully be said in the Greek tongue to be PAN, since he is our ALL. He is the god Pan, the great shepherd. The time also concurs … for this most good, this most mighty Pan, our only Saviour, died near Jerusalem during the reign of Tiberius Caesar'. Motteux could have picked up 'mighty Pan' from Spenser, who uses the identical phrase in *The Shepheardes Calender* (1579) or from Milton (who most probably did have it from Spenser) in 'On the Morning of Christ's Nativity' (1629):

> The shepherds on the lawn,
> Or ere the point of dawn,
> Sat simply chatting in a rustic row;
> Full little thought they than
> That the mighty Pan
> Was kindly come to live with them below …

The trigger for this poem was the appearance of a poem by his father Tremayne and one by Maude Goodenough Hayter in the 1906 anthology, *New Zealand Verse*, edited by W.F. Alexander and A.E. Currie. Both lyric poems were on the subject of lost love, which interested Curnow because the family believed the two had once been engaged before she broke off the engagement. In the third section Curnow recalls Maude visiting him on the occasion of his first marriage.

BIBLIOGRAPHY

Valley of Decision: Poems by Allen Curnow, Phoenix Miscellany: 1, Auckland University
　　College Students' Association Press, Auckland, 1933
Three Poems, The Caxton Club Press, Christchurch, [1935]
Enemies: Poems 1934–36, The Caxton Press, Christchurch, 1937
Not in Narrow Seas: Poems with Prose, The Caxton Press, Christchurch, 1939
Island and Time, The Caxton Press, Christchurch, 1941
Recent Poems (with A.R.D. Fairburn, Denis Glover and R.A.K. Mason), The Caxton Press,
　　Christchurch, 1941
Sailing or Drowning: Poems, The Progressive Publishing Society, Wellington, [1943]
Jack without Magic: Poems, The Caxton Press, Christchurch, 1946
At Dead Low Water and Sonnets, The Caxton Poets No. 5, The Caxton Press, Christchurch,
　　1949
Poems, 1949–57, A Glover Book from The Mermaid Press, Wellington, 1957
A Small Room with Large Windows: Selected Poems, Oxford University Press, London, 1962
Trees, Effigies, Moving Objects: A Sequence of 18 Poems, The Catspaw Press, Wellington, 1972
An Abominable Temper and Other Poems, The Catspaw Press, Wellington, 1973
Collected Poems 1933–1973, A.H. & A.W. Reed, Wellington, 1974
An Incorrigible Music: A Sequence of Poems, Auckland University Press/Oxford University
　　Press, Auckland, 1979
Selected Poems, Penguin, Auckland, 1982
You Will Know When You Get There: Poems 1979–81, Auckland University Press/Oxford
　　University Press, Auckland, 1982
The Loop in Lone Kauri Road: Poems 1983–1985, Auckland University Press/Oxford University
　　Press, Auckland, 1986
Continuum: New and Later Poems 1972–1988, Auckland University Press, Auckland, 1988
Selected Poems 1940–1989, Penguin, London and Viking, New York, 1990
Looking West, Late Afternoon, Low Water, Holloway Press, Auckland, 1994
The Scrap-book, Wai-te-ata Press, Wellington, 1996
Early Days Yet: New and Collected Poems 1941–1997, Auckland University Press, Auckland and
　　Carcanet Press, Manchester, 1997
The Bells of Saint Babel's: Poems 1997–2001, Auckland University Press, Auckland and
　　Carcanet Press, Manchester, 2001

AUTHOR'S NOTE

FROM *Collected Poems 1933–1973* (1974)

Nineteen of the twenty-two poems in my earliest volume *Valley of Decision* appear in this book, all of them revised. It may be as rash to revise in my sixty-third year what I wrote between my eighteenth and my twenty-first, as it was to publish them in the first place. I do not know that that is a serious objection. All poems are rash acts, and no less so — more, perhaps — for the deliberate care one takes. Even after forty years some poems carry between or under the lines their own instructions for revision. These instructions a poet must read as well as he can. His choice is between ignoring them and acting on them, and if he acts, he takes the risk of exceeding them. I think it is a good risk to take. If he doesn't revise, he is in effect concealing something from the reader: some part of his own better understanding.

Discontent, even disgust, with their earliest work is the common experience of poets. It is a mood. Moods don't help much, when it comes to the question: do I, or do I not, wish to suppress — or disown, since I cannot suppress — this part of my writing? I have to answer for this poet, myself, never mind what might be best for another. The impulse to revise, of itself, gives the answer. These earliest poems — like those in *Enemies* and *Three Poems*, which I have also revised here and there — have their place with all that I have written since. A hundred years ago, a conscientious editor might have covered all this with the disarming subtitle *Juvenilia*. That would not be suitable here, even if it were possible; there are too many connexions between my earliest and my latest poems to justify such a separation; they must stand together, for better or worse.

None of these early poems has been an anthologist's favourite, so the revisions should upset nobody. I do not call attention to them because I imagine many readers will notice them, but because I am accountable to the few who will. Having done so, I remember that there are famous instances of a poet's revising his life — correcting youthful beliefs or opinions — in touching up his early writings. There is no critical appeal against this, as a poet's own verdict on his work. In my case, it would be a futile exercise. In *Valley of Decision*, and after it, some crisis or change from faith to scepticism may be read, however perplexed and precarious the faith was, and the scepticism no less so. No revision can alter this. Whatever the life has been — and who knows very much about that? — the poetry is all one book.

I have altered almost nothing in *Not in Narrow Seas*. It has its own accent. It sets its own limits of a time and a place with a peculiar severity. I suppose it could be called my contribution to the anti-myth about New Zealand which a few of us poets — and almost nobody else — were so busy making in those years. It had to be done. The country did not know what to make of itself, colony or nation, privileged happy-land or miserable banishment: the polarisation was nothing new, and it is still with us, but we were the first to find poetry in it. I know that I wanted, for myself, to focus the vision sharply on a few details of a few scenes of New Zealand history, some of them distinct to me from childhood. I had not the sense of a poetic style, ready for use, that my elders Mason and Fairburn had; I had to improvise one for myself; but we had in common that instinct for a few particulars, sharpened by our antipathy to almost everything that satisfied — or seemed to satisfy — an older generation. I shared the antipathy, of course, with Denis Glover: each, in those days, wished he could write like the other, the last thing either of us could ever have done. Very soon after, I was writing the poems of *Island and Time* and *Sailing or Drowning*. I had to get past the severities, not to say rigidities, of our New Zealand anti-myth: away from questions which present themselves as public and answerable, towards the questions which are always private and unanswerable. The geographical anxieties didn't disappear; but I began to find a personal and poetic use for them, rather than let them use me up.

About the poems of the last thirty years I should have nothing to say here. They are the best I can do, so far; the little of the little I know, of myself and my world, that I have tried to add to the limitless disclosures, or inventions, that we call by the name of poetry. A collection on this scale will please, or displease, in different ways and places. Having made it, I must not make too much of it. I hope I have not finished yet.

The poem 'At Dead Low Water' first appeared in *Jack Without Magic*. I have placed it here in the later volume of which it became the title-poem. Similarly, I have placed 'A Small Room with Large Windows' in the volume which bears that title, not in *Poems 1949–1957* where it was first collected.

INDEX OF TITLES

Part-poem titles are in *italic*.

A Balanced Bait in Handy Pellet Form 195
A Busy Port 298
A Changeling 134
A Cool Head in an Emergency 204
A Dead Lamb 161
A Facing Page 312
A Family Matter 159
A Fellow Being 232
A Four Letter Word 166
A Framed Photograph 161
A Hot Time 170
A Leaf 116
A Nice Place on the Riviera 343
A Passion for Travel 249
A Professional Soldier 198
A Raised Voice 267
A Refusal to Read Poems of James K.
    Baxter 181
A Reliable Service 227
A Sight for Sore Eyes 282
A Small Room with Large Windows 137
A Sonata of Schubert 115
A South Island Night's Entertainment
    295
A Time of Day 291
A Touch of the Hand 228
A Turning Point in History 199
A Victim 73
A Window Frame 174
A Woman in Mind 29
Achievement 54
After Dinner 247
Agenda 154
All Darkens but Her Image 112
An Abominable Temper 182
An Evening Light 317
An Excellent Memory 254
An Incorrigible Music 225
An Old Hand 202
An Oppressive Climate, a Populous
    Neighbourhood 139
An Upper Room 153

An Urban Guerrilla 214
Another Weekend at the Beach 300
Any Time Now 172
Apocalyptic 16
Aspects of Monism 18
At Dead Low Water 106
At Joachim Kahn's 89
At the Brink 9
Attitudes for a New Zealand Poet 98

Behold Now Behemoth 11
Blind Man's Holiday 273
Bourdon 169
Bring Your Own Victim 206

Canst Thou Draw out Leviathan with an
    Hook? 193
Canto of Signs without Wonders 279
Capitoline Spring 145
Chief End 27
Children, Swimmers 101
Colonial Outlook 28
Continuum 290
Country School 73
Crash at Leithfield 70
Cristobal 117
Curacao 119

Darkness, Patience 105
Dialogue of Island and Time 79
Dialogue with Four Rocks 251
Dichtung und Wahrheit 203
Dimensional 100
Discovery 84
Do It Yourself 155
Do Not Touch the Exhibits 270
Doom at Sunrise 22
Dry Weather 60
Dunedin 104

Early Days Yet 308
Eden Gate 113

Elegy on My Father 119
Enemies 34
Et Resurrexit 6
Evidences of Recent Flood 131
Expect No Settlements 69

Factory at Night 28
Fantasia and Fugue for Pan-Pipe 351
Fantasy on a Hillside 59
For Peter Porter at Seventy 335
Four Descriptions and a Picture 109
Four Poems After Pushkin 337
Four Walls 11
Friendship Heights 152

Gare SNCF Garavan 278
Genesis 109

He Cracked a Word 136
His Deceit 10
Host of the Air 14
House and Land 66

Idylls in Colour Film 117
Impromptu in a Low Key 256
In Memory of Dylan Thomas 123
In Memoriam 85
In Memoriam, R.L.M.G. 108
In Summer Sheeted Under 93
In the Duomo 197
Inheritance 23
Investigations at the Public Baths 312
It Is Too Late 77

Jack without Magic 100
Jack-in-the-Boat 128

Keep in a Cool Place 126

Lake Mapourika 72
Lampoon 215
Landfall in Unknown Seas 95
Lili Kraus Playing at Christchurch 114
Lo These Are Parts of His Ways 276
Logbook Found on Ararat 131
Lone Kauri Road 151
Lone Kauri Road 171
Looking West, Late Afternoon, Low
    Water 304

Magnificat 165
Matins 10
Mementos of an Occasion 129
Morning Moon 69
Moro Assassinato 212
Moules à la Marinière 268
Mountain Elegy 32
Music for Words 113

Names Are News 156
Narita 286
New Zealand City 25
9 May 1978 223
Nine Sonnets 85
No Second Coming 83

Old Hand of the Sea 112
On Relief 17
On the Road to Erewhon 271
On the Tour 142
Orbit 37
Organo ad Libitum 258
Out of Sleep 85

Pacific 1945–1995 314
Paid Well 38
Pantoum of War in the Pacific 94
Paradise Revisited 102
Polar Outlook 65
Polynesia 86
Power of the Many 17

Quick One in Summer 72

Recall to Earth 27
Recitative 197
Remainder 36
Renunciation 5
Restraint 20
Rite of Spring 92
Rooks over Riccarton 54

Sailing or Drowning 86
Screened 13
Sea Changes 5
Second Song 76
Self-Portrait 102
Sentence 56
Sestina 75

She Sits with Her Two Children 111
16 March 1978 216
Slum 35
Song 64
Spectacular Blossom 130
Spring, 1942 90
St Thomas's Ruins 61
Statement 40
Status Quo 14
Stratagem 55
Survivors 285

Tantalus 182
Ten Steps to the Sea 319
That Part of You the World Offended So 98
The Agony 13
The Bath 55
The Bells of Saint Babel's 328
The Cake Uncut 325
The Dance 58
The Executioners 222
The Eye Is More or Less Satisfied with
    Seeing 122
The Fall of Icarus 87
The Game of Tag 301
The Kindest Thing 322
The Kitchen Cupboard 160
The Leaves Dead 37
The Letters 220
The Loop in Lone Kauri Road 283
The Navigators 87
The Ocean Is a Jam Jar 255
The Old Provincial Council Buildings 88
The Parakeets at Karekare 250
The Pocket Compass 335
The Poor 224
The Prison of the People 218
The Pug-Mill 289
The Scene 67
The Scrap-Book 306
The Serpent 15
The Skeleton of the Great Moa in the
    Canterbury Museum 99
The Spirit Shall Return 12
The Talisman 341
The Traveller 212

The Unclosed Door 293
The Unhistoric Story 56
The Upas Tree 338
The Vespiary: A Fable 287
The Waking Bird Refutes 103
The Weather in Tohunga Crescent 229
The Wilderness 21
Then If This Dies 111
There Is a Pleasure in the Pathless Woods
    171
Things to Do with Moonlight 209
This Beach Can Be Dangerous 177
Time 59
Time and the Child 61
To an Unfortunate Young Lady 176
To Fanny Rose May 109
To D.G. Overseas 105
To Douglas Lilburn at Fifty 178
To Forget Self and All 116
To Introduce the Landscape 127
To M.H. Holcroft 89
To the Reader 173
Tomb of an Ancestor 108
26 April 1478 200
Two Pedestrians with One Thought 163

Unhurt, There Is No Help 104

Valley of Decision 8
Venture 7
Veterans Day in the Metropolitan Museum
    of Art 148
Visibility Almost Nil 147

What Was That? 179
When and Where 337
When the Hulk of the World 121
Wild Iron 76
Winter Evening 340
With How Mad Steps 110
World, up to Now We've Heard Your Hungers
    Wail 98

You Get What You Pay For 231
You Will Know When You Get There 266

INDEX OF FIRST LINES

A bee in a bloom on the long hand of a
  floral 126
A bridge and a bronze creek 64
A gulp of sea air, the train 270
A man I know wrote a book about a man
  he knew 203
A man who has never visited the Uffizi 154
A poem for Lili Kraus — 114
A small charge for admission. Believers
  only. 291
A warmer latitude 341
A wood god botherer stands 156
A wood god bothering cantor 166
Absently the proof-reader corrects 249
Adam was no fool. He knew that at his age
  159
After those months 328
Against these eyes where is a man to hide?
  17
All the seas are one sea, 212
An old Green River knife had to be scraped
  193
And so the world makes you unquiet too,
  10
and to make up my mind about God before 276
At dead low water, smell of harbour bottom,
  106
At his age, he must know what it is 289
At nine fifteen a.m. 312
At ninety he told the press, 247
Awake, but not yet up, too early morning 85

Behind the eyelids the giant in the sky 312
Bishop George Selwyn grew tired of wood;
  61
Brasch wrote 'these islands' and I 254
Bush falls like waves, there is little you can
  hear 67
By night by fishes' light 152
By the same road to the same 283

Children, children, come and look 128
Children, swimmers, the whole brilliant
  harbour 101

Christ set it going and ascended 222
Circumvesuviano is the railway 223
Cleverer than ever you busy brain, 100
Clock-watchers all for whom the digits
  tick 335
Cold, limp with winter burial, 92
Come to the cliff, look over, 8

Darken, eyes, toward the day, 5
Darkness, patience at the root of the tree;
  105
Dead but to the world, Stevens, do you find
  129
Detestable gutter child, if you knew 34
Drag a star down to the office table —
  27
Drained flesh and hardened 37

Engaged too long 351
Expect no settlements or certainties 69
Extraordinary things happen every day 172

Fear made the superior sea 55
Fluent in all the languages dead or living,
  195
For Isaac the ram, 206
For pity of your own heart, think 20
Freshened by any wind, sanitised 293

Glass handle mugs the barman polishes 72
Great-aunt, surviving of that generation
  109

He cracked a word to get at the inside 136
He dressed his love in a fine dress 13
He had begun to look within 7
He will not walk in the sun, the young life
  23
Hearing my name in the barnsize bar 255
High and heavy seas all the winter 251
His letters. How can we know 220
Holy Week already and the moon 209
How is it that the thought 232
How right you are, my dear, 176

How shall I compare the discovery of
    islands? 84

I am the nor'west air nosing among the
    pines 59
I go home with my wife 36
I have lit a single lamp 29
I look from this back window straight
    across 139
I look where I'm going, it's the way 279
I met a traveller (in a sense) who said: 148
I tried from the cathedral 202
I walk to the Bryndwr bus 90
If music may save 58
If these stuck clods were blasted wide 14
Immaculate wing unfolding slowly
    enfolding 32
In summer sheeted under 93
In terms of some green myth, sailing or
    drowning 86
In your atlas two islands not in narrow seas
    40
Is it window or mirror the enormous 104
Is the word 'adult'? Utamaro's engulfing
    273
It becomes 'unnaturally' calm 229
It had to be an offering acceptable 199
It is too late 77
It ought to be impossible to be mistaken
    225
It took the sun six hours to peel 268
It was a feather of paint 214
It will be back next minute 204
Its thoughts are modular, they attach
    themselves 287

Jim, you won't mind, will you, 181

Let it be Sunday and the alp-high 267
Lift out front seat- 308
Like dry grass burning, nerves 60
Little at present, but to promise you 105
Look down the slope of the pavement 228
Look for my fingerprints. 173

Ma ficca le occhi a valle che s'approccia 198
Make it what height you like, the 155
Milton made Eve his blonde, but she is
    dark 102

Mischievous earth and sky were at their
    worst 70
Mock up again, summer, the sooty altars
    130
My fiftieth year had come and gone. So Yeats,
    178
My turn to embark. A steep gangplank
    298

National, the word, is a sign among you
    79
Necessity, now that [the] evening fog
    advances 147
Never a talking but a telling breath 123
Never turn your back on the sea. 161
Night falls on an unusual scene of public
    285
Night, will not night identical draw down
    28
Nightwatchman in some crater of the moon
    110
No ancient singing dancing infancy 113
No more burns the fire within the word.
    38
No prey for prowling keels, the south 73
Nobody comes up from the sea as late as
    this 266
Nobody less than the biggest 215
None of those was Eden 256
Normality was this car's 216
Not by voyages or accidents of ships, 75
Not him — he's where 325
Now I heard in my dream 179
Now that I am born, Sir, I suppose 61

O rational successful hands that swept 87
Often the things I see are tired, 12
Oh, some talk of Colour 142
Old hand of the sea feeling 112
Once past the icefalls and the teeth of 271
Once where the leaky 134
One more of those perfections 231
Only one night the 131
Original sea, no breath or bird, your eyes
    109
Our beach was never so bare. Freak tide,
    304
Our household consisted 218
Out of the living pit 14

Pain like cold fire binds the brows of the earth 22
Pray God and quiet take 10

Quantifiable griefs. The daily kill. 314

Rain's unassuaging fountains multiply 103
Rear-vision glass 322
Refuge in San 343
Repeat this experience 319

Scorched unforgiving soil 338
Sea go dark, dark with wind, 76
See the wide-footed, pendant-bellied beast 11
Servants of God, 6
Seven thigh-thick 301
She sits with her two children in the holy evening 111
Simply by sailing in a new direction 95
Small city, your streets 25
So they had to find somebody else 200
Somebody mistook 295
Soul, put on now as vesture 21
Spring in his death abounds among the lily islands, 119
Spring thunder thumps on Friendship Heights 145
Spring thunder thumps on Friendship, 169
Stammering wind this night 13
Stormily high the rooks soar 54
Strange times have taken hold on me, 5
Sun, moon, and tides. 160
Sun's hammer swinging at the skull 59
Surf is a partial deafness islanders 86

Tantalus, Tantalus, how are you getting on, 182
Tentative the houses 56
That part of you the world offended so 98
That silence in the hills suggested neither 89
The day doesn't come to the boil, it guards 278
The door stood wide, she stood 112
The feathers and the colours cry 250
The first time I looked seaward, westward 151

The glistening coast, field-labour and sea-faring 87
The lake's a merry bitch. 72
The light in the window blew out in a strong 306
The moon rolls over the roof and falls behind 290
The oil the blue 100
The oldest of us burst into tears and cried 108
The paper boat sank to the bottom of the garden 113
The plague's about along the street. 15
The poor publish their grief 224
The puzzle presented by any kind of a leaf, 116
The renaissance was six months old. 161
The skeleton of the moa on iron crutches 99
The slimed embrasures of old fortress walls 119
The steps are saucered in the trodden parts 88
The street's a fixed stare on the pointless night 11
The sun on its way down torched the clouds and left 317
The wistful camera caught this four-year-old 102
The world can end any time 227
Their Pole attained, bones 54
Then if this dies 111
There goes the morning moon 69
They arctic we antarctic; 65
They gave your hands a grubbing-tool 17
They were doing their thing in the burning fiery furnace, 170
They wrap mountains round my eyes, 282
Things are things carried 163
This is the rock where you cast your barbed wishes. 197
This light both whip and burden to your eyes 28
This paper is eleven and three-quarter 174
This pig of a gale 340
This was untrue, that there is division 18
Time who takes what he can use 76
Time's up you're got up to kill 258
To forget self and all, forget foremost 116

To introduce the landscape to the language
127

Together let us regain the earth's friendship.
27

Too many splashes, too many gashes, 171

Top to bottom of a skin white wall 117

Turn left at the sign. Lone Kauri Road 300

Turning its eyes from side to side, inquiring
286

Two steaming knees 55

Walking in the garden of our Father 35

WARNING 177

Wasn't this the site, asked the historian, 66

We stood at the timbered railing just one
steep 335

Weeping for bones in Africa, I turn 85

Whaling for continents coveted deep in the
south 56

What it would look like if really there were
only 137

What little do I know? 182

When I have seen a perfect flower 9

When the green grenade explodes, does the
kauri 171

When the hulk of the world whirls again
between 121

When was it first they called each other
mine? 104

Where is the world? Upstairs. 153

Where the big crowds come, the street, 337

Who hasn't sighted Mary 165

Wholehearted he can't move 122

Whose fancy fakes such crusted stuff 83

With so great wonder, at times fear, 37

World, up to now we've heard your hungers
wail 98

Yet a star will speak 16

You know the school; you call it old — 73

You move to the piano. What is it we
know? 115

Your 'innermost Beethoven' in the utter-
most isles 89